YOU
DO NOT
HAVE
TO BE
GOOD

YOU
DO NOT
HAVE
TO BE
GOOD

A Memoir

DAYNA MACCULLOCH

SHE WRITES PRESS

Published 2023
Printed in the United States of America
Print ISBN: 978-1-64742-511-1
E-ISBN: 978-1-64742-512-8
Library of Congress Control Number: 2023902902

For information, address:
She Writes Press
1569 Solano Ave #546
Berkeley, CA 94707

Book design by Stacey Aaronson

She Writes Press is a division of SparkPoint Studio, LLC.

For Billy

"The entire universe is inside your body
and you need not be afraid of it."
—Unknown

Author's Note

All of the dialogue in this memoir is taken verbatim from how I recorded it in my journal at the time the events happened. Most of the main characters in this story have been consulted prior to publication to ensure I am telling their experience accurately. That said, this is my story, and it is written through the filter of my own personal memory. Names have been changed, as well as defining details.

IDAHO

2004

My uncle decided it was about time, and in the summer he takes us back, twenty years later, to see the place where my father died. My uncle lights a cigarette and stands hunched against the car. I go to the creek and pull stones from the cold water while my sister picks flowers, white ones by the side of the road. The trees blur into darkness. I want to sing but end up crying. "So this is it, Dad," I say to the air and the ground, which, unlike me, remember him.

⇌

The butcher had come at dawn in a big white truck with the words "Bull Shooter" painted in red across the side. I watched from the upstairs window of our old neighbors, Dan and Carol. Their last memories of me are from when I was a chunky-cheeked toddler, and I have no memories of them at all. My sister, who was five when it all happened, remembers everything and has a hundred stories to tell me. "This is where our bed used to be," she said when we visited the old house— a log cabin my father built with trees that he felled himself from his land. "And here, this is where I stood when I watched Mom give birth to you," she said. "I hid here in the doorway, and I peeked around, and I saw your head coming!"

The morning air buckled with one gunshot, and I decided yes—not knowing why, but suddenly sure—I wanted to see her.

I left my sister still asleep in the bottom bunk bed and hurried down the stairs and out the back door to the field. The cow was lying dead in the dirt, eyes flat-colored, open. Backlit by the early dawn light, the butcher stooped and slit her throat, deftly across her jugular, a sound like fabric tearing. The inside of her skin was a pale, milky purple.

The day felt already too hot, the brown-backed Idaho hills leaning in on us, and the smell clogged my mouth—chewed leather and warm, fresh meat. The blood was pouring like creek water out of her neck, and her back left leg kicked gently, as if she were dreaming that she was still running.

Dan, the owner of the cow, sat on the edge of the truck and chatted amiably with the butcher, who called himself Keith the Killer. Keith the Killer—a lopsidedly fat man in green sweatpants whose wide fingers were caked in blood—scratched his head with his wet, red knifepoint as he told Dan about his niece's wedding the weekend before.

I leaned on the fence and crossed my arms, willing myself not to look away. The cow's flesh was yellow with ropes of fat, draped across white-purple sinews and rust-colored muscle that was still slightly twitching. Keith disjointed the legs at the knee—cutting halfway and then breaking—and tossed them to the side. He attached a pulley to what was left, strung her upside down, and sliced open the belly. "Looks like she's got a calf," he grunted and then went back to his story—the cousin who showed up at the wedding, who had now, much to everyone's surprise, gotten fat. A gray sack fell to the ground amid the stomachs, lungs, and entrails; he hooked it open with his knife, and the head of the calf slid out, black and slick with mucous, hooves pale yellow.

I held my arms tight across my ribs. On the drive over here last night, my uncle showed us the note that was discovered with my father's body, his hasty pencil scrawl on a scrap of paper. *What did he look like?* There must have been blood frozen in the snow. Were the windows closed? Were his eyes closed? Was his hand still holding the gun?

The carcass of the cow was clean suddenly, nothing but fat and muscle on bone. The butcher reeled her into his tall truck and shut the door. A hoof was lying near my foot, and he beckoned for me to toss it into the tractor with the rest of the remains. Trying not to be squeamish, I grabbed it just above the hoof, where the skin covered the bone. Soft and still warm, the muscle slid under my fingertips, and I dropped it with a gag.

"Do you eat meat?" Keith the Killer asked me.

"Yes."

"This is meat," he said and swung up into his truck and drove away.

⇌

As the sun was setting, we drove out to find the spot where my father killed himself. Somewhere on a forest road, we knew, but were not sure exactly where—it had been twenty years, and no one could remember. There were five of us packed into the Suburban—me, my sister, my uncle, Dan, Carol, plus two dogs in the back. Branches slid and whipped against the windows and the dogs lunged for them, cracking their noses and then their teeth against the glass. Carol, who was driving, shouted at them and laughed and returned to her story—something about herding cows, about the precise art of pushing them up hills. The sky lit in raspberry cloud rows over the trees. One dog stopped to pant over my shoulder—chewed leather, raw meat steam.

I wondered why we were doing it, wondered if we should be solemn, quiet, if we should pray. I wondered if it was okay to laugh when I was picturing my father's last moments, his careening drive on that very road, through the blizzard of snow, until his truck got stuck on a log. Then his cold hands scrawling out their last words—his will, leaving everything to us, my mother, my sister, and me, adding at the bottom, as if with a wry smile, or maybe he was dead serious: "P.S. I owe Rick a six-pack."

We rounded a bend in the road, and suddenly I recognized the spot, as surely as if I had been there with him. It was almost dark, and there was one pine tree rising, without opinion, into the sky. "So this is it, Dad," I said and began to cry, the first time I'd ever cried for him.

"You die, and then you live again, you die, and then you live again," I used to say each night in the bathtub after his death, pulling my head in and out of the running tap water over and over again.

"It was your bath-time ritual," my uncle told me. "You seemed to understand something better than we did."

What was it that I knew then? Some kind of natural dance we humans could have, but don't, with death? My uncle lights a cigarette and stands hunched against the car. My sister picks flowers, and I have my hands in the cold water, pulling up stones. I close my eyes and see the open-eyed cow, her tiny unborn child, the smell of flesh on the dog's breath.

The butcher who scratches his head with his knife and shrugs. *This is meat.*

⇌

There must be grace somewhere in all this if we look deep enough: in the gleam of the cow's purple, slit skin; in the shape of my sister's arms when she comes over to hug me; in the flowers that she's picked, circled in her fist. "What kind of flower is this?" she asks, her cheek on the top of my head, and my uncle squints at them from his lean on the truck.

"Pearly everlasting," he says.

And sometimes, I know, I actually can remember—being two years old and nothing yet, a wad of white clay that watches. I think, *Maybe I can remember what it was like when my mother took us and we left our home forever, driving long and straight into the darkness.* I was awake the whole ride, she tells me, and sometimes I can remember it: the way the night was against the windows; the way, in the omniscience of a baby, I saw my father's face, imploding into the suddenness of death. "Bye-bye," I said later when they told me, and I picked up his glasses like they were mine now, like what was his was now my job to carry.

1.

PORTLAND, OR

2006

The officer is wearing a gray hat with plastic casing over it to keep the rain off. He leans into the passenger side window and drips water onto my seat. "Where you headed?"

It is the middle of the night. I am covered in sweat, not my own sweat. "Um." I riffle through my purse to find my driver's license, trying to remember. Where am I going? (*I am coming from his house where we had sex, and it was all right. I loved only the beginning, his strong, pale shoulders, the ripple of his body, the warmth of his mouth.*) "A birthday party." I hold the license up, triumphant. He nods, plucks it from my hand and leaves me, heart pumping on the side of the road, rinsed by the red, blue, red, blue of his siren spinning. When he returns, he has only two words for me: "Slow down."

At my sister's birthday party, in a kitchen full of flowers and lemons and sliced blood oranges, my best friend, Ruby, calls from the hip-hop show in the city. She says, "Wait, there's someone here who wants to talk to you." It's a man we met at the bar last week.

"What's your number?" he shouts over the noise of the music. I am dating too many men to easily count. *Slow down,* I remind myself, but it's no use. My phone number is already out of my mouth.

This is what I do now. I am reckless with my body and other people's feelings, a sensation like standing barefoot at the edge of black, fast water. How much is too much? I want to know. How far can I go?

Ryan and I had made love in the thin light of the early evening, the windowpane above our heads turning indigo with the coming darkness. His hand was on the curve of my back. "I love you," he said, and I told him too that I loved him. I hoped that these words could be the most important thing between us, something that would go on doing the work of glowing and giving, long after I had dressed and left. It wasn't a lie, but it wasn't a promise, either. I'd loved Ryan since I first met him, since we were preteens hanging out at the high school football games. We went to different middle schools but talked on the phone every night for hours. Sometimes I'd go to his house and we'd practice playing guitar under his poster of Kurt Cobain while his parents argued in the kitchen. Neither of us had dads that were any good on paper. Mine would be in jail if he wasn't dead, and his had a temper that broke everything in its path. From those two sentences, people usually are inclined to think they know the entirety of these men's characters, but his dad also listened better than any parent to our consuming adolescent woes, and my dad was as good a man as they come until he wasn't anymore. Maybe that's why we loved each other—because we understood inherently that through every human heart cuts an incredible darkness, and no one is ever only good or only bad or only sane.

Ryan calls a few minutes after Ruby, to say he just came back from an ambulance call in which a man had two hours to live and they had to tell his wife. The man was only forty-two. Ryan says, "I want to tell you that I love you very much, and I am very happy you are in my life." They're singing "Happy Birthday" in the living room, and I press the phone tighter to my ear. "I'm feeling overwhelmed, D," he says. "I think I'm too young to be an EMT. I need more good years behind me to keep hope in the midst of all the shit this job entails."

Someone hands me a martini, but I hand it back. *Can't drink it*, I mouth.

"Sometimes," he says, "I don't feel like feeling anything in this world. And then I remember that I love you. And that's a thing worth feeling. Worth living for."

"I have to go, Ryan," I say. "I can't really hear you."

"Thank you, Ryan. I love you too, Ryan."

"C'mon, Ryan, don't do that."

"What makes you happy, Dayna?" He persists. "What do you think makes life worth living?"

Someone drops a martini, and the glass shatters across the kitchen floor. Everyone crows with laughter, and I use the noise to plead my exit again. He lets me go. We have been friends long enough for him to know my answer anyway— not much, I'd say.

⇁

At this point, I have been sick for nearly two years. No one knows what it is, though no doctor will necessarily tell me that. Neither will they tell me I will be well again. Since graduating from college, my life has been halted by symptoms that the doctors can't piece together into a diagnosis. I get pain in my bladder so bad, I scream on the bathroom floor, my urethra like it's on fire. In the emergency room, they run the tests. Can't find a source for the pain. "No infection," they say so many times that I start wishing for an infection, any kind of infection that could put a name to this, and a treatment to make it go away. Instead, they send me home with painkillers that throw me into a nauseous C curve on the bathroom floor again for hours. I keep taking them, because they dull the terrible pain. Then the pain comes back, worse. My ears erupt into throbbing pits of heat and knife fights. My throat is sore every day, my head a steady, dull throb.

"Mono," they say about my throat, so I stay in bed for three months. No change. A virus, they guess, an autoimmune disease, allergies, fungus, parasites. They keep running tests; the tests keep saying nothing. They put me on one diet, then another. I'm not allowed to eat anything that tastes good.

One summer passes and then another, and I don't get better. I refuse to stay in bed at my mother's house—I can't. I move two hours south to Portland to live with my college roommate, Ruby, and her parents. I find a part-time job nannying two girls, nine and eleven. I meet them at their school and walk them four blocks to their house and make them a snack, and then their mom comes home. I am twenty-four years old with a college degree, and this is the only work I can do, and some days I can't even do it. My whole body shakes, steady and hard, for hours every day. "You're twenty-four! You should be climbing mountains," says one well-meaning doctor. I go home and C curl on the bathroom floor again, try to breathe around the clawing terror. *I should be healthy. Why am I not? What is wrong with me?*

⇌

The day before Ryan and I break up again: Friday night in a crowded bar, downtown Portland. A man who is straight off the plane from Australia and covered from head to foot in tattoos leans close to show me pictures of his daughter in a red dress. I wonder if my father ever did this, on the nights my mother lay awake, waiting for him. "That's when I first knew I was an adult," she once told me. "Lying awake beside my two young children, wondering where my husband was, terrified of what state he'd be in when he came home. I'd think, *I am an adult now.* These are adult problems. There is no one who is going to take care of me."

To Ruby I say, "I have no patience for any of these love wounds any longer. Why even be sad about anything, really? We don't even know what death means! It's just this looming thing that happens to everyone that we're all afraid of, but what for? Maybe it's the nicest thing ever. Maybe we leave this place and go somewhere infinitely better."

I toast to Ruby, and Ruby toasts to me, and I down my water, she her whiskey. Ruby pulls my cap a little lower on my head. "Great lid," the Aussie says.

On the stage, a man plays the saxophone like we would wish any musician to play—with eyes closed and a slight smile; he makes love to all of us in the bar and then, later, in an elevator, he kisses me.

⇌

On Thursday nights, Ruby and I go to the salsa bar in Southeast Portland, down two flights of stairs, dark, tiny, and crowded with men; they all look at us when we walk in. Ruby goes to the bathroom, and I maneuver my way to the bar and

order a water. The doctors say I am not allowed to drink alcohol, smoke, or eat sugar, dairy, grains, or meat. There is
only one way left to escape the pain in my body—I dance.

The Cuban band in the corner rocks and fills the room. We
spin, moving our hips, sweating, cheek to cheek. Short, muscular men lean back on their forearms around the edges of the
dance floor, watching, waiting to cut in. To the side and behind
me, there is a dark-haired Peruvian man in an orange, collared
shirt who I kissed five days ago, with my back up against a
mauve wall, in the hallway waiting for the bathroom. I kissed
him to measure him, kissed him like a question. Did not return
his calls. He eyes me, then ignores me. Behind him is Carlos, in
a brown print button-down, his dreads tied back. He is getting
the number of one of two women who press close to him in
the crowd. We catch eyes, simultaneously wink at each other.
At the end of the night, it will be the two of us leaving for our
cars together, like it always is, when the lights have been
turned on and the last dancers are straggling out. He will wait
for me, kiss my nose and the side of my jaw. "How many
boyfriends do you have in there?" he'll ask.

I'll throw out a number—seven?—and he'll laugh and try
to count: the salsa dance teacher who looked white-hot into
the center of my body (no novice to the art of seduction, still,
I had to blink and look away); the guitar player whose lips
pointedly met the corner of my mouth when we said goodbye;
the bartender who slipped his number on a napkin into my
back pocket. "Promise?" the bartender had said, searching
my eyes. "Call."

⇄

Goodbyes come frequently. Men who will accept my terms at the beginning: "Okay, so you don't do monogamy. No problem." Until the jealousy and frustration eventually rips them into raging, red-eyed dragons. They're furious at me, and I'm furious at the universe. I want to kill the god I'm not sure I believe in. I spend hours in bed when I'm too sick to get up, drawing pictures of holding "Him" up at gunpoint. "Fuck you, God," I write at the bottom of the page. I hate the pain. I'm too weak. I'm scared. I want the men in my life to hold me and comfort me. One is not enough. Five are not enough. I want my father, but he is dead.

⇌

"When did it happen?" Ryan wants to know. He is standing somewhere outside where it is windy, and I know he is cupping his hand around the bottom of the phone, funneling his voice to me. "I want to know exactly when it happened," he says.

Four o'clock Friday morning. I squeeze my eyes shut. "There was a saxophone player too," I say instead.

"What?" There is a thump, and a quiet, windy sound for a while. Then: "What the fuck, Dayna?"

"You threw the phone?"

"Yeah."

"Did I land somewhere soft?"

"The screen's busted."

"Oh."

"What do you expect me to do now, forgive you?" His teeth chatter a little, and I imagine him in a T-shirt, the red, soft one I helped him pick out.

"Is there something to forgive?" I say.

"I can't—I have to—I don't think," he says, and hangs up. I sit on Ruby's bed, my back to the wall and my hands folded in front of me. The pain in my pelvis is back again, a looping barbed wire that makes its slow path through all of my lower organs. I grit my teeth. I tell myself I will not cry. There is only one person who I know is awake at this hour. Carlos opens the door for me without a word, still in his doctor scrubs. There is some silent thing between us, an agreement that neither of us need to name. We are not in love, and there is a spacious safety in that. I lean into his body, feeling the deep, dull sadness in me that intimacy touches. Sex is like prodding at a bruise. He holds me for a long time after it is over, kisses my face. We could sleep like this, but I rise instead to leave. He finds all of my clothes and hands them to me, one by one, then walks me to the door, still naked, and sits on the stairs as I find my shoes. I drive home as the sun rises, my body shaking again, violent, jagging in my torso and hips, like a seizure, impossible to contain. On the radio, Sarah McLachlan sings, "The world is on fire, it's more than I can handle," and I cry gasping, ugly sobs, thinking, *What is wrong with me, what is wrong with me, what is wrong with me?*

⇌

Ryan tells his family, "She kissed another man." They have heard this story before. Why he still puts up with me is a mystery they're tired of asking about. I stumble over syllables trying to explain myself to his mother, who I love, in the restaurant bathroom. She pees, looking up at me with patient, interested eyes, and I feel the cold metal of the doorway behind me, grip my fingers around the ledge of the handle. I say, "It's just that, well, I want you to know . . ." and then end up apologizing. "I don't mean to hurt your son," I say, sort of plaintively and childlike, still too terrified to say, "Listen, none of the rules make sense to me anymore."

"Everything ends," I say to Ruby. "Everything will change. We know nothing about so many things. All the rules about how to live were just made up by people from another time. We have to let go of rules and just let ourselves *be*." I am feverish with ideas. The pain leaves, in its wake, moments so still and clear, I swear I can hear the stars singing. Then it hits again, and I lose days, sweating and moaning on the bathroom floor.

Ruby and I share her childhood bed. She is just back from Brazil, where she was teaching hip-hop in the favelas of Rio de Janeiro. She is getting ready to return again for another month. I will stay with her parents, saving money to get back to Greece, where I'd spent a year living on an island when I was nineteen. Under the guise of studying writing with an expat poet named Jack, I learned instead how to speak Greek and drink and drive a motorbike and dance till the white-hot sunrise. It's the last place I felt like I was alive. *If I can just get back*, I think every day. I dream of that sea, blue as an ache.

Ruby and I believe we are inventing something important. Love Anarchy, we call it. We spend late nights talking it out. What we want is love without boundary or definition. The word "polyamory" makes us both gag. It's a term used by the hippie communities we avoided in college. We do not want the guidelines, the mutual agreements that polyamory advises. What we want is a relationship like dance: full of subtlety and deep listening, with freedom to explore the lines between things. The many meanings of a touch to the arm, a shoulder to a shoulder; that feeling when you meet a stranger's eyes, like a color poured back and forth between your bodies. We want to experience everything. We do not want our bodies to be owned, by anyone.

"It is impossible for connection to be regulated," Ruby says. "And more than that, it begs not to be. Loving another does not mean you love one less. Love longs for you to fall in love with everything."

"Yes!" I say. "Yes, yes, yes."

Fall in love with your feet as you walk. Fall in love with the man outside the tire shop, for the way he shakes the water off his broom, tiny crystal droplets cascading out into the night. Fall in love with the night, the cold body of it against your skin. Fall in love with the shape of a branch, a bundle of balloons in the sunshine. Yes, we say, yes, yes, our knees curled toward each other, the blankets to our chin. "I'll only marry you, moof," she says. And we fall asleep with our hands entwined.

⇌

She almost marries someone in Brazil. Her mom and I read her emails together with our knuckles pressed to our lips. Then we hear from him—neither of us speak Portuguese, and he doesn't speak English, but I piece the words together as best I can from my dusty back storeroom of Spanish I learned in high school. Ruby's in the hospital—dengue fever. When she finally calls, I can barely understand her. "It hurts, Day," she's sobbing. "Like my bones are breaking. Oh my God, it hurts."

I clean her room from top to bottom because it is the only thing I can think to do. I've been reading books on feng shui, energy healing, meditation. Deepak Chopra has been my friend in the darkness. If you change the outer world, it will change the inner world, he says, and vice versa. I pull out everything she has in boxes and organize it. It takes me days, and when I finish, I light a candle in the center of the floor and pray to the god I am angry with. *Please keep my friend safe. Please bring her home.*

She does come home.

She's weak, malnourished, and twenty pounds lighter. With a new tattoo of a star on her shoulder and stories about children with machine guns, drug lords, bullets through the window while she lay deep in fever on the cement floor, her bones on fire. It makes us all cry. She says to me, "All we need to do is dance."

⇌

We rent studio space in Northeast Portland and go there every day to train. I find a healer who calls my shaking "a wild animal that wants to move." Ruby says it must be a tiger. "C'mon," she says, when she's ready to go to the studio each morning. "It's time to walk your tiger."

We dance, and we dance, and we dance. Lie sweating on the studio floor, then get up and dance more. The more I dance, the less I shake. For the hours I am dancing, the pain in my body abates.

Then it catches me again.

Some days I can't get out of Ruby's bed. I wake up alone and the sun has set; somewhere, in real life, in warm homes, in happiness, people are finishing dinner. I call everyone who I am angry with. "Do you know that I am sick?" I demand.

"How sick?" they want to know, weary with their own lives. In my mind there is a list, and I am crossing people off of it. I sit in bed, wrapped in blankets, with the phone and my imaginary list, pelvic pain so sharp I can think of little else than stabbing and something screaming. I wake my ex-ex-boyfriend up, in bed in New York City. "I'm still mad at you for leaving," I say.

His voice is disoriented, climbing out of a dream. "Dayna," he whispers, and he is angry too. "*You* left *me*."

"I left the romantic relationship. You left the platonic relationship."

"You're the only one I know who is positively *militant* about maintaining friendships with exes."

"Why shouldn't I be? If you have a deep connection with someone, but it doesn't fit into the category of lovers, why just toss out the whole thing? Does that make sense to you?"

"Dayna, do you know what time it is here?"

I apologize and hang up. There seems to be a million things to apologize for, or nothing to apologize for, and I can't determine the difference. I have a sense of myself like a wheeling bird who finds herself trapped in a small room—careening, panicked, looking for an opening to get back to the wide open sky. I lie awake with my hands gripping my stomach and stare at the cracks in the ceiling, a whole crew of them in the white plaster. I imagine them a village, a gossiping community of crack people, each with names and personalities. I have spent hours staring at these cracks. There are so many days when I cannot get out of bed, the pain so deep that I can only scream, quietly, into my pillow so that Ruby's parents won't hear. I practice breathing techniques that my acupuncturist taught me, which only really serve to make me dizzy and sometimes pass out.

Everyone tells me to do different things, and no one agrees with the others' methods. I have one MD and two "practitioners" and The Healer. My acupuncturist says I have cold organs and clogged liver chi; my massage therapist says I have too much grief and should try building an altar for death. He says I should wear black. And my MD says I might have endometriosis, or bladder cancer, or both, but I need exploratory surgery for them to figure it out, and my insurance from my mother's coverage is about to run out. The Healer is a woman with red hair and big hips. She rarely smiles when I show up at her house-office, where she is always doing practical things, like pulling weeds or changing her car oil. She is confident she can help me without the others. She tells me exactly what to do, and I am so broken, so tired, I do it all without question. I drink half a lemon's juice in lukewarm water every day at exactly 4:00 p.m. I eat yams but no sweet potatoes, tilapia once a week, lamb broth but none of the meat.

I tell her about the shaking, the thing none of the others can explain—hard, rocking seizures through my body for hours every day. The Healer tells me not to worry. "The shaking," The Healer says, "is the animal that needs to dance."

⇌

I start feeling things I've never felt before.

Ruby walks into the kitchen, and even though my back is turned and I didn't hear her come in, I violently start to convulse. Nausea and anxiety rip through me. I double over and see her staring at me with open mouth. "Oh my God, I did that," she says, and I realize it's true. She had been in a high panic over a friend in Brazil—nauseous and afraid, and when she walked into the kitchen, her emotions leapt into my body. That's the only explanation we have for it, but even though I'm directly experiencing it every day, I find it hard to believe.

A man sits down next to me at the doctor's office, and my head is immediately gripped with blinding pain until I instinctively stumble to a chair across the room from him, where the pain leaves as suddenly as it appeared.

Grocery stores are sickening and overwhelming. Everyone's body feels loud and demanding of my body to carry its sensations. I pass someone and need to weep, then another person and need to scream. My left shoulder starts shaking and doesn't stop—it jerks and trembles for ten days straight. My hands crack and pop with electrical current, and they ache to be able to touch—that stranger's rigid neck, that stranger's weary knees. I'm nauseous with the amount of information that floods me every time I leave the house, terrified too, and wildly fascinated.

Ruby and I start to play with it. "Read my body," she commands. And not knowing how I'm doing it, I do. I let my eyes follow the subtle lines of movement through her body and information drops down into my brain: sadness in the solar plexus, sharp rage in the jaw, ache in the left foot. I tell her what I see. "Yes," she says. "Yes!"

Late at night, in bed, we run experiments. She thinks of a place on her body and sees if I can guess it. I get it right every time.

"How are you doing this?" she whispers.

"I don't know. I don't know." I'm scared of it. Don't want anyone to know. Some mornings I wake up so dizzy, I can't lift my head. I wrap the pillow around my ears and spin and spin in the darkness.

When I tell The Healer about it, she says "Vertigo is common when the brain is rewiring."

"Rewiring for what?"

"There's a reason all this is happening, Dayna. You're learning something infinitely important."

This is not enough information for me. I'm convinced I'm going crazy, developing Tourette's or some kind of rare neurological disease. I write to everyone I can think of to ask for help. I write to Arnold Mindell, the psychologist whose work I study. I write to my friend who is a doctor, and friends of friends who are doctors, and I write to dancers and spiritual teachers. I say, "What is this? Is this transformation? Is this sickness? Please explain. I shake and shake every day unless I dance, and when I dance, it is wild, uncontained, sometimes terrifying. The way my body becomes not my own, the way my body is literally moved by forces I cannot see but now sense, rippling through the core of all of us."

Many intelligent and kind people write me back. They pass my email around to their people. Someone in Mexico responds and then someone in Ireland. They say, "I'm sorry; I've never heard of what is happening to you. But trust it. Can you just trust it?"

I'm angry, frustrated, scared, sad. No, I can't just *trust* it. My body is going crazy. I must have some rare disease; I must need medication. There's got to be something wrong with me.

Some of the people who write back use words like "kundalini awakening" and "spiritual emergence."

"Sometimes the body gets sick to get better," they say. "Sometimes it's not sickness that causes the symptoms—it's a spiritual crisis, the body trying to show you the path for your soul."

"It's all new age bullshit," I tell The Healer in her green-carpeted office. "A 'premature kundalini awakening'? Really? I looked it up, and they tell you not to go near computers or cell phones or read any spiritual texts, because it will make it worse."

"Is it worse when you do those things?"

"Yes. But there must be other explanations for that."

"Listen, Dayna," she says, very serious, her head cocked to the side. "No one is put through the fire like this unless they are being trained to do important work. Trust the process. Let yourself not know. Don't name it. This is how we learn something new."

I break and cry ragged sobs into my hands. "Why is it so *hard*?" I ask her. The pain is back today, and I can barely sit down; I'm sweating cold water down the back of my neck. There is all this weeping in my body, this screaming. The word "help," is in the deep heart, but it can't make it to my mouth.

The Healer is patient. She puts her hand on my shoulder. She says, "Can you tell me what you are angry with yourself for?"

⇌

That I'm terrible at love. That I leave them all without explanation, in bars, in bedrooms, in foreign countries, among gleaming eggplants and oranges in narrow supermarket aisles. That I have never been faithful and don't know how to. That I am able to tear down good people like a wrecking ball that hits in the exact spot of greatest structural weakness. I write it all down on a piece of paper and give it to The Healer. "What are you angry with yourself for?" At the top of my list is "Ryan."

Ryan, who would leave through the back door of Ruby's parents' house with his hands jammed in his pockets and a grimace on his face, after shouting for an hour, "Why can't you be with me? *Just* me? Why can't you just commit to this?"

He always called later, in between his EMT shifts. "This woman stuck a fork in her vagina. She wouldn't let me near her. She was bleeding to death in front of us. Gary had to tackle her from behind to get the knife out of her hand. I'm too young for this job, D. I love you. I fucking hate how much I love you."

I'd cry when I heard these stories, hating how hard it was for him, hating how hard the world was. He'd come over when he finished, smelling of hospital soap and cigarettes. "I'm sorry," I told him, all the time.

"That's all? That's all you have to say?" he says tonight, sitting on the edge of Ruby's bed, his head in his hands.

"I'm sorry," I say again.

"You don't care about anyone or anything other than yourself. You know that, right?"

I don't say anything, so he stands and strides purposefully to the back door. "I'm gone," he says. The porch light is yellow in his straight, dark hair. He holds his keys in his fist, his white EMT shirt haphazardly buttoned. I want to touch him, but my stomach is screaming. I grip it, as though I could contain the pain. "Okay," I say, because it seems right that he should leave me.

He's halfway to his car when he turns back. "Someday, Dayna"—and he smiles, shaking his head—"someday, I swear to God, you're gonna realize you want to be with me. That you *can* be with me. And I'm gonna be getting married. And you're gonna come to my wedding, and you're gonna cry."

⇄

He will be right.

I will find a cheap ticket for Greece that week, and it will be years before I see him again. I don't go to his wedding, but I see the pictures on Facebook, their gleaming smiles, and it does make me cry. Not because I want to be her, but because I want to be *them*. Because he became what I couldn't: a shape that fits into the grid of the world.

⇄

On the night before I leave for Greece, Carlos calls and asks if I will come over to say goodbye. He opens the door in his pajamas and hugs me like I am a friend. We lie down on his bed and talk, chatting quietly about his work at the hospital, his family back in Cuba, my plans for Greece. He says, "What is this kind of dance that you love, contact improvisation?" We have danced a hundred salsa dances, but I have never shown him the form that has my deepest fascination. Contact improvisation is a dance done primarily in partners and trios, acrobatic and physical, at times looking and feeling like wrestling, other times like an intimate, touch-based meditation with another.

"There are baseline principles that contact dancers learn,"

I explain to Carlos. "Not moves, but a foundation for moves —how to stay in contact with another body as you dance, how to share weight, how to lift each other with minimal effort, how to fall to the floor with grace. And then we meet in what's called a 'jam' to improvise together with this set of shared principles."

Carlos nods, taking it all in. Then he hops to his feet on the bed and holds out his hand. "Show me."

I accept his hand up and lean my shoulder into his. "Push your shoulder into my shoulder with the exact same resistance I'm giving to you. Like we are holding a penny between our two bodies—yes, just like that. Then just follow the movement that happens—don't *make* it happen, *let* it happen."

He catches on immediately. I don't need to talk anymore, and we just start moving together—from the bed to the floor to standing to falling, with a fluid grace I have rarely found, even with experienced contact dancers. I feel myself instantly let go of all plan or expectation in order to more precisely follow the immediate path of our bodies as they move in sync. Our senses hone their perception: I know where the ground is, I know where my feet are, I know where his hands and his head and his hips are, without needing to see them. The air turns luminous, infused with the charge of creativity, as we witness the dance between us unfold.

Finally, exhausted, we find ourselves curled on the floor between the bed and the closet, forehead to forehead. I hold his dreadlocked head in my hands. Our eyes anchor softly to each other. "What makes you happy?" I ask. "What makes life worth living for you?"

"Soccer," he says without hesitation. "My mother. Swimming in the ocean." He pauses. I wrap and unwrap his soft locks around my fingers. "And this dance with you," he says. "That made me happy."

The pain in my pelvis is finally quiet as my body pulses with the strength that comes after dancing. The tiger stretches her supple body within me, offering new meaning to the poet Mary Oliver's words: "You only have to let the soft animal of your body love what it loves."

"What makes life worth living for you?" Carlos returns the question, massaging my arm with his strong surgeon's fingers.

"I don't know yet," I say. "I guess I'm going to Greece now to find out."

I think about my father. Of the moment, years ago, when he also had no answer to that question, and decided to leave us—violently, finitely. I think about all of the ways we abandon each other, creating memories that sink deep and settle in the lining of us, to hurt sometimes, with small or terrible intensity. In order to remind us that we are marked, daily, by our loves. Marked by the ways we fail or succeed at loving. Marked by the ways in which we leave. A kind of map that lives in the body, waiting for us to follow it in, all the way to the center of ourselves, to the soft animal, to home.

2.

PÁROS, GREECE

2007

It is spring, but the house still smells like the Greek winter: damp, olives, fermented grapes. It has two twin beds and a window out to the sea. Here it is—a house of my own. The first thing I had done when I arrived to Páros was to ask the owner of a waterfront bar if he was hiring. He looked me up and down with dark, amused eyes as I stood there with my backpack, literally just off the boat, and he said, "Can you start tomorrow?"

I asked him if he knew of any houses for rent. He called a friend, who called another friend, who called yet another friend, who arrived ten minutes later and took me on his motorbike up the hill. He shouted back to me in broken English that he didn't know the man with the apartment, but he would tell him that I am his friend, so that he won't jack up the price.

The landlord is a short, fat man with no shirt on, whose wife, when he asked her for the keys to the apartment, slammed them down on the table rather than handed them to him. He shows me the place, while my new friend, whose name I don't know, chats politely with him in Greek until we all end up outside again on the terrace under the lemon trees, and the tone shifts suddenly. My friend asks about the price.

The landlord says something absurd, and now my friend leaps into offense—no more polite tenses, he explodes with anger, throwing his hands, palm up, in front of him. The landlord matches him, and they argue, gesturing wildly, until a decent price is found. As quickly as it began, the argument falls away. They smile, clap each other on the back.

My new friend relays the information as we pull away on his bike. I need to meet him tomorrow morning after he calls the guy again, and if the price is still the same, we'll pick up the key. Such help! Such willingness to be there for friends of friends of friends. I am effusive with my gratitude, but he waves away my thank-yous.

And just like this, it happens.

The rain drifts down from the sky, and I am on the back of a motorbike, weaving through the rutted streets, holding on to the body of a stranger, his clean, white T-shirted shoulder against my mouth. In my veins, there's a searing kind of love, to be driving through Greece like this, through smell pockets of warm piss and then fresh rain, past emaciated puppies clambering up from someone's rocky yard. Goats are paused, watching wide-eyed, mouths open, on the terraced hillside. He stops the bike so that I can touch a yellow, rain-soaked flower. Then we are racing again, through lines of traffic, past Albanian men standing together with weathered, watchful faces, the sea, the sea, the sea everywhere around us. Just like this, it happens. A wild, dark freedom unlocks in my body. Beauty is enough. More than happiness. More, even, than love.

⇌

My old writing teacher, Jack, grabs me by the shoulders. It has been over four years since I've seen him. "You're a woman now!" he says, shaking me. "A woman!" He has not aged at all. His silver hair is cut short, and he is wearing the same black he has always worn, his shirt buttoned to the top, a tight grip around his leathery, tan neck. Four years ago, I was one of three students at a school he had just started. We lived in a giant, empty hotel that was closed for the off-season, and classes consisted of long Greek dinners beside the sea, drinking copious amounts of wine as we discussed writing, love, philosophy. During the day, we were encouraged to do whatever we wanted. One of us spent her time visiting churches as she considered becoming a nun, another wrote poetry and had her first kiss. I wrote too and learned Greek and fell hopelessly in love with a Greek boy who couldn't care less about me. It was the best education I've ever had. Now, word of Jack's school has spread, and it is an entirely different animal than what I once knew. Instead of an abandoned hotel, he has his own building now, where teachers teach classes that the students have to go to. The thirty or so of them move through town in a pack, shiny and foreign and beautiful. They fall off chairs and tables and balconies and once—"For art!" she claimed—took a shit in the middle of the dance-club floor. Or so the local Greeks tell me, with bright eyes and wicked smiles. They pretend to hate the students, but really they love the students. Besides giving them good stories to tell and spending excessive amounts of money in their bars and restaurants, they are also mostly women who are young and free and want to have lots of sex, which more than balances out the shitting and concussions.

Jack leads me back through the bar, through the crowd of

them dancing hard to Lyrics Born, and pushes me at the DJ, a skinny, pale guy in a wifebeater and a sideways-tilted cap. "Quin, this is the person I've been telling you about. This is Dayna."

Quin pulls off his headphones and grins at me. "Oh. Wow. Hi." He has a short, reddish beard and a wide smile.

"He's been talking to you about me?" I shout over the music. "How long have you been here?"

"Two years. And yeah. He's been talking about you for two years."

I am glad for the dark to hide my blush. "We're having dinner tomorrow night," Jack says. "You, me, Quin. Ten. At Christos restaurant. See you there."

Quin meets my eyes, still smiling. I can see he knows Jack as well as I do—there's no arguing with him. He shrugs. "I guess I'll see you tomorrow, then." The song is ending, so he pulls his headphones back over his ears and focuses on his computer. I watch his long fingers as they expertly adjust the levels on the soundboard. He bobs his head, pulling on his chin hair with his other hand. I'm curious about him but also don't want to stay any longer. I want to get out of the bar, where I am surrounded by too many Americans. All the art school kids know the words to the song that blares next, and they shout them: "Tried to make me go to rehab, but I said no, no, no!"

Quin catches my wrist as I turn to go. "You're leaving?"

"Yeah."

"Why?"

I smile apologetically. "Your music sucks." I mean it as a joke, but it comes out wrong.

He shrugs and says, not unkindly, "You're a snob." He

turns back to his music, and I am held there for a moment, wanting something—to apologize, or explain. His neck is pale white, his bare shoulders covered in amber freckles. I reach out to touch his hand. "Sorry. I've been back on the island for only a couple of days. I don't want to be around my country."

He's busy queuing up the next song, but he pauses to look at me with soft eyes. "I feel you, man," he says and twists his wrist so that my hand is in his hand. He squeezes it. "I'll see you tomorrow."

⇌

The next day, it rains torrential the way it does on the island in early spring, the roads turned into rivers bleeding out to the sea. I trudge through the streets to show up at the restaurant, sopping and shivering. "Do you want to go to my house and change your clothes?" Quin asks me.

"No," I say. "It's fine; these pants are quick dry."

For the rest of the night, he keeps asking me that, and I keep saying that. Jack shows up for a minute to pay for the dinner, claps us both on the shoulder, and leaves again. I've been on the island three days, and already I am on a date. It annoys me. I am cold. The pants don't dry as quick as they claim to. We drink a lot of wine. I learn that he is from Boston, a painter, who teaches classes at Jack's art school, among a million other things he does for Jack.

"Seriously, do you want to change your pants?"

After enough wine, I concede.

At his house he kisses me; it is sloppy and toothy. I feel panic rising in my chest like floodwater.

"Listen, I don't want to have sex."

"Oh." He steps back, his face closing a little.

"I'm sorry," I say. "I know this island. Where you can sleep with four people in an afternoon if you feel like it. I'm not into it right now."

"Right." he says. "Sure, no problem." But I can see that he's hurt, thinks it is a personal offense against him.

I leave feeling sad. I had liked how easy it was to talk to him, his laid-back city drawl, the way he called me "man" and listened intently to my answers to his questions. *I should have just kissed him*, I think. *Now he won't want anything to do with me.* But I don't want a lover, and I certainly don't want a boyfriend. I have been tethered by illness for two years, and now I don't want anything to touch me unless I'm sure it will not grip me.

It is just past midnight, and the rain has cleared. I pull my clothes off one by one and dive into the sea beside the road. The cold is like bright silk against my body. I feel my ring slide from my finger, the one my mother gave me before I left home. I thrash for a second, trying to find it, but the water is black, the depth unknowable. I'd loved the ring, but I realize I am relieved to have lost it. To be sucked clean by the sea like that, to be naked in the night, and alone.

⇌

After days of relentless wind and rain, the sun finally emerges. I walk the rutted, rocky streets down from my new house into town, all the farmers out in their fields surveying the damage with hands on their hips and deep frowns. Beyond them the flat, still sea, a blue rain echo.

One of the farmers beckons to me as I pass, wiping at his face with a red handkerchief.

"*Poli nero*," he says, a lot of water, and waves at the gushing creek by the side of the road.

"*Nei*," I agree politely. "*Poli nero.*"

His smile broadens into a grin, gap-toothed and excited to discover that I understand Greek. He hobbles down to the road, leaning heavily on his wooden cane, then waves it around, pointing at things. "*Na to*," he says, look at this, and he pulls me over to show me the tight green buds on the end of a thin, wiry bush. He invites me to hold it in my fingertips, first one bud and then another—hard, but also yielding, like a fist holding tight to something impossibly soft. He motions me very close to him, down, next to the buds on the branches and whispers, "*Ih Aniksi*."

"What is it that you love so much about Greece?" Ruby wrote in her last letter.

I have spent days answering her in my head.

I love the wailing Greek pop music people play loud from their radios in public spaces with no regard for others around them. I love the very small, very attentive ways that beauty is created, like fresh flowers in the vase on the café table beneath the sloping almond tree and the perfectly sliced strawberry on my margarita glass. I love the sea—its cold embrace of my body, the two million blue shades of it, the ever-changing moods of it, the stillness and the thrash. I love the sage smell of the hills, the rustle of lizards in the stone walls, and the shape —like a sound you might make with your mouth—of the round, blue church domes. I love the food that comes drenched with flavor: the rich buttery olive oil, still slightly green; the eggplants that taste like they have had wonderful, full lives beneath hot sunshine; the cheese that is sprinkled with oregano and unfolds, cold-sour, in my mouth. I love the late-night heat that collects in the plastic-awning–wrapped patios of the restaurants and outside of them, the fresh, cool breeze up from the water.

Most of all, I love the feeling in my body when I'm here. Like all of me, every part, can finally come to the surface, take a breath, bloom.

"Yes," I say to the farmer as he squeezes my hand in his weathered one. "*Ih Aniksi.*" The spring. Which means, literally, "the opening."

⇌

Quin is having coffee on the waterfront when I walk by, and he beckons me over. "I've been thinking about what you said . . . about having sex with four people in an afternoon," he says with no preamble. "I realized this island has fucked with my head."

I laugh. "This is Páros. It exists to fuck with your head." I adjust my heavy bag from one shoulder to the other. "I lived here for a year. I can only imagine being here two."

He nods. "Yeah. Yeah. Well, I just wanted to say thank you. And . . . can we be friends? Do you want to hang out?"

"Sure," I say, surprised and touched. "When?"

He looks around and then pulls out the chair beside him. "How 'bout right now?"

"All right," I say, laughing.

He'll tell me later that it was the moment he knew he was in love. "Like getting kicked in the face," he'll say.

I didn't know yet what I felt. Not attraction, not exactly.

But something like a deep relief when I sat next to him—
dropping what I was carrying and just sinking in beside him,
my body like a room that's been silent, suddenly flooded with
the warmth and the comfort of music.

⇌

Also, I love the nights.

The bars that burn deep into the darkness like long, slow
candles.

My work at the café finishes at 3:00 a.m., and then my
night begins. I head down to the place Quin DJs, a whitewashed, sea-facing bar called Club Marie, with a small dance
floor that is always full. *This is what it's like to be in my twenties,* I think as I walk, tired, a little bit drunk, my pocket full
of tips from the long work shift. I finally get to be that—in
my twenties—not sick anymore, thanks to the slow and
steady guidance of The Healer, though not yet climbing
mountains like that doctor said I should be. I still shake every
day, and sometimes the pain comes back, but most of the
days, most of the time, I now get to be something so completely normal: *twentysomething.* A hanging, waiting age,
where you're not anybody yet, but expected to be. So you
wait in the bar. Dance, until nothing else matters. *I'm in
Greece, and nothing matters.*

At 4:30 a.m., Club Marie, in accordance with the law,
shuts its doors and turns out the lights. Everyone inside stays
inside, the music fueling our secret dances in the darkness
while the police cruise slowly down the road, watching for
slipups: shreds of light or a few notes of wild, naked music in
the now quiet streets. The sun turns the sea morning, every-

thing copper red, and I dance. I dance till it is not me who is dancing anymore, till the whole group of us is churning and replacing each other. A girl beside me, her belly slipping somehow gracefully over the top of her jeans, places her finger over her lip like a mustache as she dances—it's Eminem singing, "I'm Slim Shady, yes, I'm the real Shady," and I do it too, grinning, our finger mustaches some kind of acknowledgement that we spin back to each other.

At 7:00 a.m. we go to Café Mira for breakfast and beers before bed. I sit in the crook of someone's arm, Quin on my other side, slumped with exhaustion, drinking Mythos from a two-pint mug. Sweat and dark blue under his eyes, he touches my skin where my shirt has pulled up from my hip. "Dayna?" he says.

I close my eyes, smell morning—crepes and salt and oregano from the turning-hot hills. The girl with the finger mustache orders a salami sandwich. "You see," the Irishman is saying. We are having a conversation, though I have forgotten what about. He puts his finger on my knee. "Seattle would be here. And this"—he traces up my femur bone—"this is San Francisco. Fourteen-hour drive."

"Eighteen," I say, remembering.

"And you call it your country!" he laughs.

I open my eyes. Sitting up, I turn back to see that I have been in Petros's arms, a Greek who Quin calls Hercules. His arms are as sculpted as the statues. He shakes his head, amused by our ridiculous conversation. "You have very beautiful feet," he says. I put my head back on his shoulder.

"Ice cream sandwiches," points out the Irishman. "I have one every three hours of the drive. Then count the wrappings. Four and a half. Every time."

"What do you do with the last half?" This is Quin's inter-jection.

The Irishman shrugs. "Throw it out the bloody window." He turns to me, grinning. "Seeing as I've already been eating them for the last fourteen hours!"

"Like a model's feet," Petros continues. I wiggle my toes, breathe in the faint sweat of his body. He whispers in my neck, "Where will you sleep today? You must be too tired to walk that steep hill all the way back to your house."

I shake my head. "You're just like Morgan Kelley."

"Morgan Kelley?" Petros repeats.

"Morgan Kelley was a boy in my kindergarten class."

"Another beer?" the Irishman interrupts me. Vangellis, the owner of the shop, is poking his head out the door. I wave no at him.

"And he was *the* man," I continue. "Every girl wanted to be with him—"

"Just one," the Irishman yells back to Vangellis.

"Girls would worry about it and cry, 'I want Morgan Kelly to be my boyfriend.'"

"So you were giving me a compliment." Petros grins.

"But I knew that he would come to me, eventually. Be-cause Morgan Kelly kissed every single girl in the class. One to the next. One to the next to the next."

"Ahhh." Petros crosses his arms behind his head and grins again. "So you're calling me a pimp."

Vangellis brings the beer. "I need you all to get the fuck out soon," he says. He's been here all night. His eyes are framed with red. The finger-mustache girl pays for her sand-wich and sets off with it. She winks at me first, before she goes. I want to run after her and ask her something—how she does it, that going-home-alone thing, that graceful beauty with a belly. I always wanted to say screw Morgan Kelley, but I never did. I went behind the play plastic kitchen cupboards just like everyone else. And kissed him when I should have been playing with dolls. Or girls. Or both.

"I'll walk you home," Petros offers, standing.

"Yeah, okay." I accept his hand up.

"C'mon mate," groans the Irishman, shaking his head. He'd been angling toward the same thing of course, everyone desperate to not go home alone.

Quin downs his beer. His eyes hold mine. "Dayna," he says again. You don't have to, his eyes say. He inclines his head ever so slightly toward his own house down the alley behind us.

I nod. It is not the first time he has saved me from a bad decision. "No, actually, I'll just sleep at Quin's tonight." Both men groan and turn to glare at Q, who shrugs.

At Quin's house, we listen to music and talk until we have wound down enough to sleep. And then we sleep, not lovers, just quiet, just safe, in his narrow bed, holding on to each other.

⇌

"Why is it so impossible to leave this island?"

Quin and I, in the afternoon, are hanging our feet down from the walls of the Frankish Castle, looking out at the flat, turquoise water.

"I think there's something buried beneath us," he answers. "Some kind of ancient scrolls that explain the nature of everything. And we *sense* it here. Keep thinking that if we stay just a little longer, we'll find that secret, know that secret."

"That's it! That's exactly it." I lean into the comfortable, soft yield of him.

"Otherwise, why else would we stay here? It's the island of broken toys, man."

I laugh. Nearly every resident of the island is some degree of crazy. Even the language itself is bizarre and often impossible to translate. "How from here, morning, morning" they say, and "slow the eggs." I have spent the early part of my work shifts each day trying to improve my Greek—a slow, painstaking process with thus far very little return. Toothless Vacillis, my favorite regular, always sits at the narrow bar and watches me as I copy words from my Greek dictionary onto a notebook. "You are very beautiful," he tells me often. "Very"— he makes curves with his hands—"chubby?"

He is the only one I know who was born and raised on this island. "Ever go anywhere else?" I once asked him.

"One or two times to Athens," he said.

I make him bacon-and-cheese sandwiches, and we talk about *The Little Prince*. Or try to. My Greek: I spit out broken sentences like unchewable pieces of meat. "Was . . . good . . . a book . . . the book . . . an books?" Greek has five different articles: *to, ta, tis, ih, o*. I don't know the correct way to use any of them.

His English: "Is good, one book, very. . . ." Trails away. "I am shy," he says. I applaud his sentence structure. He has the beginnings of a beard, and purple moons under his eyes. True to his nickname, he is missing several teeth, and his front tooth has gone completely brown, like it was just pulled from the mud and stuck into his mouth. I can't tell if he's crazy. Some say he hit his head, hard, some years ago. He doesn't have many friends and still lives with his mother. He wears a red helmet with stickers when he rides his motorbike. "I think I love you," he said last night as I served him a cup of sage tea, and then he blushed deep red.

"Again, perfect grammar." I clapped.

He stared at my mouth and wrinkled his eyebrows as though my words might appear again, suddenly in Greek, printed across my lips.

I can't tell if he's crazy, because all I have to compare him to are the other islanders, each one of them quirkier than the next. Yourgos from the sandwich shop next door is another regular; at noon every day he orders a frappé and a beer and drinks them simultaneously as he begs me for a date. "Just one coffee," he says.

"I'm still saying no."

"Why? Why do you keep doing that?"

Next to him is often Tomas From The Bakery, a short, balding man who is Greek but speaks English with a British accent. He comes with his Polish girlfriend, who doesn't speak Greek or English. "A mail-order bride," my boss, Dimitris, has whispered to me. "One of those women you can buy from the boat and then take her anywhere." She is pale and plump. She sits with her chin on her hands and stares out the window. I always try to smile at her, but she never looks at me.

Just before sunset, an American kid named Chris, from Jack's art school, stops by and says he's taking a poll of all the cafés. He wants to know what our theme song would be. Dimitris is bringing a crate of Heinekens in from the back door, the receipt in his mouth.

"What do you think, D?" I ask him. Yourgos From Next Door is fiddling with the music, attempting to mix a reggae beat with trance. Outside on the patio, the Albanians are drinking Mythos in two-pint mugs, talking quietly in accented Greek.

Dimitris takes the receipt from his mouth, thinks for a moment. "I like to party, everybody dance."

Yourgos and Chris begin to sing, dancing in the narrow floor space: "I like to party, everybody dance. Make love and listen to the music. Just let yourself go, go, go, go. . . ."

⇌

"That could be the theme song for the entire island," Quin says when I tell him the story at the Frankish Castle. He takes a drink of his frappé and squints out at the sea. "Mashed with the song from *The Twilight Zone*, of course."

We lean together on the castle wall in the sunshine and laugh till we cry.

Thank God for Quin, I think every day. Our conversations anchor me, our laughter reminds me of who I am and where I come from. Because I also know that the longer you stay on this island, the more likely it is that you too will go crazy.

⇌

I dream I am trying to help my sister dance, but her arms can only move in a cramped, ghoulish kind of way. When I pull at her arm to try and extend it, an energy snaps through her, at me, and her face is that dark evil that I have dreamed of before—*what my father's face looked like when he reached for his gun.* I rocket out of sleep with a scream, and Quin grabs me tight against him. "I'm here, it's okay, I'm here," he whispers.

He told me at dinner last night of his first love, a girl who had a mental breakdown and walked naked into the fountain of a hotel lobby. A girl he proposed to—red-cheeked and skinny eighteen-year-old that he was—in the dirty bathroom of a Montreal bar. "I was crazy too," he said, and I watched the light from his body recede, a little deeper into him. Quin is the child of two schizophrenics who slept with each other in the psych ward. He was adopted by Italian Americans who already had two biological kids, and he grew up with them in a suburb of Boston.

I touched his chest lightly over the table. "What do you feel here?" I asked.

He was taken aback. "What do I *feel?*" he said. "Um. Your hand?" Then he stopped. "A tightness," he said, and a bit of his chest released just to admit it.

"Sadness?" I asked, and he nodded immediately.

"A lot of that," he said.

Later, in his dark basement apartment, we danced. He played me his favorite dancehall songs, and I did impressions of all the island characters—Jack and Yourgos and Toothless Vacillis—dance portraits. Then he asked me to do him. I tried on his body, imitating his movement, and what came surprised us both. A sweet, searching quality—a sincere and urgent desire to give, a sad longing for someone to accept his offering. "Wow," he said, shaking his head with tears in his eyes. "That's it. That's me, man."

In bed later, my head on his chest, sliding into sleep, he said, "I understand why you didn't want to have sex. This is so much better." He kissed my hand, my knuckles and my palm. "I've never had anyone feel me like that. My sadness, I mean."

I squeezed him tight, and he squeezed me. "I feel so

much, I don't know what to do sometimes," he whispered. "I can't let myself feel it, 'cause I'm scared. But I think I need to feel it."

"I know. I'm here," I whispered back, right before I dropped into dreams.

Hours later, when I wake screaming from the family demon, he holds me and whispers the same thing.

⇌

We are not lovers.

I come home to him with hickeys on my neck, from a Greek man after work.

"Was it something?" he asks.

"Nah, it was nothing."

We sleep with the island clasped between our bodies— our shared, impossible love for this place.

Sometimes we stay in bed until the sun sets, until we both have to go to work again. He plays me the music he loves, and I play him the music I love. I introduce him to Fat Freddy, and he wants to hear it over and over again: "Something magic in the way you touch me."

"It's so good, it makes me want to fuck the speaker," he says.

I ask him about the home in the Boston suburbs he swears he'll never go back to. "It could have been a museum of middle-class things, man. Doilies with hearts. Little plaques that say cheesy things about the house. I remember one of the last times I was there. This spider, size of a flea, had strung a line between my glass and the pepper shaker. Right over my bowl of cereal, you know, just the milk left. It's 3:00 a.m. I can't sleep for shit. And this spider, it sets out over this giant canyon of milk. I watched it for an hour. It was the most intensely beautiful thing I've ever seen."

I find him intensely beautiful. I rarely go home to my own bed anymore, consumed by slow pulling in my body, wanting to always be close to him, wrap myself in him. I try to hold back, terrified to imagine the intricate, artful, exciting friendship we have built placed in the wrecking ball path, doomed to implode like all my other romantic relationships. I know I could not, and I do not want to, give up my free nights—kissing sweating, muscled, dark-eyed European tourists on the dance floor as the sun rises and finally no one, absolutely no one, harmed by these actions. He knows this, agrees with me; he holds back too. We both try to hold back. We hold back for as long as we can.

⇄

And then one day, we just don't anymore.

It's our day off, so we buy apricots, cherries, milk chocolate, and a bottle of water and rattle up the mountain in his beat-up blue car to Kolymbithres. To a house that stands in the lonely, windswept way that houses do here: square, whitewashed, hunkered down against the backdrop of bare, brown hills. The house belongs to his friend who is away in Africa. We sit on the patio and contemplate the rolling, rocky land in silence for what feels like hours, days. There's one donkey in the corner of the field, chewing slowly on thistles, the water sound of the goat bells trickling up from the valley. It is early summer now, hot in the days and cold at night. When the sun begins its descent, we retreat into the whitewashed stone bedroom, and he draws me with charcoal while I read with my back against the red velvet cushions. Wind washes through the open window, the room deep orange with the last of the sun. He brings the drawing to me when he is finished, and it is beautiful to see how well he sees me, my double chin as I read, the softness in my shoulders, my tired eyes. "Ah, my weak chin," I sigh.

"It's beautiful," he says, running a finger from my chin down my throat. Our eyes meet and then, finally, we just let it happen—let it seep out of our skins and into the other, the love we've been building. He kisses me, and he kisses me, and I kiss him back, my hands on his shoulders and the back of his head, threaded through his russet hair. We kiss, and we kiss, and we kiss, until the sun has set, and we can take no more of it, the emotion cascading and overwhelming between our bodies. Without a word, he takes my hand, and we emerge from the house into darkness. We pick our way quietly through the stones of the field and then stand so still that the donkey forgets us and wanders close, the sound of her chewing like comfort—the sound of sustenance.

He says, "Listen, I just realized that this, between us, is too important. It's more important than fear. It's more important than jealousy."

"I love you," I tell him. "But I can't be anyone's girlfriend. I don't like it. I don't believe in it. I'm not good at it."

He grips my hand. "I get it," he says. "I really do. Your heart must be allowed wings."

"If you can say that, and mean that, then you will have all of me."

"I don't want to have all of you. I just want to love you."

We kiss again, the stars burning fierce holes through the

quiet night above us. "Then let's do that," I say. "Let's do that together."

⇌

I talk to my mother on the phone for five minutes before the connection is lost. She does not try to call back. I am not sad nor homesick. I go to take a shower and come out to Quin spooning hot lentil soup into a bowl for me, and I feel it—he is my home now. We kiss each other desperately and hungrily in the kitchen. "I love our relationship," he says, finding my eyes. "It's like having a best friend who I'm attracted to. I love making love with you. But I don't care if we don't do it. I'm just as happy to kick it with you."

The days are full of him. I move out of my own place and into his—to save rent, we both say, but know it is really because we can't stand not being together. I come home to him after work, exhausted at 5:00 a.m., and he listens as I recount the night, meaningless stories and conversations with customers unwinding from my brain. "I asked one of our regulars how he was when I gave him his beer. You know, '*Yasu, Yourgo, ti kannis simera?*'"

"Yourgos From Next Door?"

"Yeah. So he looks at me and he goes, 'Rabbits.'"

Quin chokes on his laughter. "You asked him how he was, and he said 'rabbits'? What does that *mean*?"

"Another customer grabbed me by the arm and said in English, 'Screw the sardine. Take the white snapper.' And then he chuckled his head off. I have no idea. I have no idea."

We laugh until I'm too tired to laugh anymore, until sleep overcomes me, and then, when I am deep in dreams, he draws me. Says he likes it best if I am drunk, because then I don't move.

In the morning, he shows me his paintings, and we think up names for them: *The World Gets Bigger*, *It Went Quiet All of a Sudden*, *Marital Sex*. He tells me about his painter obsession with light in college. Every day at a different time, painting the view from his window. Every night at 2:00 a.m. on the streets with his headlamp, trying to understand how to capture the colors of the darkness.

He makes eggs with rice and fresh salad, and we eat it in bed among his canvasses. "You know that I have never felt this before," he says, grabbing my hand, making sure I hear it.

"Yes," I say, "me too." And I mean it.

The word "love" has finally become fluid, unweighted. I love him, and I tell him I love him, and it means nothing more than it is. On nights when I don't work, I go to the bar where he DJs, and he plays songs for me while other men kiss me on the dance floor. He laughs when I ask him later if it was okay for him. He says, "That's what I played the song for."

But sometimes we talk about the winter, about buying a small house on the cliffs above the sea, planting a garden, raising chickens. Having children. These longings emerge from a place in me that I don't all the way recognize, a younger version of myself that expects my adulthood to look a certain way—house, husband, kids. I close my eyes and imagine Quin and me finding a place where we both could arrive at and stay, finally safe, together. But all I can see is how quickly I would abandon it all for the experience of a wilder thing.

⇌

We hear the child screaming before we see him, tugged by his mother, her hand gripping around his upper arm, and she is nearly lifting him. His feet tangle and scrape along the cement road. I sit at the edge of the street with my boss, Dimitris. Work has not yet begun, and it is that slow hour before sunset, when even the man who walks the Paralia all night with a fistful of balloons doesn't care yet about anything but the rose rinse of the light on the sea and the hilltops. He stands, ten feet down from the crying boy, whose mother has sat him on one of our chairs and is waiting, with arms crossed, for him to stop wailing. The boy screams and shakes and kicks his heels against the wooden chair legs. The balloon man closes his eyes and lets the light wash his face clean.

"Let's close early today," Dimitris sighs. "I feel like that boy." He nods with his chin at the wailing child. "Or that guy." He nods at the tired balloon man. "You know, sometimes you just don't want to do it anymore."

Dimitris is tall and reminds me of Gregory Peck's Atticus: his broad shoulders, his gentle and serious eyes, his even, mild temperament. Besides the bar, he owns another restaurant on the beach, and every hour of the summer days is spent working there or here. I often ask him how he does it, and he shrugs, "Eh, it's only six months. And then. Beach. A nice whisky. Bliss." He is one of the rare ones on the island who appears to be entirely and completely sane. Sometimes his wife, a beautiful Italian, and his wild-haired, precocious two-year-old daughter will visit us at the bar. He'll sit quietly at a table with his wife by the sea and drink coffee while I entertain his daughter. I chase her among the tables and chairs as she shouts questions at me in Greek: Why do you speak funny? Why is your hair curly? Why are your shoes so ugly?

"Closing early" means that tonight we lock up at 2:00 a.m. rather than 3:00, but it doesn't mean work is over. It's now time for what Dimitris calls "public relations"—in other words, going to as many bars in Parikia as we can in order to have a drink and say hello to the owners. "Public relations" is the only marketing tool on the islands. If you're friends with the other business owners, they'll send tourists your way. If you're not, watch out. One person who hates you will close you. I have seen several bars fade into oblivion from the rumors circulated to unsuspecting tourists. "Don't go there, the owner drugs girls and takes them in the back room; don't go there, the cook ejaculates into the soup." None of it true, but on an island with new boatloads of tourists every day, it doesn't matter. People will believe anything they're told.

So we do the rounds. Smiling, chatting, talking business, making fun of the tourists. The summer is in full swing now, and the streets are crammed with them. Crowds carrying backpacks and water bottles, their Teva sandals clunking on the white-painted stones. They take pictures of everything— the red geraniums in pots on the doorsteps, the fat stray dogs, the bedraggled kittens, the overgrown ruins—so ubiquitous that those of us who live here barely see them anymore. Everyone wears stripes—red and white, white and navy blue.

I was nineteen when I arrived in Greece as one of them. I had left my own country for the first time to come to a supposed school here, and I was terrified—young, unworldly, with a suitcase full of my mother's shirts because we assumed that all of my own tank tops would be too revealing for an orthodox country. I stepped out of the Athens airport that summer into blistering white heat and throngs of knife-thin women wearing miniskirts and halter tops, and that was the beginning of feeling wildly embarrassed and huge and foreign for months on end. "Don't worry," Jack had said to me at dinner that night, at a tiny table in the Plaka, beneath swooning purple boughs of bougainvillea. "Just stay here a while. More than most Americans do. Then you will become European."

Though I was only supposed to stay three months, I followed his advice and stayed the year. Up until that point, I had done everything right by American standards. I was a straight A student and a dedicated athlete. I had spent nearly every single weekend of my childhood, from age eight to age eighteen, competing in volleyball or soccer tournaments. My best friend was a football-playing Mormon whose wealthy family I adopted as my own. Every day after volleyball practice, I was over at his house, eating frozen pizza and watching sports on his big-screen TV. I didn't allow any of my friends over to my house, where I thought I was poor because our house was small and the cupboards were always understocked with food, compared to my friends' houses. My mother was obsessed with being outside, and the decor of our home resembled a tent. My sister and I literally slept in sleeping bags every night. Whenever she could, my mother was out backpacking in the wilderness, dressed atrociously in ripped hand-me-downs. I knew I didn't come from normal. And then, of course, there was that story about my dad to keep on the DL.

When I got to Greece, none of that mattered. No one knew where I came from, and if I did tell them, it didn't mean the same thing here that it did at home. In Greece I came from no story and could be anyone I wanted to be. The freedom was intoxicating. I drank and had sex and stayed out till sunrise; I plunged off the good-girl ledge I'd been perched on and learned how to swim in a much more complicated ocean.

That year, Greece, and who I was there, became as comfortable as a favorite dress, one I never wanted to take off again. I wanted to see every season on the island and then see it again. I wanted to bind the land and the people around my body, the beauty and the beauty's shadow—the empty rattling streets of the winter, the waves crashing up over the parked cars and dragging them out to sea, just the locals left, in it together, crazy together. I learned that I did not want to just pass through a place, be a tourist, take a picture and go. I was consumed with a feverish need to crash into the entirety of people and places, to know them fully, love them fully. I left Greece that first time with the realization that the surface of anything would never be enough for me. My own country on return felt bland, tired, desperately uptight. I fought hard to get back to Greece, and now that I'm back, I long to never leave again, but it is not for the same reason that the tourists say it. The tourists all "absolutely love it here." They want to stay forever, they say. Tonight, an art-school mom with her son, at a table beside Dimitris and me, is talking about buying a café. "Why not?" she says, shrugging. She holds her cocktail straw with peach, manicured fingernails. I imagine her in the winter, sweeping floodwater from her café back into the street, and I know that she doesn't actually want that, it's not what she's looking for—the winter that lies forgotten on the other side of this heat, that only those who stay beyond the summer know. The bars and restaurants boarded up, save for a few small ones that stay open for the bedraggled locals who come and drink until they fight—lovers gripping each other by the hair, screaming, until someone thinks to separate them. Most people don't want to see or know that shadow. But for me, it pulls like a siren song.

The last winter I was here, out in front of Club Marie one night, I saw a man standing on the seaweed-strewn beach, speaking intensely to a woman who was on her knees, crying very quietly. His voice rose, and he hit her, his whole body thrown into the movement. She crumpled onto her side, and he hit her again, across the other cheek, but she didn't scream, her sobs muffled by her hands across her mouth. On the street, a Dutch man was passing—a rare winter traveler, on the island for a night before moving on. He stopped and stared at the couple for a moment before starting toward them. "Hey!" he shouted. "Hey!"

"*Ade yia gamesu*," the man cursed, go fuck yourself, and yanked his girlfriend to her feet. The Dutch man shook his head but obeyed, backing off.

"He shouldn't do that," he muttered to me, and I nodded but said nothing. What is unacceptable in my country, or in the Dutch man's country, is not what's unacceptable here on this island. I had once bumped my head on the corner of a door one drunk night, and for weeks after, when people saw the bandage, they said, not joking at all, "What did you do to piss off your boyfriend?"

The woman I saw on the beach five years ago is our bartender now. She has dark curly hair and big, bright eyes, and she doesn't mind when I hug her for no apparent reason. "Maria," she tells me is her name. I'm tipsy enough to tell her the story, how I saw her, how I wished I'd done something, how I would do something now. She purses her lips and shakes her head. "But what could you have done? Nothing. He was just an asshole. All the men, they hit or cheat or both."

"There is something different about you," Dimitris says

after Maria has left to refill someone else's drinks. He regards me with his quiet eyes. "You are very . . . free in yourself."

"I'm free here," I say, shrugging. "It's the island."

Dimitris nods. "The heart can live an open life here."

"It is only with the heart that one can see rightly," I say, quoting *The Little Prince.*

"Yes! Ha, I like that!" He stands and goes to the corner of the bar where the DJ booth is. "I want to play you a song," he shouts across to me, picking up the DJ's stack of minidiscs. I follow him, lean on the bar.

"Do you cheat on your wife like all the other men here?" I say, not thinking about the question, only wondering. He whips his head up in surprise and then drops all the minidisks he is holding, *crrrunk*, onto the floor. Stands there, his empty hands frozen in space. We are reactionless for a breath. Then we howl with laughter.

"Shit, I'm drunk, Dayna, I'm *kunupithi*," he gasps between laughs.

"Fifteen years!" Maria says, shaking her head.

"Fifteen years!" the men sitting at the bar echo, toasting their glasses, grinning.

"Fifteen years?" I ask Dimitris. He is looking down, still laughing.

"They are talking about our friend," he says. "He is waiting for the perfect girl, the one he dreams of in his head. He calls her Juanita."

"Fifteen years I have been waiting for Juanita!" Maria mimics, holding her head with mock distress, and the others laugh.

"That is what our friend always says," Dimitris explains. "'Fifteen years I have been waiting for Juanita.' Everyone here is looking for the perfect love, and it's never the one that they have."

⇌

As the sun is rising, rich red on the lip of the sea, we stumble home, our public relations finally complete. "To answer your question," he says when we reach the crossroad of our separate directions home, "no, I do not do what the other men do here." He rubs at his eyes and stares out at the brilliant blue water. "*Ah re*, Dayna, now we can go home. I miss my garden," he sighs, and claps me on the shoulder goodbye.

⇌

I wake with the bladder pain again. Quin finds me curled on the bed, shaking, dismantled by it. He pulls a chair into the bathroom and rubs my back while I pee, a sharp, blistering trickle that makes me moan. He kisses me. "I can't kiss you while I pee," I protest.

He holds my head against his mouth. "Let's cross all the boundaries," he says with a smile.

Later, when the pain has passed enough to work again, he comes to visit me at the bar. Petros, who we call Hercules, sits at a table by the street. He is there for me, waiting for me. I'd caved and made out with him two nights ago and then told Quin, almost as a test, to see if he could really do what he'd promised. He winks at me now and goes to sit next to him. T. I. P., he mouths when I give him a look (this is Páros), and then he proceeds to have a long conversation with Hercules, spanning topics from globalization to art history, judging from the snatches I overhear each time I have to pass their table. "Cool guy," Quin tells me when he kisses my cheek goodbye.

"I love you," is all I can say in return, watching him, a little mystified, as he strolls away down the street to work.

"What is it?" Dimitris asks me, noticing the confused look in my eyes as I stand in the doorway to the bar.

"I think I found 'the one,'" I say, inclining my head toward Quin's disappearing back. "I found Juanita."

"Oh, is that all?" he nudges me with his shoulder. "I promise, here, you'll find another one."

⇌

It's my night off, but we go to my work so I can pour the tequila shots for free. Quin and I talk heated and fast, about art and dance and the outer world as a mirror of the inner world, while the house music pumps and the warm wind blows up from the sea.

It's the first night of work for the boy who Dimitris has hired to help during peak times and cover my days off for the rest of the busy season. He comes over to our table to introduce himself. He is wearing tight, white jeans and sports a slicked-back haircut, his lashes long, his teeth tiny. "I'm Stellios," he says, taking my hand in his.

"I'm Dayna."

"Yes, I know."

"You know?"

"Of course. When you see something you want, you find out what it is."

Beside me, Quin chokes back a laugh mid sip of his tequila.

Dimitris beckons for Stellios from inside the bar. "Ah, I love this song!" he says, wiggling his hips as he walks away, singing along with the music, "Girl, you're so sexy, I like your flow, let's do it later, out of controlllllll. . . ."

Quin is shaking with silent laughter against my body. "This island kills me," he gasps. "Dude. When I was talking to Adonis yesterday about going to Israel, he said, 'Eh, Quin, but be careful. In Israel, the devil comes up from the ground.' And he *meant* it!"

We are laughing hard and can barely pull ourselves out of it when Dimitris comes to stand beside our table. He waits patiently for us to settle. "Dayna," he says finally, without sitting down. And then, in Greek: "Can we go around together? Public relations. Just you and me?"

"Oh. Um." I'm not sure why he's said it in Greek so Quin won't understand. "Dimitris wants us to do some PR work," I say to Quin. "Okay if I leave you for a bit?"

"Sure, sure." Quin is still laughing, wiping at his eyes. "I love you. Find me later."

⇋

Instead of taking me to the usual bars we visit, Dimitris turns his motorcycle on the street out of town and drives to his now-empty beach restaurant.

I get off the bike warily, standing among the naked tables and chairs on the patio. "What's going on?"

With no preamble, he pulls me to him, clumsily, like his body has gotten tired of waiting around for what it wants and has snapped, desperate for the quickest route. He kisses my neck forcefully, my ear, my jaw.

I push him away. "Dimitris. What the *fuck*? I can't kiss you."

"Why?" he says, his face a child's suddenly, open and awash with a thousand currents of fear, desire, remorse, hope. Beside us, the midnight sea slips like silk back and forth across the sand.

I count the reasons on my fingers. "Your wife. Your child. You are my *boss*."

"But what if none of those were true?" he says and in the same breath, kisses me, hard, steering me backward, toward the kitchen of the abandoned restaurant.

"No," I say. "No," I pull away, disentangling.

He lets me go. I sit on a table on the patio, angry, scared, sad. From across the restaurant he says, "Listen. I'm crazy for you. You're making me crazy. I can't work. I can't go two minutes without thinking about you."

My body feels deep down on fire and eerily quiet too, from layers of tequila stilling my nerves. I'm thinking about Dimitris's daughter, her wild hair and her fierce eyes.

He comes and puts his hands on my shoulders. "Listen. I respect you. I want to travel with you. You have me thinking crazy thoughts; I feel *crazy*." He cups my face and kisses me again, tenderly, gently, and I can't find the words to stop him this time. In an instant, he has lifted me and carried me to the wall, and I'm fighting my own self now, wanting him and wanting to stop at the same time. I push him off me again, and he stands, breathing hard at the doorway, his back to me, trying to quiet himself. "Are you attracted to me?" he asks.

I cringe, but tell him the truth. "Yes."

He is quiet. Then he says, "I think, Dayna, we have ourselves a problem."

⇌

"Where did you go? That was some PR. It's almost morning."

"Quin. We went to the restaurant. He. . . ."

"Oh my God. Dimitris too?"

"I'm sorry."

"Did you fuck him?"

"No."

"What about his wife?"

"I didn't. I said no."

"Jesus, Dayna."

"I'm confused. You look mad. You don't usually look mad."

"I'm just getting sick of this. We were having such a good night together. And then you left me for *him*. I don't think I can do it anymore."

"I didn't know it was going to happen. I thought it was for work."

"Are you attracted to him?"

"Yes."

"Oh Jesus. Fuck you, Dayna. Really. Fuck you."

⇌

Drinking his usual rum and coke at a seaside café, Jack beckons to me, then pulls me down to sit beside him. "I'm concerned about you," he says. He signals the waiter to bring me a drink. "I heard you've been saying things like 'I just need freedom' to Quin and showing up with hickeys on your neck."

I don't need to ask how he knows this. There are no secrets on this island. "Is there a better way to do it?" I ask.

He leans forward and pins me with his sharp eyes. He is one of the best poets I know, crazy, and a genius. I realize I'm prepared to do whatever he tells me. "Dayna," he says, "you're a *real* woman. You have to remember that. It's selfish and stupid to think that you could ask such a thing of a man you are with—because he will almost always be weaker than you." He runs a hand through his silver hair, smoothing it. "You must lie," he says. "You must learn how to lie. Because to be so honest, well, that is only putting unnecessary stress on the hearts of those who you love."

⇌

Closing the bar, it's just Dimitris and me. The stars are wild and everywhere above the sea, like diamonds flung from Zeus's hand. I lean against the doorway looking out, and he rubs my shoulders. For a moment, I let myself sink, just for a moment, into his touch, but it is enough, a cave in my boundary. With one smooth movement, he scoops me into his arms and then sets me down gently on his lap. I feel small and safe. This is everything about my father, the attraction so obvious it makes me cringe—the grown-upness of him, his tall, strong body, the very sure confidence in his touch. I do not know how to avoid him. I feel stupid, helpless, weak.

In the shower later, the panic seizes me. I shake in near hysterics against the slick wall, my fist pressed against my mouth to keep quiet as it all washes through me, the whole gray world of it: the ripped-up letters to my father that I used to write, that I could never finish, never give; the attention I've gotten from men for as long as I can remember; the way my married college professor would touch my knee, the nauseating mix of desire and repulsion; the slightly sick quality of all of my sexual relationships, that kneading-at-a-bruise feeling, that fascination with the wound and the pain. I can't breathe, naked and shaking against the cold bathroom tile. Quin hears me, and without a word, he climbs, fully clothed, into the shower and holds me. He kisses my shoulder again and again. "It's okay, it's okay, it's okay," he whispers, but something deep inside me knows that it's not, and might never be.

⇌

Dimitris calls again and again. I have four days off work. I ignore him for three. Finally I answer, in the evening, when Quin and I are about to watch a movie and he has gone to the kitchen to make popcorn.

"I have so much to say to you," he says. I can hear the wind whipping in and out of the telephone. "I can't say it like this. I need to see you."

I close my eyes. "Okay," I say finally. "Tomorrow. I can meet you tomorrow." I'm consumed, as I always have been, with the need to play water for the man who says he's dying of thirst.

⇌

He shows up late to meet me, in ripped jeans and Converse shoes, looking like a goddamn skateboarding Atticus Finch, and my body leans into his eyes, forgetting all danger and the downright stupidity of what I am doing. On his motorbike, I speak into his ear sternly. "Just talking, nothing else."

He nods, saying, "Yes, yes," and when we arrive to his

restaurant, he leads me to a table on the patio closest to the sea. We talk for a while under the stars, laughing and sweet like we used to be when the lines between us were clear, when I was his employee, he was my boss.

I say, "See, we can do this, we can just talk, be friends," and he leans over and kisses me. I don't know how to say no this time, and he feels it. He picks me up and carries me like a small child into the restaurant—finding the key in his pocket as he effortlessly holds me—and I feel again the father-fucking Freudian mess of it all. He sets me down on the bed in the back room, and I pull something from underneath me—his daughter's pacifier. I hand it to him with a moan—"Look, ugh"—and I remember what we're doing and pull away from him.

"Shh," he says and hands me a plastic bag, hands me a shirt, saying look, they're just objects to hold. "Shhh." He kisses my neck, touching me, until then it is a new feeling, licking like fire through me.

After that, it's nothing new.

I come home with that same empty panic in my stomach, after having sex with a man who I couldn't look at, lest the guilt devour me, lest the voice escape from the cage I locked it in, which screams: what the fuck, what the fuck, what the fuck, Dayna, are you doing?

Not new, either, is the concern on Quin's face. His confession—"I'm feeling insecure, you're gone all night, I don't know who you're with"—is followed by his shock and withdrawal when I say it: "I slept with Dimitris."

Not new, the ensuing monologue—he can't be intimate with me anymore, he needs to go, he needs a walk, he can't handle this—while I cry on the bed. I want to talk about my own experience, how sick I feel, how scared I am, why can't I say no to Dimitris, that there is something wrong with me, there is nothing wrong with me, am I fucked up, is this normal. . . . Quin is not listening, not able to, as he stands alone in the ruins of his hopes for our relationship—a ravaged field of marriage, kids, travel, eternal happiness together.

Not new.

He leaves, and I am alone. Alone with the memory in my muscles—so that they seize when I think about it, and cry out—of Dimitris entering me and the way I lurched away from him, wanting to cry but closing my eyes instead and continuing, and the sick horror I felt watching myself. *Who is this girl who is doing this?* Who didn't know what to say when he asked, "What do you want? What can I do for you now?" Didn't want anything from him, really, and when he was finished, I said, "Okay, let's go now," because he was just another body I needed to get away from.

⇌

Quin comes home and crawls into bed at 5:00 a.m. "Will you just hold me?" he whispers, and I do, wrapping his pale, sweaty body in my arms. With every cell in me, I want to never stop doing this; I just want to lift him, comfort him, feed him, protect him, be with him forever. "Why can't I just love you, and do it well, as well as you deserve?" I say.

"I don't know," he says, his mouth in my neck. "Why can't we do it for each other?" I kiss his damp cheek and his ear. "My best friend, in Boston," he whispers. "He was starting to lose his mind. We all saw it. The way he was dressing. His nails bit down to the cuticle. He started talking a lot about buying a gun. To 'extinguish' himself. I didn't know what to do. I was scared. Every day. I didn't know how to be there for him, how to love him better. I think I wasn't strong enough. We're all so close to the edge, man."

"Like your spider on a tightrope."

"Exactly. That grand canyon of milk is the madness we all could fall into."

Despite ourselves, we both laugh. "Poetic."

"Would make a good T-shirt."

"Did I ever tell you the story of my dad?" I say.

"You told me he killed himself."

"Yes. But there's more to the story. He did something else that we don't really talk about."

Quin listens with his head resting on my chest. About the whiskey my dad started pouring into his coffee in the mornings. About the time he kicked my mom out of the car and left her, heavily pregnant with me, on the side of a mountain road in the middle of the wilderness. About the time he pushed her, and the things he said to her, and the way she asked the neighbors for help, but no one believed her. He was too good of a man to do those things, they said. He was quiet and smart and calm, the kind of man you trusted instantly. He could build anything, grow anything, make the most skittish horse eat out of his hand. She must be overreacting, they said.

"The only person to believe her was an addictions counselor, and he advised her to get away as fast as possible," I tell Quin. "Then three days after she took us and left him, my dad got his rifle and walked through a blizzard to our friend's house. He opened the door and shot him in the face while his wife stood there and screamed and his kids slept in the back bedroom."

Quin, his face against me, makes a soft, sad noise.

"The story is big, and it hits people hard when they hear it," I continue. "But the thing is, it has never felt that way to me. I always knew the full story, before I knew what right and wrong were, I knew the full story, and it just . . . was. My dad killed someone, and he killed himself. I never thought of him as a bad person for it, and I still don't, but if I tell anyone what he did, they immediately label him in their minds. I grew up spending every summer at his mother's house; she was the best grandmother, his brothers the best uncles. I grew up hearing all the good stories about him, the way he was the favorite brother, the eldest, the one everyone looked to. So what happened? How did he fall off the edge and do something so horrific?"

Quin pulls back from me and finds my eyes and holds on to them. After a while, he says, "And you wonder if you have it too, inside of you?"

I duck my head and cry hard for a minute. "I think you're the first person who I've told this story to who understands."

Quin pulls me into him, and the rise and fall of his breath is as comforting as the steady waves of the Aegean sea outside our window. "You know about my birth parents, right?" he says. "That they were both schizophrenic . . . schizophrenia doesn't really come on noticeably until your late teens. Those were the scariest years of my life, when I was seventeen, eighteen, just watching my own mind, waiting. . . ."

He tilts my chin up gently and kisses me for a long time. Then he wraps me up again, tight in his arms. My breath syncs with his, our chests rising and falling together. "Dayna," he says. "When I'm with you, it's the only time I don't feel alone. And that's something, man. It's really something. Let's not sweat the small stuff; none of that matters. Hercules, Dimitris, Vesicles. . . ."

I snort. "Do you know a Vesicles?"

"I might." He chuckles and sits up, stretching his long pale arms over his head. "Look, man, it's morning now. Don't move. I'm going to make you breakfast."

⇌

Dimitris opens the shutters in the back room, and the thin light of early dawn floods in, the hills pale violet and green. "It's almost morning," he says. "We don't have much time." Both of us a little drunk and not yet tired, we dive into each other with ease, not rushing, though we know we should. He gently eases off my shirt, slides my bra strap off of my shoulder. This time there is no "no" in my mouth. I don't know where it went to. This time I want it, for our bodies to be together.

"Was it worth it?" I ask him that night, when he tells me at the bar with bright, wired eyes that he has not slept yet, not even for a minute, that he had gone straight from being with me to opening the restaurant to coming here to the bar, and he is running on coffee and cigarettes.

"Worth it?" he says. "No."

I mock a punch to my stomach, thinking he is joking, but he says, "No. Really. There are really important things I need to be doing. I have to be careful."

I straighten up, nod. It is true. He smiles softly at me. "See you," he says, quietly. I watch him as he saunters off toward the port, 2:00 a.m., to meet his mother arriving on the next boat. I watch him, feeling helplessly attracted to him, his broad shoulders, his white shirt with the rolled-up sleeves, his motorcycle helmet resting on his long forearm.

The repulsion and terror of him wanting me has somehow transformed into me wanting him, my curiosity and desire overriding all other things. "I resolve to be finished with this, and then I see you and forget everything," I confided in him last night.

"Me too," he sighed, "me too, baby," in the bright yellow light of the early morning, after making love.

He is a man with a wife and daughter. This is the first time I have done such a thing, and the way feels uncharted; the only thing known is that it will end, however it ends, in disaster.

⇌

See Something I Want Stellios leans back with his elbows resting on the counter as he watches me clean the bar. "No girl is perfect," he tells me. "It is natural, you know, natural for a man to always be looking for someone new. With each girl, you get something better and better."

I stop and stare at him from where I am, on my hands and knees, scrubbing the inside of the refrigerator.

"What?" he asks.

Yourgos From Next Door sits at the corner of the bar, his chin in his hands. "I'm done with love," he says. "No drinking, no sex, no love, no nothing."

"Good luck," Tomas From The Bakery says beside him, stirring his orange juice with a pink straw. His Polish girlfriend no longer comes with him. He says she just wants to stay home, but I pray it's because she has run away.

"Really," See Something I Want continues, "if I ever do get married, I am going to make my wife sign one paper that says, 'I will not gain any kilos more than what I weigh now.' And if she does, I will divorce her. Divorce her. Ehhh, you know, I can't take that." He leans with one leg crossed over the other, his foot bouncing idly. "My wife, you know, she must be beautiful. Men are always settling in the end, just because it is time, you know, but not me." He twirls a saltshaker on the counter. "Greeks, they hate the city, they hate their jobs, they do not love their girlfriends, but they marry, because, *ach*, is there any other way, you know? Like Dimitris's wife, you know—there she is, walking by now—she used to be so pretty, but now, after the kid—"

"Okay! Enough of that," I interrupt, standing fast, and he stumbles to get out of my way, knocking over the saltshaker.

"*Ach*, spilled salt! *Ellare*, Dayna, now you've given me bad luck!" he shouts after me as I untie my apron and walk away.

⇌

Toothless Vacillis finds me at the port windmill, hunched over my journal, scribbling unhinged thoughts as I stress eat hot baklava fresh from the bakery. "Be careful to eat those," he warns, pointing at the pastry. "They make you to be fat. And you, I think your body, you must to be careful."

"*Yiasu*, Vacilli. Nice to see you too."

He sits beside me with his stickered motorcycle helmet perched on his lap. "What do you write?" he wants to know.

"Not sure," I say. "Thoughts. Questions about love."

"And what do you think about love?" he asks. "Is it . . . good?"

"Fuck if I know."

Young boys are racing on motorbikes across the square, shouting out to each other, steering with one hand, holding their backpacks steady with the other. A bright red backpack zips by a bright red car; a mother helps a small girl into her bright red bathing suit. It is sunny, and beyond them is the brilliant blue sea.

"Oh! Tomorrow is my *indervenda* day," Vacillis announces, nudging me with his shoulder. "My *interpendi* day?"

"Independence day?"

"Yes." He smiles his cigarette-stained smile. "This," he says.

"Why?" I ask.

"I stop to everything," he says.

"Your job?"

"No."

"Smoking?'

"No. Dayna, tomorrow"—he leans close for emphasis—"I am *free* of everything." He juts out his chin and grins like a baby.

I hug him sideways, trying not to laugh. "That sounds really good, Vacillis." I think of a painting an art school student brought into the bar last week. It was of a couple sitting at a table, a newspaper between them and an empty coffee cup. The woman sat with her knee up to her mouth, the man had his head in his hands. "What?" the woman was saying in a white bubble over her head. "Will we never get out of this kitchen?"

"I'd like an *indervenda* day too," I say. "But I don't know how to get out of the kitchen. Can you tell me how to get out of the kitchen?"

Vacillis's eyes are narrow with concentration as he tries to comprehend I don't know what—my English, my obscure reference, or maybe just whether or not I'm looking particularly chubby today. Then he shrugs and laughs. "Oh, Dayna, you are funny," he says. "I think you must to marry me."

⇌

The end of summer: I get an infection in both ears, and Dimitris brings me weed for the pain. I haven't smoked since early college years, but I try it out of desperation and discover that not only does it cure the hot knife stabbing in my ear drums, it softens everything else too. Suddenly the fact that nothing makes sense is a very normal and floaty thing. Conversations with Greeks are much easier. "Have you seen where I put my beer?" I ask Yiannis the bartender, and he says "Mashed potatoes." I nod, because it doesn't matter. I can spend hours feeling the way my feet sink into the wet sand. I can say "oh" and "I guess that's bad" when Dimitris tells me that nearly everyone is suspicious of the two of us now and that sooner rather than later, someone is going to inform his wife, in which case everything in his life, and my life—at least here— will be destroyed. "Mmm," I say, and twist my water bottle in my hands so that the water sloshes. I like this sound, and giggle.

Jack and another writing teacher from the school, John Pearl, come often to our bar, and it's slow enough now for me to join them at their table by the sea. I tell them everything. We have long discussions on monogamy and morality, Love Anarchy, the jungle of the heart's desires, the guilt, the fear, the inability to have a "normal" relationship. Jack keeps telling me to lie to Quin about my affair with Dimitris, and I finally agree with him. "I will probably never stop being in relationships that are impossible," I tell them one night, after enough wine. "Just as my father will never come back and be in my life long enough for me to stop trying to find him all the time in other people."

Jack, his wine glass poised midway to his lips, reaches out very quietly and puts the back of his hand to my cheek. "I hope that will not always be true, Dayna," he says.

⇌

Dimitris meets me at the junction to Punda and Alyki and takes me down to a beach where there are six small boats tethered. Into one of these boats we climb and float on the still water under the stars. He holds me as he tells me Greek jokes, all of them as nonsensical as this island: about a frog who has all his legs pulled off and then can't jump, about Makis and Takis who go climbing up a mountain and fall and decide they want chips. Dimitris chuckles as he tells them as I rest with my head in his lap. He smells of cigarettes and Greek aftershave and something dusty—the shelves in his closet where his winter clothes have sat all summer. He presses his hand into the curve of my neck, and we rest in silence like that for a while, the only sound the ripple of the waves beneath us. After a while, he kisses me, very slowly, his fingers admiring the curve of my hip bone, cupping my breasts tenderly, as though he has never touched me before. We make love, and a ripple of pent-up, glittering sadness moves through me like swallows in the sunset. Tears blur my eyes, and he stays very still beneath me, witnessing, rubbing my back gently with his fingertips. I curl into him, helplessly loving this man, this stranger, this unconquerable, separate being, who I will never have as my own. Merging, for a moment, with such an opposite is as tantalizing as connection to God, as doors opening that once were locked, as Greece itself, this foreign, beautiful country, embracing me.

"You need to get the fuck off that island," Ruby told me on the phone last night. "It's pulling you under, like a drug. You need to do your goodbye, your ceremony to the land, whatever, and then go."

"Yes," I said. "I know. I will." Knowing, even as I said it, that what I wanted most was for the island to make me stay—to croon me down into its arms and let me forget everything.

⇌

Late afternoon at the beach and it's getting cold, the breeze coming up off the water. I pause on my way out of the bathroom, mesmerized by the bougainvillea growing across the balcony railing. That color—a cacophony of pink. Everything so brown from the summer, and then there's this, flowers like a clap of sound. Yourgos, who still asks me out every day at work, stops playing ping-pong to inform me that beside the flowers I am "unbearably beautiful."

"What does that mean?" I snap at him. "You're bearing it."

To the side and up from me, Dimitris stands, leaning against the pillar of his restaurant in an old plaid farmer's shirt with the sleeves rolled up. He catches my eyes, and everything softens. "Listen, I'm telling you this because I like you," Yourgos says, leaning close. "If anyone else sees you look at each other like that, things are going to get very, very bad."

But we can't stop or don't know how to. We lie down on the bed in the early morning hours when it is still dark, the wind urgent against the windows. The music is slow violin with a beat behind it, and I touch his stomach where there are strings of tension tangling—a sick, guilty nausea. With my head on his chest, I hear the quickening of his breath. I move his worry and his confusion gently with my fingertips. That I can do this still surprises me. That I can, with my hands, slowly strip away all of the things that cloud him, and bring him down to what is simple underneath—bring him down to just that beat, breath, beat of his body. As I move the terror from him, his heart floods and his breath slows and he tells me he feels dizzy. "*Tin afto?*" he whispers again and again, what is this?

There's no easy way out of what we have anymore. Maybe there never was one. I know I will have to leave him, regardless, and carry with me all of the stories: the weariness in his wife's eyes, what she knows and what she doesn't know; the wild rage in his daughter and her fierce will; the despair of Dimitris, who doesn't know how to be with them the way they want him to, the way they deserve.

His wedding ring was two bands of silver, one of the bands broken since I've known him. He goes to get it fixed and adds a third band, white gold. "Three," he shows me when he comes back to the bar after the jeweler, with a shy smile, holding up his hand.

"What is that supposed to mean?"

His face gets very serious, and he leans close. "It means I love you, Dayna." Throwing it out of his mouth like he was trying to get rid of it, this thing he'd discovered.

"Don't say that," I say, walking away from him.

"I told you I never cheated on my marriage, and that was true; it was true until I met you. And now when I look at the sea, the moon, the trees, the fucking bushes, it's Dayna, Dayna, Dayna. The only other time I felt this was with my wife, and I married her!" he shouts across the empty bar.

I take off my apron and keep walking away. "Please, please don't say that."

⇌

I have moved into my own house again, my tiny one-room flat above the sea. "I just need my own space," I told Quin, and he has tried to be kind about it. He pretends to not worry. I will leave for Israel at the end of the month for a contact improvisation dance festival, and he will meet me there two weeks later, after the end of the art school semester.

It gets colder, and the rains come. The hills flare into radiant green. Quin and I drive to the other side of the island, to a tiny beach in Drios, one of the only places we can go where we won't run into someone we know. In the windy sunshine, he wraps himself around my body. "You know, I would ask you to marry me if I thought you'd say yes."

I rest my head on his shoulder. I want to say something but don't know what to say.

"I just don't want to lose you, Dayna. I don't want to be another ex-boyfriend."

I close my eyes, hating the word. *Boyfriend.* The way deep love, when it doesn't go a certain way, has to end. "I don't want that, either," I say.

That night there is an island storm, the first one of the season. The waves rise up over the street and tear into the empty patios of the bars once full with tourists. I cry with my forehead pressed to the knife edge of a table top in the art school computer lab after reading emails from friends far away. "I've been bored with love and sex, but I feel a stirring again, with this new girl," Ryan writes. "We have not kissed, but it is in the works. And I feel like she'll make me crazy. Not unlike you did, not long ago."

Outside, the wind cracks the shutters against the white-washed walls, an eerie, persistent noise that echoes through the empty art school. Meanwhile, down the street, in the cold wind off the boiling sea, he is sitting drinking coffee with three wedding bands on his finger, wanting most, same as me, to be able to be happy in his garden, to know how to sit quietly among the rose bushes and the eggplants.

I call him when I am done crying and ask him to come over later so that I can end things gracefully. It has to end. With tourists gone, the island is too small. I cannot stand lying. I want quiet nights with Quin, and long mornings of just us. I want to talk about our future—Israel and whatever next —without this grip of guilt on my throat.

Dimitris shows up at midnight, drunk, wavering on his feet, and before I can muster up the right words to say, he has found and smoked all the weed I have in the house and can barely keep his eyes open. I start to cry again, and he laughs at me. The day before, we'd thrown a party for the bar's birthday, and I'd watched him and his wife play with their daughter on the beach all afternoon as I got drunk in a white sun lounger alone. He says with a smirk, as he smokes the last of the joint, "I liked watching you on the beach."

"Fuck you," I say.

We make love all night the next night. He says his worry

is making him sick. "This island is too small for me to love you like this," he says, panicked, and it's true. I hold him to comfort him. He talks for a long time about his wife. "Everything is perfect with us. Perfect. Except just this one thing." I wonder if the lack of sex in his marriage is really the thing, or if it is just the reason he has pinned to the nameless emptiness inside of him. He tells me he doesn't have any friends, no one to talk to. He says he's never finished anything in his life.

I say, "This conversation. We have to finish." I say, "From now on you and me only see each other in public places. No phone calls. No texting. No showing up drunk at 5:00 a.m."

He nods, his eyes drooping, fighting sleep. "Dayna," he says. "Remember what you said: the heart is the only thing that can see. We will do what's in our hearts in the moment."

"No," I say. "No. We cannot do that anymore."

⇌

Quin stops by my house to get his headphones on his way home and finds the voice recorder we'd borrowed for an art project we started a couple months ago in July. It had been sitting in my drawer, and some gut pull urges him to charge the battery and rewind through it. It had been accidentally left on for weeks, recording everything: drunk conversations, hours of sex sounds, a terrible moment when he calls and I lie to him about where I am and what I'm doing.

I have been out at a restaurant listening to my friend play *rebetiko* music, and I have her drop me at Quin's afterward. I slide into bed beside him, and he wakes sharply, sitting up fast. In an instant he has me by my wrists and is shoving me across the bedroom, across the kitchen, and out the door. "Get the fuck out of my house, you fucking whore," he says. He slams the door hard, locks it, and presses the voice recorder up to the window. "You are a lying bitch," he says through the glass.

Panic blurs through me. I can't think, but I know I can explain if I can just get to him, touch him. I grab up the nearest rock and punch open the window of the door. There's glass everywhere, and my hand is bleeding like a motherfucker, and Quin is so stunned, he stops shouting at me for a second and just stumbles back. "I'll tell you everything, I'm sorry, it's over between me and Dimitris. . . ."

He snaps out of his surprise fast and is then sprinting with his rage, words cutting deep, furious, aimed to kill. My knees give out. I sit down hard in the middle of the glass, thumb wound spurting. Like Jack advised, I'd thought that in lying, I could save him from the unsafe sides of me. But now he says he sees the real me—sees the real me, and it's ugly.

"You're *disgusting*," he spits. "I can't believe I ever thought I loved you. What about his wife? What about his *daughter?* You *lied* to me. I thought honesty was all you cared about. Who *are* you?"

I'm done, *I'm finished*, *it's over*, I think through the spinning terror. If I lose Quin, I lose everything. He is my home. I pick up a shard of glass. Press it through to the vein in my wrist—not to kill, just to numb. The pain blurs out the sound of Quin's voice. I'm dimly aware that he's shouting my name, but it's too late; somehow I'm gone. Looking back, I remember it so crisply and so distant at the same time. I was not there. I could see myself only from a great height, as though hanging from the stars, gazing down.

Quin tries to get the glass out of my hand, and his arm gets cut, a four-inch gash along his forearm. He sees in my eyes that I'm nowhere, and he tries to shake me out of it. I don't respond, and panic eclipses him; he's suddenly right back there with his first love, her mind gone, wrestling her naked body out of the hotel fountain. He logics that the only thing to do is knock me out to keep me from killing myself. He cracks my head against the ceramic floor. I'm above us, watching all of it, the glitter of glass, the crimson blood. He can't bear to do it hard enough, and I won't let go of the glass, trying to push it deeper into my arm, keep me far from myself. He's shouting my name and telling me he loves me as he brings his knee to my forehead as hard as he can. The blow stuns me back into my body, and the wound that blooms instant on my forehead stuns him. He backs away, and I sit up, confused, a cupful of blood dropping from my face onto the pink tiles.

⇌

The doctor who sews my face is wearing flip-flops and grips an unlit cigarette in his teeth. "Was it this guy who did it to you?" the doctor asks, nodding at Quin, who holds onto my hand with both of his. I widen my eyes at Quin. "T. I. P.," he whispers. This is Páros—that the doctor assumes it, and even more, how casual the assumption is. The doctor tugs at the final stitching and grunts. "Ten. You're going to have a huge scar. Pity." He pulls back to study my face. "I can see that you used to be pretty."

Jack and Quin have spent the morning scrubbing the blood from the apartment. They tape a piece of cardboard over the broken window. When we go back there, it looks almost normal, but for the red spatters on the ceiling.

"Jesus, how'd it get on the ceiling?" I say.

"I have no idea," he says tightly. "Nor any idea how to clean it off."

We wrap up in blankets on the couch and just stare at each other for a long time. "You're really a narcissistic person sometimes, you know that?" he says. "Do you know that about yourself? Maybe you do. You're incredibly narcissistic sometimes."

I nod with tears. "Yes." I'm in pain and oddly grateful for it, the ugliness in me finally directly on the surface of my skin.

He smiles and huffs a little from his nose. "You know, I think I love you more for it. You are so many things." He leans forward and grips my hands. "Dayna, I'm sorry I said what I said. It was horrible. I'm so sorry."

I wipe my eyes. "I get it. You needed to say them." The words that come next surprise me, how real and true they feel. "I *am* so many things," I say. "I am good, and I am everything opposite of that. I think all humans are. I'm trying my hardest to understand the darkness in myself, so that I will be able to understand the dark in everyone else. Does that make sense? I want to understand and forgive my father. I want to know how to love everything, everyone, their whole selves, without condition."

Quin, with his strong heart, nods with tears also. "I understand. I really understand." He puts his hands on either side of my face and looks into my eyes. "I love you so fucking much it's terrifying."

"I love you like that too."

"Feels like getting kicked in the face, man."

"Or kneed. . . ."

"Oh shit, c'mon. . . ." He giggles, which makes me giggle too, and then we are laughing, hard and hysterical, the way we always have.

"Narcissus," I say when I can finally speak again, wiping at my tears. "At least Narcissus is a story that ends well."

"Truth. There is a flower," Quin concedes, curling into me, pressing his face into my neck. "A beautiful one. A really fucking beautiful one."

⇌

One week later, at my goodbye dinner, Jack reaches across the table and pats my hand. "You're doing fine, kid," he says. "Totally fine."

Seated at the table with us are students and teachers from the art school, a few Greek locals, some of them my friends from when I lived here five years ago. My head is bandaged, the wound still fresh. I have not seen Dimitris, though he saw me, walking sometime after the hospital with a bandage on my head. He sent me a panicked text. "Is that from Quin? Did he do that to you?" I didn't answer. It will be seven years before I see or speak to him again.

I tell everyone at the table the story of what happened from start to finish: the affair with Dimitris, the decision to lie, the voice recorder, the glass fight. Quin chimes in with a few details at the end. No one is appalled or surprised. This is how I know I am on Páros. "I think there's something buried beneath us here," Quin had said. "Some kind of ancient scrolls that explain the nature of everything." Something like what I knew as a child, pulling my head in and out of the running water: a natural dance we humans could have, but don't, with darkness.

"You know," says John Pearl, the writing teacher from New York. "I'm sixty-five, and I still haven't found a system for love that works. Lying, truth telling, forewarning, compromise—the outcome is always the same. You can't sanitize or safeguard against the desires of the body, of the heart."

I groan. "Great. At sixty-five, you have found no solution, and at twenty-five, I have already run through them all twice."

"Perhaps that's the point," Jack says. "For us to discover that there is no solution. That it cannot be placed in a neat package. As the great poet Mary Oliver says"—he waves his arms at us and puts on his deep poetry voice—"whatever the name of the catastrophe, it is never the opposite of love."

Down the beach, at the dark sea's edge, two fishermen are standing over their catch. In the dull circle of yellow from their flashlights, I see a glimpse of an opal tail, arcing upward, then down again. Their words carry over to us in the wind, tender and reverent, "*Orea. Orea einei.*" It's beautiful, they're saying.

The Greeks say that when the earth was all water, Greece was the first mountaintop to emerge. The sun fell upon the peak, and from this came the name for the land. *Hellada*—"touched by light." *It's true, it's true*, I have thought every day of living here. The way everything secret from my body is pulled up as though by the unseen hand of an unseen fisherman—to dangle, awkward and gasping and suddenly beautiful, in the rich light of the blue-church-dome rising hillsides.

3.

ISRAEL

2007

I.

On the plane, I sit next to an American man who is going to Israel to make Aliyah. Aliyah, he explains, means literally "to rise up, or ascend," and it means to become a citizen of Israel. This is available to all Jews: the right to return to the homeland. He asks me if I am Jewish. To say I'm Jewish is as strange as saying I'm Russian or Irish—I've got some of all that in my blood, but what it means, I have no idea. I try to tell this to my neighbor.

"Is your mother Jewish?" he asks.

"Yes," I say, though that sounds strange too. My mother rarely spoke about it, and what I knew was only from observation—the Yiddish words she used, or her easy recitation of the Jewish prayer when we lit candles at Hanukkah parties. They were never our parties, but friends' parties, who were unequivocally Jewish, with yarmulkes and stories of ancestors who were in the Holocaust.

"Well, do you know when Yom Kippur is? Or Rosh Hashana?"

"Uh. No."

He laughs. "Yeah, okay, you're not so Jewish."

But when we're off the plane, before he disappears into

the crowds at border control, he says, "But you are, you *are* Jewish. Maybe you will see, when you feel the land, now that you are here."

The land looks like the pictures on the pamphlets the Jehovah's Witnesses hand out door-to-door back in the States— rolling, rocky hillsides and small, tough-looking pine trees. From the window of the train, I watch as we pass camels in garbage-riddled fields, power lines and decrepit factories and huddled-together houses that are grubby white and flat roofed, surrounded by barbed wire and lookout towers. After the sparkling white and blues of Greece, the churches, castles, and taverns by the sea, I rub my eyes, my perception reeling.

I arrive under a red setting sun to the kibbutz where I will stay for the next few days—a small housing development built on the side of a rocky hillside, fenced in with barbed wire and overrun with chickens, pecking and squawking between the small, uniform houses. The dance studio has big windows and clean wooden floors, and the dancers I meet are mostly from Europe. I am the only American. "Did you come all the way here for this dance festival?" they ask.

"No, I was in Greece."

"What were you doing in Greece?"

I have to think: What *was* I doing in Greece? Twenty-four hours gone, and my time there feels like a dream I can't fully remember. Only Quin is real, a throbbing absence in the center of my chest.

For the opening night of the festival, an Israeli dance company does an informal performance. The choreography is fast, emotional, at times violent. I'm struck by a particular man, tall and tan, with strong shoulders and messy black curls. He stands in the center while the others circle him and throw themselves at his body in turn. He catches each person, effort-lessly, and then drops them again, their bodies thudding into the floor. His utter lack of emotion juxtaposed to the other dancers' full, desperate emotion is striking. I think for a mo-ment about the conflict here in this land—this conflict that I know very little about, except that it is happening and people are suffering. But I am tired after my long day of traveling, and the tiredness makes me soft, keeps me from putting too many thoughts together too quickly. All I can think is, *Here I am. Israel.* As I felt in Greece, I want only to slide deeper into this land, forget where I came from and where I am going. I want only to wrap myself in the just-right-now moment, the sound of the dancers' bodies meeting, as a woman begins to sing The Cure in accented English: "You-ou, soft and only, you-ou, lost and lonely, you-ou, strange as angels. . . ."

Just like heaven.

This new, alive, throbbing place.

⇌

I'm on the beach in Ashkelon; my new dance friend Tal is teaching his ballet class at a conservatory down the road. I've been in Israel for three weeks, and I'm trying to figure out if I can stay. I'm writing in my journal, trying to organize it all, see what I have, see what I need. Home: Sharon in Tel Aviv, check. Transportation: a neon yellow bicycle given to me by a fellow dancer, check. Dance: a list of classes and contact improv jams, check. At the bottom of the list: work. Question mark, question mark, question mark. *How the hell are you going to pull this off, Dayna?* my brain begins to shrill. Two young Arab men wander over and offer me vodka mixed with orange soda. I stare down at the hopeless question marks in my lap.

The boys say again, "Vodka?"

I close my journal with finality. "Thank you, yes, please."

We drink out of thin white plastic cups and watch the wind in the waves. They teach me how to count to one hundred in Hebrew. After some time, they invite me back to their tiny apartment a few blocks from the beach. Their younger brother lets us in, a skinny boy in his late teens who tells me immediately in English that he loves break dancing. He plays Black Eyed Peas on his cell phone and asks me, with kind, dark thumbprint eyes, "Do you need something for to eat?"

"No thank you; I should go," I tell him and text Tal the address where I am. When Tal lets me know he is outside, the youngest brother insists on walking me down to the street. "Where he is?" he asks, and I point, feeling suddenly embarrassed, to Tal's Mazda MX-5 convertible idling a little ways up the road.

"He's rich," I say, like an apology.

The boy nods. I hand him my half-finished beer because I know Tal won't let me have it in his immaculately clean car. "I don't drink," the boy says, but he takes the beer anyway and walks to throw it in the dumpster, giving a shy, polite shalom to Tal as he passes the car's open window.

In the car, Tal won't speak to me. Then later, he explodes: "You can't just go home with any boy you meet on the beach! It's not safe! You don't know this place! I have no tolerance for your poor decisions!"

I stay quiet. I know those boys were about as unsafe as a field of flowers, but there's no easy way to explain this to Tal. The Dayna that I was only eight months ago in Portland would have snarled at his comment, fought back with a firm boundary: you can't tell me what I can and cannot do; you don't own me; you're my friend, not my boyfriend; and even if you were my boyfriend, you *still* couldn't tell me what to do . . . and so on. But there is someone new inside of me now—patient, more willing to just listen. I sense there's something else going on beneath his anger, a cultural norm that I've unknowingly trod on, which I don't and might not ever understand. So for the first time, I just stay quiet. And it feels good, to let it be.

When we are almost to Jerusalem, Tal puts his phone against my arm. "I'm sorry," he has typed out in a text message. I nod and touch his hand. I realize my earlier worry about the future has been eclipsed by helpless fascination for where I am now. *How did I get here?* Making friends with childlike ease—because we are together in the same place at the same time, without preamble, we begin to play. In my own country, I had not made a new friend since college, since Ruby. I had no idea how to make friends. Now, unleashed in the big world, everyone, no matter how different from me, is suddenly someone I can talk to, listen to, dance with. I follow them wherever they lead me—like Tal, this young modern dancer from the company who performed for us the first night. When he found out I was considering staying in Israel after the festival ended, he took me home to his parents' house and told me I could stay there for as long as I wanted. His mother cooked me grilled chicken and steak, fresh hummus, and *shakshuka*; at every dinner, the table was so full, there was barely room for our plates. "Jewish people take care of Jewish people," his mother told me, brushing off my frequent thank-yous. "You'll find this anywhere you go."

"But I'm not really Jewish," I protested. "I wasn't raised Jewish. I don't know anything about it."

Tal's mother shrugged. "You have the blood in you. You are Jewish. Whether you want to be or not."

"If you've got enough in you to be killed for it, you're Jewish," Tal said with a grin, reaching for more steak.

"Tal!" his mother reprimanded. But shook her head. "Well, yes, but it's true."

⇌

Tal played piano and sang Tom Waits songs all that night while I drifted in and out of sleep under a down comforter on the couch. In the morning, I left him to wait for a bus to Tel Aviv with a crowd of young soldiers on the side of a dusty, four-lane highway. The desert stretched out beyond the road, long, yellow, empty.

Sharon met me at the station in Tel Aviv and kissed both my cheeks. She led me to her house and handed me a spare key. There was fish stew bubbling on the stove and sage tea brewing. "Come when you want, leave when you want," she said. "I'm not asking you here for any reason other than to help you be happy."

Sharon had hugged me for a long time after our first contact dance at the festival. "Do you want to come live with me?" she asked when she finally unclasped her arms from around my body.

I blinked in surprise; we had spoken very little. In fact, these might be the first words she'd ever said to me. "Yes," I said and then laughed at myself. "But I can't."

"Why not?" she asked, her dark eyes serious. "I think you need to stay here. This should be your home." *Why not?* The question nudged at me, persistent as Sharon's Israeli, no-

nonsense stare. I had a plane ticket to Italy for the following week and a plea from my mother to come home for Christmas. I had not heard from Quin since I arrived, which could mean anything. On Páros, he would often duck out to the kiosk for cigarettes. "Be back in five minutes," he'd swear and return five hours later. Goldfish, I called him, his memory of what he'd planned to do, where he was going, dissolving within minutes of setting out on his own.

"I'm not asking you here for any reason other than to help you be happy," Sharon said in her apartment.

And I thought, *Happiness is dancing.*

After three straight weeks at the contact improv festival, muscles strong and used and supple, a need to dance, and dance constantly, has overcome me. But the *how* feels impossible, unpaved by anyone I know—my friends back home all settling into jobs, finding partners, having babies. The thought of that life makes me shudder, and yet I have no idea what other way to go except staying, dancing, living. "I want, I want, I want—" I tried to tell Tal on the last night of the festival, fumbling to articulate, frustrated nearly to the point of tears.

He nodded, understanding anyway. "Yes," he said and hugged me, and took me home to his mother.

⇌

We arrive in Jerusalem as the sun is setting. Tal wedges his tiny sports car into a spot beside a graveyard, next to a man with a face as blank as stone who is peeing against the corrugated metal fence, "Know Hope" scrawled in black spray paint above his head. Tal leads me across the street and into a dark building. "*Yalla*, Dayna, we're late," he whispers, climbing the stairs two at a time until we arrive at a small studio on the top floor. The performance has already begun. We ease into the back of the crowd as four dancers advance toward us, stomping their feet and shaking. As the music rises to a crescendo, their torsos begin to retch—erratic and violent shaking somehow in harmony with the music as they come forward, arms outstretched, faces infused with euphoria.

It is too much, suddenly; it is all too much. I am nauseous, dizzy, tongue thick in my mouth. Without a word to Tal, I stumble back down the stairs and blindly clutch my way to the back of the building to crouch in the dust and the weeds, the night full now, the darkness draped over us. My body is wracked with the spasms I have not felt since being sick, since all those hours I spent shaking, and I realize it is a movement exactly like what the performers were doing in the studio.

I shake, in a back Jerusalem alley, as the years of being sick rattle through me, memories of gripping pain on the bathroom floor, my list of beautiful things I kept by the bed—lavender fields, sound of rain, hot baths—my feeble attempt to ward off my terrible despair. I think about broken glass in Greece, the way it felt to press that sharp edge to my wrist. I think about what it would feel like to be in love with my life as I have been these last few weeks—to dance every day, all day. To get stronger, better, to learn how to fall, lift, be lifted, jump, fly. To dance like those men were dancing, fierce and free and wild.

I retch, my body shaking and shaking and shaking me. *This is just the animal that needs to dance.*

And I know then, with a deep-bone sureness, that I will not be going back home—not now and maybe never. "Let the soft animal of your body love what it loves." Mary Oliver's words shimmer through me, and in that back alley of Jerusalem, I say yes. Yes I will.

It doesn't matter *how*. From now on, *yes*. I will give my life to dance.

⇌

Hey D,

Yeah . . . I'm struggling here. I came to Rome for a gig, and so far it is a bust. I've been couch surfing for the past few days, but this is proving hard and bothersome because the people here are not the most hospitable of people, I am finding. I spent one lovely night sleeping in a twenty-four-hour kabob place 'cause no one I was with was willing to let me crash. These two German girls said I could stay with them, even called me and said to come over, gave directions and everything. And then when I finally get over there, which was on the other side of the city, they say I can't even come in, cause their roommate doesn't want strangers over. I swear I was ready to cry.

My gig Friday was lame. The regular DJ was a total malaka. Really pretentious and hiding behind a machismo facade. I felt lost among strange people. I got on the mic at one point and was so fed up with the whole scene, I started making fun of everyone, and guess what . . . nobody even noticed. The DJ started playing "YMCA," and I was screaming, "Why not? Whatever works!" and, "Keep acting like you're dancing." The worst thing right now is that I have no one to talk to. I'm leaving as soon as I figure out where to go. I was thinking Africa. Don't know yet. Rome has left me so cold and bitter, all I want to do is join some real people living close to the earth and I don't know, raise cattle.

I couldn't call the last few days, but believe me, I wanted to, actually needed to. But everything shuts down here around Christmas and finding an Internet phone center is really a challenge. Can you sense my frustration?

I think about you constantly. Tell me something good: a joke, something beautiful in your life, anything inspiring. I just hope I can make it out before I turn to dust here. I'm almost finished with A Hundred Years of Solitude, which I think is a pretty appropriate book for me to be reading right now. It's incredible, almost had me in tears at a few points. It's my only refuge at the moment. I keep having ideas, thoughts, jokes, inspirations, amusing stories, pop up in my head. And then I look up and realize that there is not one single person that I can explain them to who will even come close to understanding. And lo, a single tear rolls down my cheek and lands in my lap. Ha.

I miss you. You are an amazingly beautiful person . . . and I realize this more and more every day, when I meet people who aren't you.

Sincerely,

Lost in Rome. . . .

~

Q! I'm so sorry things are so hard for you there. COME HERE. What are you talking about, Africa and shit? COME HERE.

I want to write you more, but I have absolutely no time right now. I love you and I miss you, and I will try to write to you soon, okay?

And um . . . COME HERE. . . .

Love you,

D

D,

I do want to come out there, but like you said, when it feels right. I'm just a little reluctant to jump into your world, not knowing if I'll have some of my own stuff going on as well. I don't know if I could live with you again at the moment (don't take it personally). I just don't want to be in a situation where I have to depend on you. But I really want to see you and be close to you, so maybe visiting for a while is the best idea. Madrid is only twenty euros one way, so after I pop over there, I'll get a ticket to Tel Aviv. Really, baby, I want to play with you in Israel too and many other places as well. But first I need to get Quin settled and taken care of. I know you understand. Shit, time's almost up, I better hit send. Love.

So now I live in Israel.

In my class this morning, the teacher plays Death Cab for Cutie and we dance while the rain clatters against the windows. I tell her afterward that the band is from my home, that the music made me feel like I was back there again. "You must miss it a lot," she says. I smile, realizing how much I don't miss it, not at all.

I spend two weeks compiling a study schedule for myself that will be my own intensive dance program. I race from one end of the city to the other, exploring all the options—release technique and butoh and contact improvisation, yoga, Pilates, and dance improvisation. Something called Biodanza, and something else called Gaga. I pedal my hand-me-down neon yellow bicycle at top speed down the narrow streets crammed with children, cats, dogs, rabbis, cars, buses, soldiers, buskers, and beggars—weaving, then accelerating, through the color and the noise. I sing as I speed, my voice lost in the horns and the shouting, feeling awake and in love with this complicated, dirty city. This morning, I race by a homeless man passed out on a bench with three well-groomed poodles at either side of him and at his feet. I turn my head to get another look at the absurd image and then crash into a wooden flower bed, landing on my feet on the other side of it. My bike wheel pops, but me, I'm still singing.

All I need is dance, and I know it now. Nothing else matters.

After much bartering, finagling, interviewing, and budgeting, I have a schedule that I am happy with. Weekly classes in Aikido, Pilates, yoga, and contact improvisation. Three hours every day of Gaga—a technique training created by the choreographer of Israel's famed dance company, Batsheva. Gaga is a dance technique that has its foundation in, of all things, shaking. In my first class, my teacher begins by instructing us to let our bodies shake for ten minutes. "Find where the movement isn't going through, and let it through," she says. "Shake in your ankles. And your fingertips. The shaking allows you to feel the subtle connections in your body—ear to toe, tailbone to eyes. The space in your hip joints."

I laugh out loud. I realize I'd already been studying this for years, believing there was something wrong with me, when in fact, my body was just trying to teach me how to dance.

⇌

Someone is staring at me all through Gaga class. I keep catching him watching me—an older man who I have seen here a few times before. His attention flusters me after a while. As we are packing up our things to leave, I finally just ask him. "What? What is it?"

He laughs. "Your shirt. I want to know what your shirt means."

When I left the states for Greece, I brought only as much as I wanted to carry: one T-shirt, one skirt, one pair of jeans. The T-shirt I chose was a favorite that used to belong to Ruby, but it became mine when I wore it more than she did. It was well cut, had a perfect drape, was a vibrant shade of turquoise. I never paid attention to the words printed on the front, and no one in the States ever commented on them either, so when I packed it to be my sole T-shirt for my open-ended trip, I thought it to be just another innocuous article of clothing. I was wrong.

Shortly after I touched down in Europe, I got what would be the first comment of many, from an Italian security officer in the Milano airport at four in the morning. As I passed through the metal detector, he read the words aloud: "Stop Genocide in Sudan." His brow furrowed. He leaned forward to see if he had read it right. He looked at me, then looked at the shirt again. "How?" he said finally. "How stop it?"

Now the Israeli man in my dance class is also furrowing his eyebrows as he reads my shirt. "Really, what does that mean?" he asks again. He goes on to say that he just came back from filming a documentary in Sudan, and he is now wondering, very politely, if I know how one would go about stopping genocide. "Does it help, to put it on a T-shirt like that?" he asks, really wanting to know.

The more time I spend in Israel, the more I realize how sheltered my life has been, how tiny my perception is. Every day, Israel—loud, direct, hot, dirty, angry—presses into me, and at the most unexpected moments, asks me to look close at the things I never knew I wasn't seeing.

Two weeks ago, the short-lived truce between Gaza and Israel ended abruptly, with Hamas shooting rockets into the city of Ashkelon, where Tal lives. Yesterday, a rocket demolished the roof of a house across the street from his parents' house.

I now spend my afternoons reading every book I can get my hands on about the conflict. Slowly, I let the story of this place grow in me. I let the ache and the throb of the land knock on me, until I vibrate with it—the history of wars, the UN rulings, the negotiations between presidents and kings, the Israeli body parts in the trees after a bus bomb, the Palestinian homes bulldozed to the ground. With each book, the city of Tel Aviv peels off one more layer, revealing a more and more naked, complicated history—one that I can scarcely comprehend, for I am still so new here, my eyes only just barely opened.

The Israelis I meet don't like to talk about it, and I understand why—the necessity of letting this conflict go unresolved is excruciating. Many an afternoon has found me crying over my books, as I read personal accounts from both sides of torture, terror, the houses they had to leave, the homeland, the safety, the rest they all desperately long for.

Over breakfast this morning, I read about a Palestinian terrorist with a machine gun, who killed a handful of students at a school in Jerusalem yesterday. A Scottish friend from dance recently returned from the West Bank with stories of protecting a playground from being bulldozed by the Israeli army. A *playground*. These are not stories that are new to me. I've read the news; I've paid attention to the state of the world. The difference is the stories are real now. They are not just words on a T-shirt, reports on the radio, pictures on TV. They are happening next to me, on every side of me. *What can I do?* is the mind's natural response. Longing for an answer when someone asks, like the man in my dance class, "How? How would you stop this incredible suffering?"

I walk home from Gaga with my sweatshirt over my embarrassing T-shirt, despite the heat. I'm sweating buckets down the back of my neck when I come upon a man who has collapsed beside a kiosk. A teenage boy beside him, perhaps his son, is screaming while three people, two men and a woman, work feverishly to restart the man's heart. There is nothing I can do, and I just stand there with eyes wide and tears. By the time the ambulance gets there, he is dead. Walking away, I am behind one of the men who had been helping. He pukes against a ragged city tree, wipes his mouth, and keeps walking. It had been his breath that he'd pushed into the dead man's mouth. I fall into step beside him. "What do you do after such a thing?" I ask him quietly.

"Tell someone," he says. "Cry. Go back to work."

It will be the best advice for living in Israel that anyone will ever give me.

When the world roars too loud, when all I want to do is throw it, break it, blow up its intensity, when I want to close my eyes and ignore it, all the suffering that I cannot fix, I think about his advice. Then I wake in the morning and dance. I dance so that I might know, someday, how to tell these stories and tell them well. So that I will know how to cry, and in that crying, cry well. Cry well enough to go back to work, again and again, back to the work of keeping my heart open, willing, listening.

⇌

I spend New Year's Eve with Sharon and her friends from the army: three bright, bubbling Israeli girls with names I keep forgetting. We sit at a bar called the Hoodna on the corner of Vital and Frenkel while a three-person band with tuba, cymbals, and accordion parades around and around the block playing circus music. A few minutes after midnight, I sneak away to meet Hassan, an Arab man I met last week at the market. I am horrified after Sharon, speaking to him on the phone to give him directions to where we were, covered the speaker and rushed to me hissing, "Dayna, Dayna, he's *Arab*. They're different. Not safe. Don't meet up with him."

I sneak away to find him waiting for me in his silver Range Rover down on the corner of Salame Street. He shakes his head with heavy eyes when I climb in. "I don't hide that I'm Muslim," he says. "I'm not going to give a false name. Yeah, I'm Arab, so what? I was born here in Tel Aviv. I have a lot of friends who are Jewish. My last girlfriend was Jewish."

"I'm so sorry," I keep saying because I have no idea what else to say. I think about the boys I met on the beach in Ashkelon, how angry Tal was with me, the way he too told me it wasn't safe. I've just gotten into a car with a man I don't know, and I'm willing to admit that there's nothing safe about that, but I refuse to believe there is any danger based on his race. I keep apologizing, emptily, for something that I can do nothing about, for history I barely understand, the same way I apologized for Tal's expensive car to the Arab boy who loved breakdancing.

Hassan takes me to a sandwich shop in Yafo where we eat shawarma—shredded gyro beef with hummus and pickles and tomatoes—and we talk about what I am doing in Tel Aviv, while the shop bustles around us with late-night, hungry Arab men.

Later, in his car, he kisses me goodbye, pushing his fingers into my mouth along with his tongue in a way that is okay at first and then annoying. I pull back, and he, a man who up until this point has shown nothing but gentle kindness, commands me to "come" and kiss his fingers again.

I roll my eyes. "No."

He says, "You're a woman. You're supposed to. . . ." His voice trails off. "I am a man."

I nod, feeling patient. I think of Sharon. *They're different, Dayna; they're not safe.* Traveling, I realize, has afforded me the ability to start seeing how *different* does not mean *unsafe.* The more people I encounter who think and act differently from me, the clearer it is becoming that all the norms of a certain place, of a certain group, are merely man-made—often absurd agreements between humans who happen to share the same land they call home. I do not need to be afraid of what is normal for someone else, but neither do I need to subscribe to it.

"I don't agree with that," I tell Hassan. "I do what I want to do, not what you want me to do."

He nods and apologizes. "I don't want to offend you. But maybe you don't understand what I'm wanting," he says. "Maybe you *want* to do what I want."

I shrug. "Maybe. But probably not." I climb out of his car. "Happy New Year," I tell him and wish him well before I close the door.

⇌

I walk home through the crowded, confetti-strewn streets. 2008. Another end and beginning. And I smile to myself, my whole body flooded with relief, because I am alone, finally, and it is exactly what I want.

At home, I pull out my Hebrew book and begin the process of teaching myself a new language. I select a list of words from the thousands available. I make flash cards on torn-up scraps of notebook paper. I feel frustrated and tired and excited, imagining Hebrew decoding and dropping open as Greek once did. I long for it as much as I long to dance— for new sounds to be natural in my mouth.

I am slowly finding new movement to be natural in my body, though the process is as slow and arduous as learning a language. I have discovered that my body is terrified of changing the way that it moves.

When Tal took me to the corner last night after Gaga class to give me some tips, I felt real, heart-pounding fright. I did not want to try what he was suggesting. I sat instead and watched him, feeling slightly nauseous. "Put your hands here, your shoulders here," he said, and I went to write it down, but he pulled me to my feet. "No. *Do* it."

The simple act of tucking my solar plexus in brought the full weight of my shoulders onto my spine. I realized I never wanted to feel it, the weight of my body. A sudden grief seized me, and tears came to my eyes.

Tal saw it and groaned. "Dayna. Get over it. It's just dance."

"Dance is never *just*," I said, shaking myself out of the feeling. My eyes snagged on his chest and impulsively, I reached out to touch it.

He knew exactly what I was seeing. "I know. Dead," he sighed. "Like a tin can."

Now it was my turn to advise him. "Let it up," I said. "From here." I touched his tight diaphragm. Before I could say any more, it had already happened. A light burst up into his empty chest.

"I did it. Feel!" He grabbed my hand and put it back on his sternum, his face triumphant. It was true—where once there was dead space, something now hummed. He tried a few leaps across the empty studio. "*Chuka!*" he shouted, his nickname for me. "Look what you've done!" He began to dance, moving his body with a tentative freeness, a little goofy, with a glow of delight on his face. I saw him suddenly as he was, no longer what he appeared to be. This opinionated, often-arrogant, disciplined dancer, who did not smoke or drink or fall in love, suddenly unpeeled to reveal his most tender self: afraid and curious and testing his muscles in the world. His movement was honest in a way one is when they are dancing alone in a dark room. My heart ached for him as I watched—wanting to hold him suddenly, rock him, celebrate him.

"Why do you get to feel like that when you learn, and I keel over and cry when I learn?" I said, laughing, not really complaining. I could feel Tal's joy exploding in my chest.

He stopped leaping instantly and came to wrap his arms around me. "Dayna, that was so small, but you really moved something in me. You've been moving something every time you work on me, and then that, it just . . . shifted everything. You need to ask money for this. At least *try*. It's your *work*."

I shook my head. "I have no idea what I do. I can't ask money for it. I can't even explain it."

He held me at arm's length and nailed me with his eyes. "*Chuka,* this is your work, and you are strong enough for this. It already is running through you. Just follow the current."

Later, I got a phone call from another dancer in his company. Her English was shy and musical. "Tal gave me your number. He's dancing so different, and he told me it was because of you. I'd like to make an appointment with you?"

My heart rattled, and a blurriness came down between my eyes. "Oh. I. Um." And then I was just doing it. Saying yes. "You want to come to my house tomorrow?"

"Great!"

"I live in Florentin. Benbenishti Street."

"Okay. Yes. *Tov meod.*"

Just follow the current.

Beyond my open window now, I hear singing and a few stray notes from the circus band. People laughing in the new year, which is not actually considered the new year here, but still it is a cause to celebrate. One more opportunity to begin anew.

⇌

Hey D.

Thanks for writing back promptly. I had trouble sleeping last night, thoughts racing, about you, about life, yada yada. I'm happy to hear you want to see me. That's all I want. I don't know what we're meant to be to each other—friends, lovers, maybe I'm supposed to catch your child's foreskin at his, umm . . . christening??? That can't be right, I clearly need to brush up on my Jewish vocabulary. The biggest truth is that it doesn't matter what's happened or what's happening on the surface—what we title our connection as. Because underneath, we have something so strong, and it is bigger than any title anyone has invented. I've never felt this with anyone else. It's something that can't be broken by Dimitris or Kostas or Yannis or Nikos or Vangellis or Yourgos (I think that covers all of them, ha ha ha ha ha).

Baby, you've got me.

My life situation is confusing at the moment. I don't know where I need to be right now. I'm feeling it out. I'm in the streets like a lamppost trying to make some contact with the extraterrestrials in Madrid. Maybe I'll find my community here, maybe not, who knows, not me. It sounds like you've found your place in the sun for the moment, and you're dancing. Good. That's the most important thing. Without dance, even if we are together, it's not gonna be fun. And who knows it could even get . . . DANGEROUS. I don't want any more scars. Ha.

But I mean it, I want you to be happy, and I want me to be happy.

I love you. So much.

Don't forget that.

Keep telling me all of it, I can handle it.

Peace.

⇌

It only takes one night for everything to change.

I lie on the floor in the corner of the contact jam. Around me, the bodies of the contact dancers tumble and whirl, their hard breath and moving feet an echoing, soothing music. I close my eyes—that vertigo again, consuming me, shaking, but just barely under the surface of me. A man I don't know comes and puts his hands on my head, the way people often will in contact jams—silent offerings of help, from one body to another. I feel the knowledge in his touch. I close my eyes. He works quickly and gently, and the shaking smooths out, the vertigo evaporates. I open my eyes to thank him, but he is already gone. A new man sits at my feet. He has a shaved head and arctic blue eyes; without a word, he pulls me to my knees, and then we are dancing.

For an hour, we move without stopping, a long unwinding story. We dance longing and we dance lust, we dance fear and fury, the emotions rolling through our movement and away into space. He is far better than me, and I must rise to his level, meet him. He flips me around his shoulders. I let go, trust the height, and the speed. Trust myself to fall from his body, but he does not drop me.

When it is over, Tal comes to where I am gulping water. "*Chuka*," he says, "you were just dancing with the best dancer in Tel Aviv."

"Who is he?"

"His name is Alon. He is amazing."

I turn to catch sight of Alon, his bag over his shoulder, slipping out the door. He meets my eyes and raises his hand, just slightly. A goodbye and a thank you.

We should leave it at that, I think. *God, I hope we can leave it at that.*

But he gets my number from a mutual friend and calls later that week.

⇌

I wait for him outside the café around the corner from my apartment. He crosses the street to me, carrying a plastic bag of milk and what looks like pasta. He wants to stay sitting outside so he can smoke a cigarette. I can't stop staring at him—his startling good looks, his sharp eyes, his black sweater stretched taut over strong shoulders. I am aware of the humming in my stomach, the slight, grappling terror in my chest. "What is going on with you?" he asks. He feels my nervousness. I brush his questions aside, ask him questions instead. He tells me about his time in the army. Ten years in Israel's top unit, where he did things he can't really talk about. Then he decided to quit and learn to dance in London, where his now ex-wife was also studying dance. He tells me about her, about their seventeen-year relationship, the last half of it an open marriage.

"Wow, was that hard? How did you pull it off?" I ask.

He shrugs. "I work my emotions the same as I work my body."

I realize this man is stronger than me.

We sit close, our knees touching. He talks, and I try to listen to him rather than the rattle of my thoughts: *You have been so happy alone. You will lose yourself to this, the same as you always do. . . .*

I focus on my breathing. He touches me often, which helps.

"I'm talking too much," he says. "Will you share something?"

"Like what?"

"I don't know. A story."

I feel shy. "You lived in London for several years?" I re-direct. "Tell me about that?"

On the street, as we are saying goodbye, he says, "It's funny. You make me want to see you more. You have some kind of power. . . ."

I laugh. "*Me* with the power."

He kisses the side of my mouth. "I'll call you," he says. I stand on the corner as he sets off down the block. I feel soft and shaken with my feelings, the longing and the desire and the fear.

⇌

It storms for days, the wind tossing itself against the windows, pushing through the cracks and smashing through the neighbor's wind chimes, a sound like glass shattering. On my bike ride to the contact jam, I am nearly knocked to the ground by the force of the rain. The sea is drained of color. At the jam, Alon and I dance again, as full and rich as the first time. When we are finished, we stay locked together in embrace for a long time. "Do you want to come to my house?" he asks me. His body is compact under my arms. *It's just a dance; we should leave it in the dance* some part of me begs, some part I don't know how to listen to.

His apartment is only a few blocks from mine. When we get there, he doesn't say much. He makes tea in the kitchen, and I watch his body. I see something troubled in his solar plexus, a kind of subdued, withholding hum.

"Listen," he says, bringing the tea over to where I sit on

the futon. "I have just separated from my wife. I would like to move slowly. I do not belong to you, and you do not belong to me."

He is ten years older than me, and I can feel it, how dropped down and centered he is in himself. He knows how to be clear in a way that I do not.

All night he holds me. We do not kiss. We turn in and out of each other's embrace as though continuing with our dance. He stays close to my body, seeking to find where I want to be touched. When he finds it, he keeps his hand there, waiting for the muscle to release—my knee, my hip, the side of my neck. There is heat and throb between us, so palpable that it is as though another entity is with us in the bed also, dancing. I start to shake, and then he does too. I feel fear, and he holds my face in his hands. "It's okay. Give it to me. Give what you feel to me. I can take it."

As I am learning to do in Gaga, I open the channels of my body and allow the movement within me to pour through and into him. He shakes, his forehead to my forehead. "Yes," he says. "More."

And I let it all flood out, the tension and worry and panic and memory. He takes it without question or fear, until a deep peace blooms through me and I sleep, rose-colored, quiet, in his arms.

In the morning, he rises to take a shower and I admire his body: a rippling eight-pack, broad shoulders, a square jaw, and eyes blue as a glacial lake. We have barely spoken. And yet our bodies lock into each other like they love each other, like our cells are drinking from the water of the other. I feel a tangle of excitement and caution and detachment. How many beautiful first nights have I had? What does it mean anymore to connect in such a way with someone? Can I maintain a balance in myself as I open again to having a partner? Or am I headed fast for the same cliff edge?

"What happened?" he asks me as we say goodbye at the door, touching the scar above my eye.

"I got kneed in the head."

He raises his eyebrows. "Sounds like a good story."

"Sometimes it is."

"Listen," he says, taking my hands. "I go to Japan next week to teach. I feel something for you. But we must go slow. You must be free. Be with other men. Do whatever you want while I am gone."

I laugh at the irony. I finally find one who wants me to have many, just as I am finally wanting none.

"All I want to do is dance," I say. "I'll be as single as you left me when you return."

⇌

It only takes one night for everything to change.

Quiet shabbat evening, full moon, eclipse, and it's Purim. I drink a lukewarm Heineken beside a stone urn in a corner of the Yemenite neighborhood, the only place in the city I could find that was quiet. Not much sleep and an entire day of lying in bed with another person has left me off-kilter and half out of my body. Talked to Quin for an hour tonight, finally, and felt buckled-knees relief to hear his voice so close. He has gotten a job teaching English in Madrid. Shares one tiny room with three Latin Americans. "But who cares," he said. "Life is a jungle, and I'm alive in it!"

How I *love* him. My whole body shouts it.

But what does such a thing mean?

And so I am back to this. Had a short break, but here I am, again. With so many loves. So many different kinds of loves.

⇌

I saw Shai the moment he walked into the party. Big dark eyes, and clothes that looked like he'd picked them up from a pile on the floor, gotten dressed in the dark. He sat beside me on the sofa and asked me question after question, his English impeccable, his eyes attentive and patient. I'd never been listened to so well before. When he leaned in to kiss me, I stopped him with a shake of my head. "Why not?" he asked with a curiosity as gentle as all of his earlier questions. Alon would return from Japan in a few days, and as I had proclaimed before he left, my time *had* been full of nothing but dancing, early evenings in bed alone. But on this night, Sharon wanted to go out, and she had convinced me to go with her. *It only takes one night.*

Shai's gentleness, coupled with something blocked and terrified in his chest, had my hands aching to work on him, bring movement back to a body that looked like it was in pain. He said, "Do you want to go downstairs to my apartment? We can just keep talking."

I thought about putting my hands on him, and finally I said, "Okay."

But in the end, it was he who touched me. Lovingly, skating his fingertips over my skin and whispering in my ear. "I just want to hold you; can I just hold you all night?" he said.

In the morning, he rose early for work and did not wake

me. He left granola and yogurt on the table and a note. "I loved sleeping next to you."

I ate the breakfast he'd set out for me, sitting on his couch as I looked through the photo album on his coffee table. A younger, skinnier, grinning Shai in various parts of the world—Central America and Indonesia. A small blond girl reoccurred in several pictures, and I realized it was his ex-girlfriend—an Australian he almost married, he'd told me last night, but then there was a terrible breakup. He didn't say why and I, for once, didn't ask. There was something that hurt in me when I looked at the pictures of him—his softness and his pain. His house too throbbed with the same feeling, the walls dark with tapestries, a single piece of art above his bed: a painting of a monster embracing an angel.

⇌

We met at our neighborhood bar, the Hoodna, the next night. "Sleeping at your house, that can't happen again," I told him. "But we can be friends, I think."

"Why?" He leaned close to me, his dark hair rumpled and his eyes soft. "Why can't it happen again?"

"I told you, I started dating someone who I really like. And he comes back in four days. I don't want to date more than one person. I've done that. It's not as fun as it sounds."

He nodded. Then smiled. "So we've got four days. . . ."

"That's not exactly what I was saying."

He touched my hand, and my skin lit into fire. He made a small noise, not expecting it. "You feel that?" he whispered.

"Yes."

He leaned closer, his lips inches from mine, his hands on

my face now. "Dayna, tell me we have four days." I closed my eyes. His touch was like a brush with an electric fence. "Okay," I said finally. "Okay."

⇌

I finish my Heineken in the Yemenite neighborhood and then walk slowly toward Shai's house. The streets are lit up with people partying for Purim, everyone in costume and drunk. The stated goal of this holiday is literally "to drink until you don't remember." It reminds me of the ancient Greeks, who had a god for everything: a god for jealousy and a god for wrath, a god for blind, mad, raving drunkenness. If you honor and acknowledge every aspect of your shadow self, Greek mythology teaches, it is less likely to harm you. I pray for it to be true, as I knock on Shai's door.

He opens it and without a word, embraces me. That same electricity engulfs us; my body becomes one color, one sound, blending into him. It is too much, almost immediately. We push back from each other, blinking hard, shaking our heads.

"What the hell *is* that?"

"I don't know."

"Let's just take it slow."

We sit on the couch, one cushion between us. We talk about our days, about nonsense, about language, about nothing. It gets late, the Purim street party in full swing beyond his closed door. I've only had one beer, but I feel it happening anyway—my mind can no longer remember anything. The past does not exist. There is only this now: I am alone in a room with a man who makes me feel like I'm wrapped in fire.

Finally, we sink into it. Into the white-hot, deep running

flow of desire between us, our bodies bending and wrapping in delirious sync, mouths pressed together, passing breath back and forth like words. He lifts me effortlessly, and I wrap my legs around his strong waist as he carries me back to the bedroom.

⇌

We wake wildly cheerful in fresh morning sunlight.

He kisses my nose and my ear, and we wrestle until we are both slick with sweat and we laugh and cave into each other and kiss. Meanwhile, some stern voice knocks patiently and persistently on the back door of my mind: "But Dayna, but. . . ." It cannot finish its sentence, not in the midst of such love, the happiness it is creating in our bodies, the air around us, the way it makes the world hum.

He walks me four blocks home in the early afternoon. "Oh God, back to the sinks," I groan when we arrive at my apartment door, remembering. The kitchen and the bathroom sinks have been clogged for weeks, and neither Sharon or I know what to do about it. "They're starting to smell," I tell Shai with a grimace.

He pushes the hair back from my face and kisses me. "Sometimes you just need a man around," he says.

He follows me up and goes immediately to the kitchen, where he begins pulling things out from underneath the sink. He rolls up his sleeves, unscrews the pipe, and lets a wash of black water pour out into the bucket. I watch, marveling at the ease with which he has released what seemed so impossibly stuck.

Afterward, we sit on Sharon's tattered red couch with

sage tea, and I have to tell him gently. "Listen. Alon returns tomorrow. From now on, we can only be friends."

He cuts his eyes at me. "You think that will actually work?"

"Yes," I say, "it has to."

Something snaps in his chest, a flash of rage. "I don't understand. If you really liked him, then you wouldn't be able to be with me like this. He'd always be here. In your mind. In your heart."

Where is that *function in me?* I think. *Broken? Obsolete?*

"You love a lot of people, don't you?" he says, his eyes softening slightly.

"Yes."

"How? How do you have room to carry all of that?"

"I don't know. Maybe I don't?" I hate the conversation, hate that I'm having it again. I reach out and touch the anger beneath his collarbone.

"Ugh. Dayna. What am I supposed to do?" he says. "Now it's happening again! No matter how angry I am, I just want to get closer, and now I *can't*, you *can't*. But what we have between us, we can't walk away from this, either—"

He goes on like this for a while, saying the words I've heard so many times, bringing back slashes of sensation with Ryan, his dark hair in the yellow porch light, or Quin, the voice recorder smashed against the window. It feels unbearable and horribly sad until I finally just wrap my arms around Shai. And then we are holding each other, lying together on the couch. His anger, as quickly as it came, dissipates, our bodies soft and relieved and humming next to each other. He massages my shoulder where it is aching, following the muscle down my back. He takes a deep breath and then laughs for a while, and I laugh too. "It doesn't matter; it doesn't matter, does it?" he sighs. "We can just let it be."

⇌

And yet when he leaves, when I am alone in my room, my own voices come loud and furious. *Who do you think you are, some fucking* love *parade? You're selfish, you're self-centered, you're a whore. How many men do you need? How can you love so many? That makes each love* less, *don't you know? You* are betraying *the ones you love by loving others. You can't just walk around being so open. People fall in love and get* hurt. *And it's your fault. It's your responsibility to take care of them. There must be something horribly wrong with you.*

All of this. Rattling around too fast to catch or stop. So many men. A fucking *glut* of men. Is it normal, my longing to love them, their desire for my love? Is it okay, what I am doing? Or will it all crash, will I be punished, fail terribly? I glimpse it again, that thing that drove me to put glass to my wrist—the terrible, terrible self-loathing. There is something horribly wrong with me. There is nothing wrong with me.

And yet, what failed? Quin and I, even in our distance, love each other now more than ever. I accept and love myself, now more than ever. I have seen the shadow side of Love Anarchy. I have touched its center, and it has not broken me. It has not broken anyone.

I remember the sink in the bathroom, and I go to it, rolling up my sleeves. I face the pool of black water. Then I unscrew the pipes like Shai did and let the black, sulfur-reeking liquid cascade over my hands and into the bucket. *I do not need a man, I do not need a man, I do not need a man.* I reach into the pipe and pull out the ratted hair, the thick, black slime. *But it is okay to love a man. It is okay to love many men. It is okay to love everyone.* And with my hands full of this shit, I let the clean water take it; I let the clean water rush through.

⇌

Alon flings open his apartment door with a grin and stretches out his arms. I step into his embrace but have trouble hugging him, his body all angles I do not know how to wrap myself around. When he kisses me, I feel like I'm putting my mouth to the edge of a box. I keep thinking about Shai.

Alon does not notice. He says, "In Japan, I realized I am ready for this. I am ready for you."

He leads me back into the bedroom. "What do you think, should the bed be against the window like that, or the wall?"

"I don't know, *motek*. What feels best for you?" I say. Then I realize the way he's looking at me.

"I want to change it to however *you* will sleep best," he says. He holds out his hand, a key to his apartment in his palm.

What does it mean to care for others' hearts? I think. What a terrible responsibility. The feeling of carrying someone else's glass palace across a cement floor strewn with obstacles. Why did I pick up such a thing in the first place? And can I not just set it down and dance?

"Alon," I say. "I met someone else, while you were gone."

The hurt on his face is more than I expected. He tries to mask it with an even voice. "Did you enjoy it?"

"Sort of. I mean, yes. But I don't want it to continue."

"Okay. But it can. If that's what you want." He slides the key into my front pocket and kisses my face. "Open your body, darling," he laughs, putting a hand on my rigid chest. "Just let go. Let it all go. What you need will come back."

His words seem to bypass my mind and go directly into my body—as he speaks, I feel something deep within me release. And then I do, suddenly, I do let go, of everything: the thoughts, the doubts, the worry. A bright, white calm surges into me where his hand presses against my heart. He pulls me down onto the bed, and in an instant, it is as though we are inside of each other with our clothes still on. It happens that fast. Holding hands, our foreheads pressed, my mind blurs out. My body becomes my mind, and it takes me far. Light years I am traveling, diving into another dimension, dimly aware of Alon beside me, going there with me. Though it is of the same shocking, new quality of connection, it is different from the way I felt with Shai. This world is so quiet, rose colored, gentle. A vision, as palpable as a lucid dream, eclipses my mind's eye. I am in a winding maze of underground passageways. I am brought to a door. The door opens. I am in a cave. The cave is heart shaped—insistently heart shaped. *Why is it heart shaped?* I ask in my body. I am brought closer and closer to the crystals hanging from the ceiling—closer, until I am inside the crystal, and it explodes with light. Alon keeps right next to me, feeling me, whispering, "You're safe, yes, go there, go there," until I shatter and he does too, with me. Our clothes are on, we are side by side, our hands have not moved from their grip, and yet we are somehow orgasming together.

"How, how, how, why?" I gasp when the glittering shards of sensation fall away and I can see straight again. I look for his sharp blue eyes and hold on.

He laughs at me. "Darling. Darling. Enough questions. Let it go."

In the shower, later, he tells me that the energy our bodies create together is like the Sakora he just saw in Japan. "The cherry blossoms, they make you so starving to climb inside of them. At the same time, they are washing you, holding you, floating you."

He washes my body with a white loofah, and my skin delights at everything—the water, his touch, the scrub of the sponge.

"I can feel everything so clearly," I tell him. "I've never felt my senses so awake, it's like I'm on a drug."

"Better than a drug," he says, dabbing my nose with a tuft of soap bubbles. "It's clean."

⇌

After lunch, it happens again.

His body locks into my body on the couch, and we go sailing through that electric force field with our clothes on and our eyes open—a feeling like a full-body earthquake, shaking me and shaking me. When it finally loosens us from its grip, he says, closing his eyes and catching his breath, "What *is* it that you have inside of you?"

Something about the question rings a chord of unbearable loneliness in me. Wishing someone could *know* what it is and then tell me. Because the intensity of it is not just beautiful but also terrifying. I curl into the couch, trembling a little. He feels my mood and puts his hand tenderly on my head.

"You know the story of Samson?" he asks, pushing the hair back from my face.

"Samson and Delilah?" I talk into the couch pillow. "She figures out his strength is in his hair, so she cuts it off."

"Yes. That's *their* story. But his story, do you know about him?"

"No."

"When he was a young child, he was walking with his parents in the fields and a lion came at them. He was very, very young. But he reached out to stop the lion, and with one hand, he killed it. Instead of saying, 'Wow, you are amazing,' and, 'Thank you for saving our lives,' his parents were very afraid. They said, 'How could this small boy do that?' And he was very afraid too. To have that kind of power and not know what to do with it."

I roll over to look at him. Tears blurring my eyes. "You understand."

He smiles down at me. "I do, darling, I do."

⇌

The shaking in my body doesn't stop, so I leave Alon's apartment with the idea to walk on the beach, hoping the sea will calm whatever it is that is knocking through me. I go one block and find myself at Shai's instead, thoughtlessly, as though sleepwalking. His door is unlocked, and I just walk in. He is sitting on the floor, his computer open on the coffee table in front of him. He smiles up at me. "I was just thinking about you," he says.

I go to hug him hello, and it is instant, the white heat blurring through us. Within seconds, we are both on the floor and also rocketing through light fields. This quality is different than with Alon, more physical, our bodies so willing to blend into each other. But we do not kiss, we do not pull at each other's clothes—rather, we just grip each other and hold on as the electricity cracks through us.

We land, eventually, on the other side of something, and I wrench myself away from his body. "See you later," he mumbles, lying on his back in the middle of the cream-tiled floor, his eyes closed, his hand on his head. We are beyond asking what it is, or why.

I stumble out of his house, dazed, and someone calls my name—Shai's neighbor Oren. "Dayna. I hear you have a magic touch. Can I get you to work on my back?"

I'm blinking hard, the sun like a knife. "Yeah. Yeah. Of course." I back away. This time I really do go to the beach, to the calm back and forth of the sea on the sand. I sink down, my knees to my chest. Thinking of the questions a young Samson must have asked: *Am I normal? Are there other people who feel this intensely? What am I supposed to do with it?*

From Yafo, the sound of the muezzin echoes down the beach—a call to prayer. I notice a man sitting near me, staring at the sea, as though also looking for an answer. He sees me see him and nods hello, then stands to leave. But he hesitates, turns back, and sits beside me.

"Shalom."

"Shalom."

His eyes look like he's been crying. "You okay?" I ask, and without a word, he collapses into my lap, his face in my belly, his body rounded over his heart. I hold him. He weeps. The sunset breaks open on the water, magenta and pale pink. Two men play paddleball along the shoreline. I hold a stranger on my lap, feeling it all, the wonder and the terror and the questions. The abject confusion. And most of all, the love.

Blooming like water from a deep wellspring within me, pouring through my arms and hands and into this man who, when it is over, thanks me with a long, quiet look into my eyes and then walks away into the twilight.

⇄

By the time I get home, I am exhausted. Alon is out teaching a dance class, and I call Ruby, crying panicked, explosive sobs. "What's going on? What am I supposed to do with it? Is it okay? Is it real? I don't know how to talk about it."

"It's okay, it's okay," she says. "I'm with you. I believe in you. We'll figure this out together."

"I can't tell anyone. It's not even a good story. It's too over the top. I just had *three* extremely intense connections with *three* different men in less than three hours. This isn't *normal.* I don't even know if it's safe. My body is so charged with electricity, I feel like I could pull lightning to me. My touch seems to literally electrocute people. I don't know if I'm being irresponsible. And why only with *men*? Ruby, I'm freaking out."

"I know. I know, honey. It's intense. I get it. This is something we don't have a lot of understanding about. But that doesn't mean it's not right. It doesn't mean that in other cultures, in other languages, it's not completely normal. Just because *we* don't know it doesn't mean it's not real or okay."

"Okay. Okay." I take deep breaths, drink water, my hands still throbbing and shaking. "I just wish someone would tell me what to do. Teach me what to do."

"Maybe you *are* being taught. You just have to recognize your teachers."

"You're so smart."

"So are you."

"I love you endlessly."

"I love you too. I'm with you. Don't forget. I'm always with you."

⇌

That night, I babysit for an American friend's daughter in north Tel Aviv. It's an hour bike ride from where I live in the South, and by the time I get there, I am considerably calmed from the physical exertion. As soon as I walk in, the little girl leads me downstairs to show me her room. She is four and petite, with clear, wide eyes. When I tell her I like the giant stuffed orca on her bed, she asks her dad if she can give it to me.

He looks at me with raised eyebrows. "Honey, that's your favorite animal. Are you sure you want to give it away?"

She nods, slipping her little hand in mine. "If it would make Dayna happy, I want her to have it."

Now it's me, widening my eyes at my friend. We laugh and shake our heads.

"Your daughter is magical," I tell him and his wife up-stairs as they put on their jackets to go. She is sitting at the counter in the kitchen, humming a song to her grilled cheese sandwich.

"She's not like that with just anyone, actually," my friend tells me. "She likes you."

"I like her."

When they have left, she climbs into my lap and I read her book after book, my hand cupping her round belly. I real-ize my hands are still throbbing with light and heat from the encounters of the day, and, thinking it might be too much for her, I move it to the arm of the chair. When I turn the page, she takes my hand back and places it again on her belly, with her hand this time on top of mine. The gesture is so poignant, I have to stop reading, and for a little while, we just sit there and glow together in the chair. Then she says, "I want you to read my favorite book, and after that, I will go to sleep."

Her favorite book is about a giraffe who can't dance until he learns to listen to the music of the moon. *Sometimes when you're different, you just need a different song*, the giraffe is taught.

"This is an important book," I say when we have finished reading.

"I thought you would like it." She crawls off my lap and into her bed.

"How old are you again?"

"Four."

"Wow."

"That's what my dad says."

I laugh. She asks me to lie down in bed with her for a little while, and I do. "What does acidic mean?" she asks. "What makes my arm move? Does the moon really make music?"

I try to answer as best I can. But the questions don't stop, and eventually I have to tell her I have no more answers.

"What happens when there are no more answers?"

I laugh, because this magical four-year-old has now gotten me to answer my own deepest question. *You just have to recognize your teachers.* I kiss her on the forehead good night. "When there are no more answers, we rest."

⇌

Shai stops by in the late afternoon when I am cleaning the house. He lies on the couch as I sweep and chatter—about a bodywork session with a new client, about a girl in my Hebrew class whose boyfriend kicked her out for bringing home a goldfish.

"*Gedol*," Shai croons appreciatively, laughing at all the parts of the story that I too find funny. When I am finished cleaning, he sits beside me on the bed and helps me with my Hebrew homework. Alon calls, and I go to the kitchen to talk to him. He says he's going to bed. Asks me about my day, but when I start to tell him, he interrupts. "Darling, darling, I'm too tired to try and understand English right now."

"Okay," I say, and we get off the phone.

I walk back to my room slowly. Shai is where I left him on my bed, leaning back against the wall. The night is warm through the open balcony door, and we can hear the band across the alley practicing. A saxophone joins the notes of a guitar. I know I should tell him to go home now, but instead I return to my place beside him.

"Alon?" he asks.

"Yep."

"How was that?"

"Fine."

"Can I kiss you?"

"No."

"I thought he was okay with it?"

"They always say that at the beginning."

He nods, holding my eyes in his. "I won't push you," he says. "I do think we can be just friends. Do you want to watch a movie?"

"Sure." We put one on, some slow French film, and I fall asleep in the curve of his arm.

I wake in the middle of the night, my body throbbing, loud, like a drumbeat. Without thought, I reach for his mouth, and in sleep, he responds instantly, rolling onto my body. We make love in underwater, slow, delirium, coming together in silence, our foreheads pressed. His weight relaxes into me, and as quickly as it began, we drop back into separate dreams.

The guilt is waiting for me in the morning like a disapproving father—mouth a tired line, heavy arm on my shoulder. *Do you want to repeat the same story?* it asks me. *Maybe you will not survive it this time.*

⇌

Shai calls me that night, when I am walking home from Gaga. "Will you come over?"

I am just passing his door, so I stop, with dread pulling at me. Inside his apartment, I sit on his couch and attempt to explain all of the things that don't need explanation: the wreckage of my relationships before him, how I want to give this thing with Alon space and peace to grow. . . .

Shai watches me with glazed eyes and a sick smile, drinking whiskey quickly as he smokes cigarette after cigarette. I think of Dimitris on one of our last nights together, smoking weed and laughing at me as I tried to end things with grace. This time, I realize how stupid it all is. There's nothing graceful in a goodbye. I just have to get up and leave.

But when I stand to go, he says, "Wait." He wants me to read something he's written—poems, in English. They are as sad as a child in a locked room: "I do not expose what I do not have. I do not expose what I do have. I am a petty, full man."

I sit for a long time staring at the screen after I have finished reading. He has gone very quiet on the couch behind me. Outside it starts to rain. When I turn to him, his eyes are back—looking at me straight and deep. Something in the stare is so reminiscent of Dimitris again that I feel like screaming but also like going to him. I go to him. I lie down on his body, and this is when the pain hits, that old, familiar screaming in my pelvis. I shake and shake. He grips me hard and rocks me. "Shh," he whispers.

Whose pain is this? Who's comforting whom? I wonder. I don't want to wade through these battlefields of other people's lives, emotions, memories. Don't want to be the one they see as their savior. And don't want to see myself as that, either.

And yet, I can't stop loving him. I hold his brown, taut body against mine as the pain grows like a tree through my center. With one hand, I start to work on the churning in Shai's chest, and he leans his head back and closes his eyes. "What is this thing that you do?" he whispers, his breath grounding and deepening from the touch.

"I don't know. It started a couple of years ago. I was really sick. And then I just started seeing. The way things move through bodies. The way things want to move but get stuck."

"When you were sick. Was it this pain you get?"

"Yeah. Except it was all the time."

"I've only felt pain like that twice. In the army."

"What happened?"

"I don't want to talk about it." He keeps his eyes closed. "Do you love me, Dayna? Because I'm fucked up. Do you know that I am fucked up?"

"What do you mean by fucked up?"

"It means I'm mad. Sometimes I go crazy. I have to close the door and not see anyone."

Somehow I do know this. I could see it and smell it in his apartment, in his clothes. I take a deep breath. "I care about you. And yes, I do love you."

"Then why can't you be with me?"

"I need to give space to see what it is between me and Alon. But I can be your friend. I'm a better friend than girlfriend, anyway."

He listens with a small grimace. "I've heard all this before. And don't say love. I hate that word, it scares me."

"Then why are you asking?"

When I stand to leave, he stands also and puts his hands on my hips. His grip is strong on my pelvic bones. "Do you trust me, Dayna? If you trusted me, you'd stay." His eyes are dark, and for the first time I glimpse inside him this madness that he speaks of—a blazing, wild violence in the deep pit of his body. I am face-to-face with his darkest self until, with great struggle, he wrestles it back and slams the door of his eyes, leaving them as blank as they were when I first arrived. He unclenches his hands from my waist and lets me go.

⇌

By morning, I am so full of fire I can barely see straight. I bike to the contact jam, hoping movement will settle me, but when Alon, leading the warm-up, tells us all to open our centers—let go in the hip joints, breathe deep into the belly— the intensity that comes with doing it is so extreme, I nearly pass out. I hold my head in my hands, the room spinning. I try to feel my feet and wait for it to pass, but it does not pass.

Soon I am in the corner, convulsing, biting my hand to stop from crying out, while Alon coaches me. "Darling, darling, open," he says, pulling on my arms and my feet until finally whatever is pulsing through me drains out. He rests my head in his lap. "Listen, I want to tell you about when I first started working with my body's energy," he says. "At first it felt bigger than me. I was terrified. But finally, I learned that the key to harnessing it is simply to allow yourself to get bigger. Open your eyes, and widen your body, and breathe, and walk through the crashing."

I think about what I have learned with the pain attacks—how to open to the sensation, rather than fight it. I nod with my eyes closed. "I think I understand."

A glow has begun between our hands, entwined on his knee. I listen to it build and pour into me. "Wow," he says.

"You feel that?"

"Yeah. Your touch. Darling, there's something in your touch. You just have to learn how to harness it."

Slowly, I am understanding that it is not only with Alon or Shai that this heightened, palpable energy exchange can happen. I am beginning to see that it is the way my body wants to communicate with everything, and, if I allow it, I can have that level of connection with everyone. The fear is that I do not yet know how to turn it off, and the intensity of what it does to me, and others, is more than any of us can understand or explain.

In the container of dance, though, I know I am safe. When Alon goes to speak with a friend, Tal pulls me up to dance with him. Here, I can play with what I am understanding, and there are no consequences or questions, no falling in love. Immediately, Tal and I are moving, also, in that delirious light exchange. But because it is dance, it is clear that it has nothing to do with sex, nor affection even. It remains strictly focused on the art: a finely constructed ode to connection. *How could I describe this to others?* I wonder, wildly happy inside of a perfect flow of movement with Tal. I imagine a thousand sticky cords that jet from one body to another, tethering us to each other, and there is no movement, no matter how it appears, that is not in accordance, in rhythm, in answer to the other.

The pain in my pelvis remains jarring and persistent. I try to let it open, as Alon counseled. Let it pour into the dance. Let the dance be the pathway for it out of my body. Tal drops into my rhythm without question, and we move in perfect sync, swirling and sweating across the floor, down together and then rising, my body spinning up and over his shoulders, then his body up and around my shoulders, until finally we collapse with exhaustion. He rests his hand on my back, and I let myself be huge with the energy that throbs through me. I feel the light pulse and radiate, two feet out from my skin and thick. He feels it. "My God, girl, what are you carrying?" he whispers. I let the pain and the light slowly open me, move me, while Tal watches. From across the room, I am dimly aware of a man rushing toward me, wanting to jump into the dance that is happening, but Tal reprimands him sharply. "*Lo lahikaness.*" Do not enter.

I find my way out of the pain, moving with my eyes closed, while he waits beside me, patiently. I find my way out, and he joins me again. We dance a deep, throbbing, hungry, terribly sad dance, and I feel Shai releasing from me, and

I feel Alon releasing from me, as Tal stays fierce beside me. He plays the role—he is the sadness, the heavy, the black fear, and I am hating him, loving him, tangled into him, seeing him, inside of him. We embody it, we move it, until it is all finally gone, and I can feel myself, finally, just me, alone again. Wrung clean.

⇌

On the morning of Memorial Day, which will, later in the night, fade into the celebration of Independence Day, there is a nationwide siren in honor of all the people who have died in Israel's wars. The tradition is to stop everything when this siren goes off and stand for two minutes in silence.

When it begins, I am walking down Allenby, one of the busier streets in the city. In accordance to the custom, all of the cars stop in the middle of the road and everyone piles out into the street to stand with arms crossed and heads bowed while the siren pours through the otherwise silent city. Everyone stops except for one car—an Israeli–Arab driver, who is trying, without much luck, to maneuver through the swamp of stopped cars. What the Israelis call Independence Day is also what the Palestinians call "the catastrophe" because the independence of the Israeli state meant that the Palestinians didn't have one anymore.

He honks and waves his arms out the window and yells, and honks some more while the Israelis in the street refuse to move, waving their arms too in total outrage.

"There's a siren!" they scream, and the Arab driver lays on his horn.

I stand alone on the sidewalk, crying, as I witness each

side beg for the same thing: a moment to remember what was lost.

⇌

It is dark in my bedroom when Alon arrives. He sets his bag down by the door and pauses, one hand extended out from his chest, a buffer. I call him toward the bed, wanting just for the simple things, the way our hearts open when we lean them together. When I ask him how he is, he says he's nowhere—in nowhere land. "Some days my chest is completely empty," he says. "I'm afraid for how I feel about you. I'm excited too. And annoyed." He tells me he has felt homeless and disoriented since separating from his wife. "There's no structure anymore to tell me what decisions to make." I hold him in my narrow bed. He is hard to find. There are several patterns of vibration happening in his body, and I can't determine which is which, what he wants, what is most true. After two back-to-back Gaga classes, I am feeling strong and patient in my own body, so I just stay quiet and keep listening until eventually, his chest settles under my hand and grows very calm. We are face-to-face, but it is so dark, I can barely see him.

He says, "I love you. I don't know what that means, but I know that I feel it. And I'm very afraid."

He untangles himself gently from my embrace and stands again, his body disappearing into shadow. "I would like to stay here with you, but for now I am too frightened," he says. I nod, wanting, also, for him to go. There is a very careful regulation device in my heart for this man—I am afraid of too much time spent immersed in him, terrified of racing headlong into a relationship that maybe I don't want, cannot hold or protect.

He does not kiss me goodbye, just turns and leaves as quietly as he came.

I've been tiptoeing around his requests and Serious Talks for weeks. Unwilling to face the terror that rises in me when I think about having an Ordered Life, a Healthy Relationship, a Set Schedule, a Predictable Path—despite wanting, very much, all of these things.

"You'll never be happy in a safe place," The Healer once told me.

I refused to agree. "But I want a garden! Children! Cats!" I said. But the reality is, I have boxes of my belongings strewn across three different countries, and the closest thing to a garden I've come to is some scrawny mint plants growing between the cracks of my balcony. I have very little order and no schedule, and when everyone else is at their day jobs, I am stalking the streets thinking about poetry and God and art and war and peace, feeling simultaneously useless and completely free.

"Your center is strong," Tal keeps telling me when we train. "But you're gripping it." He holds up his fist to show me. "You won't let your movement out; it stops at your elbow. So there's all this force, but no follow-through."

I cringe every time he tells me. "You're saying I'm not committing to my own movement?"

"Yes. You go halfway and then stop. You're not committing, and so you're not able to do anything new with your body."

After the third time of hearing it, I decide to spend the month focused on my own studies, alone—working from home, three to four hours of self-practice a day, with additional yoga and Pilates classes every morning and night. *It is a perfect way to prove my own commitment to myself,* I think.

If I truly wanted to continue having a life that was devoted to art and dance, then I would have to know how to also be practical, focused, and dedicated on my own in order to sustain it in a world that is full of distractions and time warps, where losing track of what you love is as easy as losing your car keys.

Thus begins Discipline Month.

I have dreams every night about the word "commitment"—a woman is baking a cake for me, but she won't give it to me unless I sign a contract that promises I will stay for dinner, and so on. I wake up sweating. I vaguely see the humor in all of it, but not really. I get myself to my yoga and Pilates classes every day, welcoming the relief of someone telling me what to do, but then feel miserable during my hours of self-practice. Most days I finish my work flat on my back, fuming—at my body for feeling so stubborn, at my heart for being so fickle and afraid. Dancing is suddenly not fun at all; it is a chore.

"So you hit a wall," Tal says as I lie in the grass and watch him stretch in the park. "And there's only two things to do with a wall. You face it and you face it until it becomes a door. *Or* you escape. And you *really* escape, to a place where there's no wall, there's absolutely nothing, and eventually you start all over again."

I try both.

Some days I just stand there and watch my body fight with itself.

Move.

I don't feel like moving.

Move anyway.

No.

Then, for the Memorial Day–Independence Day holiday, I give up everything and go running around for four days with no schedule, getting lost in the tangle of street parties and wild, disorderly dancing on crowded street corners to the music of violins, drums, and electric guitars. I sleep till two every afternoon.

I decide that structure and discipline completely demolish the urge to create, because that urge is, in essence, wild, manic, unpredictable. It wakes you at four in the morning shouting about swamps you must wade into, luring you to give up sanity, happiness, green salads, to search instead for the art that burns like fire beneath the black water. It's why so many of the great artists have been drug addicts, alcoholics, or just completely insane.

And yet without the discipline, the structure, nothing is created from the creative urge—it remains raw material, throbbing within me, threatening to explode.

I become paralyzed with the split inside of me. I stop going to dance classes. I abandon my Hebrew lessons. The days spin.

On Thursday night, I convince Alon to go out with me, to a club on the beach. As I used to do every night in Greece, I give myself over to the music, the sea, the blur of alcohol. I am inside of all of it, moving as one with black-haired women in short skirts and tall boots, muscular men with shirt sleeves rolled up, the stars flung wide in the deep night sky, the waves crashing forward and sucking back again.

Alon's ex-wife, Mirav, is dancing across the bar, and I can see everything that she is in the way her body slides in and out of the music. I do not know her, but I love her—her pale, slender limbs and dark curls. We had met her on the stairs coming into the club. I took her hand warmly in greeting, relieved to finally meet the woman I had heard so much about. Her face was quiet and amused, also a little sad, looking from me to Alon. "It is nice to meet your girlfriend, Alon," she said to him in Hebrew, and he just nodded, his hands in his pockets.

He worries about her now, if she is okay, if she is comfortable with us all being together in the same place. He stays close to her side, talking in her ear, dancing with her.

He brings me a shot of tequila and over the pump of the beat and the sound of the sea below us. I shout, mostly joking, "Where is *your* clarity now? Who are *you* with?" He looks fiercely out to the ocean, and I am surprised to see a tear catching on his cheek before dropping. He takes a deep breath, and then in the crowded bar he gets to his knees. "Dayna, I have been trying to tell you. I am ready for this. It is just you. I am here."

I pull him to his feet. "Don't do that. You don't need to do that."

From the crowd, Tal suddenly rushes at me and pulls me back to the dance floor. I forget everything immediately, sinking back into the music. We do lifts, we spin, we dive at each other to the beat of the blaring hip-hop. I am vaguely aware of Alon, as he slips in and out of the crowd, looking tired, bored, sad. He does not want to dance with me when I motion him over. He has a wary look in his eyes.

⇌

He is very quiet when we get back to his house.

"What happened tonight?" I ask him finally. "Was it because of Mirav?"

"No." He goes to the bathroom and undresses for a shower.

I lean in the doorway. "What is it, then?"

Alon steps into the shower, the steam parting, then closing around his body. I follow him to the edge of the tile. He crosses his arms and levels his eyes at me. "The way you were dancing at the bar tonight. With Tal—"

"He is a friend. No attraction. None."

Alon shakes his head. The water cascades over his shaved head and pours over the cliff of his jaw. "It's you," he says. "You don't get it. It's *you*. I do not like the difficulty of our relationship today. And I am afraid."

Memories of Quin knock at me, and I am suddenly nauseous. I realize I could just keep doing this—living with one foot jammed in the exit door, one eye focused on wherever I could go that's not here. Slipping from bed to bed in a series of split-second loves—holding as many as possible till everything shatters and I start over. Half-happy. Half-terrified. Half-wildly satisfied. Half-numb.

Or, I could commit. And maybe this too is half. To be mostly content. To know how to fix his coffee in the morning. To make love the same way I might clean the kitchen. A cheerful, necessary obligation. This is not what Alon and I have yet, but I am wildly afraid this is where we'll end up.

"Have you ever been in a relationship where things are just simple and peaceful and nice?" he asks, reading my thoughts with his smart blue eyes.

"No."

And I don't know if I want it. Neither do I want the wild, unstable world of Love Anarchy. It is the fear of both paths that keeps me from being able to move in either direction, fear that one way will cancel the other out. And so my body becomes a mirror of this country—two opposite sides, unable to move or make room for each other.

⇌

I am ungrounded and unfocused when I wake the next morning, and stay that way all day. I race on my bicycle through the noise and the dirt of Tel Aviv. I meet Tal to eat hummus in the sun in Yaffo. "Dancing with you last night," he says. "Wow. You know what you are? You are *meshAgaat*."

"What does that mean?" I dip the pita in the warm hummus, hoping the food will calm the throb under my skin.

"It means 'so gorgeous, you make people crazy.'"

"C'mon. I'm not *that*. Especially here." I nod my head toward three women laughing at the table next to us. The Israeli women are among the most beautiful women I have ever seen: wild curly hair and strong, lean bodies; mystical eyes and fine, delicate facial features; confident, proud walks. My head turns daily on the street, in awe of them. I am the girl next door in comparison, their shy, doughy younger cousin.

Tal nods. "Yeah, sure, you're right. So many women are beautiful. But it's something else about you. An energy you have . . . I even slipped into it for a minute. I mean, you are like my sister, but for a second I also fell into what everyone falls into around you." He shakes his head and takes a bite of the hummus. "Complete craziness. The feeling, really, like I could go mad. I lost my balance. You kept gripping your head."

"I feel crazy. I make *myself* crazy."

Tal pushes his messy black curls back from his face. His skin is dark, and glows rose around his high cheekbones. "It's about to get hot here, Dayna. Really hot. Then you'll see this whole country go crazy." He smiles, but when I don't smile back, he leans forward and takes my hand. "Listen, sweetie. Here in Israel, we see so many people come here trying to change the situation. All these activists shouting how bad us Israelis are. All these Zionists shouting how bad the Palestinians are. And most everyone, you know, they have no idea what is happening. There's a joke about how every writer comes here, and if he stays for a month, he will write articles about us. If he stays for a year, he writes a book. If he stays for two years, he will swear to never write again. Because it is only then that he actually starts listening and realizes it's so complicated, one can barely say anything about it at all.

"Almost everyone who really lives here believes that there will never be peace, that there is no solution to the conflict. And this is just where we are at. Maybe if everyone could just let us be where we are at, without trying to *change* us, maybe then things will change."

The sun is hot on my face. Tal's strong hand is on my hand. And it is one of those moments—I am starting to recognize them. Those moments while traveling, when someone—a stranger, a child, or this dancer, my dear friend—says something so true, the moment stops or seems to stop. There's a sensation like color. I see a quality to the light, am aware of its changing as I hold the words given to me. It's like God has pressed a gift into my hand, directions to someplace sacred.

"Yes," I say. "What you are saying. Yes."

"Let the lover be," the poet Rumi wrote. "Disgraceful, crazy, absentminded. Someone sober would worry about things going badly. Let the lover be."

Maybe the first step in happiness is the acceptance of

misery, the first step in peace the acceptance of war. An agreement to stop fighting the way things are and listen, instead, to simply what *is*. Listen to the complexities of the human experience, and try, in some small way, to stop fighting the fact that we are fighting. Settle instead into the only thing that we *can* do: have compassion for where we are.

⇌

In Gaga class later, the teacher says, "How can you be truly happy with wherever you are, no matter where you are? If you're not happy with where your body is at, then a part of you is asleep."

⇌

A dancer from Tal's company sends her cousin Arya to me to work on his shoulder. He has obsidian eyes that curve up at the edges like a smile and a shock of unruly black hair. Something about him is deeply familiar, like I should hug him instead of shake his hand hello.

He is taking a course in Jerusalem to fulfill a requirement for his Austrian medical degree and is in Tel Aviv just for the weekend. I feel nervous, as I always do when I work on new people.

"You're going to be a doctor," I say. "So you might not like what I do. Because I can't explain it. Like . . . scientifically."

He shrugs. He has brought me a bag of dried fruits from the *shuk* and he places them on the counter. "I trust you."

He lies down on the mattress on the floor, and I begin to work on his shoulder, which my hands eventually show me really just means holding his heart for a while. I sink into the meditative space that comes when I let my body communicate directly to another body. No need for me to be involved. Just let it happen. Time stretches out, and there is deep quiet. When it is finished, he nods and meets my eyes. "I guess you can't tell me what you did. But I felt you doing something." He pulls himself up to sitting and leans forward, his elbows on his knees. "When you had your hand . . . your hand on my. . . ." He stops. His dark eyes fill with tears, and he looks away quickly.

"You can talk about anything you want." I touch his arm.

He shakes his head. "No, it's fine. I'm fine."

"Okay. Do you want tea?"

He nods. But when I start to stand, he grabs my wrist. "There is something," he says. He looks away. Looks back at me with his curved, black eyes, then away again, his mouth working around the words that won't come. He laughs. "Silence is also a way of talking, no?" he says.

I feel patient and relaxed from working on his body. I watch him wrestle with it. When it seems that nothing will come, I start to rise again, but instead of letting go of my wrist, he pulls me to him—his body moving slowly and deliberately around what the rules in his mind are clearly telling him not to do. I let him sink into me. His head goes to my collarbone, his hand to the nape of my neck. I feel him like a brother in my arms. He does not grip, but his arms are tight around my body. I hold him like that for a long time. It is late afternoon in Tel Aviv, that special time when the birds are the loudest noise in the city.

Eventually, I say, "You felt very familiar, after five minutes of talking with you."

He says, his mouth muffled by my shoulder, "After so long? I knew the second I saw you."

"Really?"

He nods into my body. "Your eyes. I saw them recognize me. They greeted me with delight. Like an old friend."

I laugh. How good and right it feels to connect with people like this, to feel us both relax into it, without confusion about what it might mean or not mean. In the context of these body sessions, as with the dance, this deep intimacy has safety, a container where I can just let my heart do what it longs so desperately to do: give love.

But when we eventually rise, when he is putting on his jacket and straightening his messy hair, my body seizes with worry. What was so clear minutes ago I am afraid will become unclear. He sees it in me and puts his hands on my shoulders.

"There is a connection between us. Do not be uncomfortable. I will not make it more than it is." The cleanness of his touch and his words are immensely relieving. When we hug goodbye, it is as old friends.

⇌

Alon is in Japan again to teach, and I am at his house using his Internet to check my email. Shai messages to say he stayed home from work today, and do I want to come over? I have not seen or heard from him in weeks, since he shared his poetry with me. The water is shut off, and the eggplant I'm roasting directly on the flame from the stove is burning, bleeding metal-colored juice into the spaces between fire. Shai's instant message hangs on the screen of my laptop, and

I try to remember if I've eaten today. Chocolate cake that Alon's mother baked me—that's it. Not a good place to make decisions from. And yet I will go, I realize; I cannot say no. I am consumed, as always, with the need to get close to the darkest thing—in myself, in others—as though if I could just touch it, then it might dissolve, free me to finally live quietly.

I shave my legs with the water that is left in the teapot. I say, "Yes, okay," to my face in the mirror. She is looking drawn and strange. She does not say, "Yes, okay," back to me.

Alon's house is clean, but I make his bed again, better, in ridiculous hope that it will somehow protect our relationship despite what I'm about to do. On my way, I stop at Shai's neighbor Oren's studio on the corner to record my voice for him on a new song he's written. He wants me to talk about Tel Aviv—doesn't care what I say, he just wants the English words, the American accent. He says, "Can you say it sexy?" and when I blush, he says, "This is the Dayna I know. You might not know it, but I know it."

"What's your song about?"

"It's about a woman. A sweet woman, in the city, who can't stop devouring men every night."

I cringe. "It's about me."

He considers this for a minute, then nods. "I'm renaming it 'Dayna's Song,'" he says.

⇌

Shai, when he answers the door, looks terrible—unshaven and hair greasy. His orange shirt is dirty, and he smells like cigarettes. He barely gives me space to come inside before his rough mouth is on mine. It is not about love, this time; it is about business, finishing something. I try to relax, try to find him. He will barely look at me. He pulls off my clothes and pulls off his clothes, and then he's deep inside of me and doing what he knows how to do, which is looking for and listening with his body for my most secret, most vulnerable places. When he finds them, he pushes so carefully and persistently into them, again and again, until I break, the desire to cry unbearable. And if I trusted him, I would let it come, this sadness and this wanting. I would lose myself to him, promise him everything. But I do not trust him, so instead I grip my jaw and shudder and hold his body which is already, slowly, beginning its gradual retreat.

"We're sweaty," is all he has to say and stands immediately to take a shower. I am left alone on his bed, staring at the painting on his wall, the monster embracing the angel. My hands on my stammering heart, listening to the panic, as my will to do anything, including breathe, seeps slowly out of my body.

He gets out of the shower to find me exactly where he left me. "Why did you come here?" he asks. He has put his pants on and is leaning against the doorframe, his arm behind his head. "You're looking for something you lost?"

"That sounds like a good explanation for it."

"Is it here?" His eyes are clouded in that terrifying distance, darkness between us.

"Why are you so gone like this?" I say.

My question brings him back for a brief instant. "Because you have a boyfriend. We say in Hebrew it's a *metaxola*. A sick bed."

"Okay. You're right." I gather my clothes to leave.

But when I am dressed, he takes my hand and pulls me

into him. His hair is wet, and he smells like his apple soap. He draws me back down to the bed, and I lie beside him, trying to concentrate on calming myself, the sick, sad feeling in my belly. I open my heart to the pain, and his body beside me responds instantly. He moans softly. A muscle in his stomach jerks. His shoulder shudders, and we are on the brink of falling into an electrical ocean when he says, "Enough," and shoves me from him, and this time he is really gone. He goes to his computer, and I put on my shoes and turn the keys in the door and step out into the street, into the sunshine and the noise.

⇌

I come out of the Hoodna's bathroom that night to find Shai kissing a woman, a slight blond in a blue-and-cream flowered dress. He tries to catch me as I slip past him. I don't know what I feel, but I know I don't feel like saying anything, and I dip away from his touch to dissolve into the packed street party. He calls and calls all night, and I ignore it. He texts, "I'm so, so sorry, I didn't mean for that to happen."

I assure with a text back that it doesn't matter. "We don't belong to each other."

⇌

He finds me again at the Hoodna just before sunrise and pulls me into the alley, away from the crush of the crowds. "The truth is, I really, really love you, Dayna."

"I thought you hated that word."

"I do. I do hate it. But it's the truth, so I have to say it."

He takes my hands. The sky is turning dirty white. Down the alley, reggae music from the Hoodna blares.

"What do you want?" I ask him.

"Someone who will love me. Accept me. Who I can feel safe with."

I nod, knowing this is not me, that safety in a relationship is the last thing I can provide.

He says, "I'm emotionally attached to you, and it's scaring me."

"Why?"

"Because you will leave."

I feel my heart as it pushes against my ribs, strains toward him. Shai leans in to kiss me, and I squeeze my eyes shut. "No."

He apologizes. "I want to be with you," he tells me, his stare intent. "But I don't want to destroy you, either. Your life, your happiness. Because of who I am."

"Yes," I say. "Me too."

He closes his eyes and rests his head back on the graffitied wall of the alley. "I've been so tired," he says, his voice defeated, weak.

I touch his stomach. "You've got a lot going on here."

"I know."

I feel the layers of shifting qualities inside of him, sadness and anger and fear cutting up against each other under my hand. "Your body's freaking out."

"Really freaking out." He keeps his eyes closed. "I need help, I think."

"I want to help." I pause. "You know that, right?"

He presses his hand gently to my shoulder without opening his eyes. "Yes," he says. And then: "I was stationed in

Gaza when I was in the army. I hated it. I fucking hated it. I didn't want to point my gun at anyone. And then. . . ." He turns his face away from me. "Then my whole unit died. Everyone but me. They all fucking died. I had to move their bodies, what was left of them." He keeps his hands jammed deep in his pockets, his eyes closed.

My hand is still on his stomach; I hold him there. I want to rip what I feel from his body, that dark starving animal of pain. But all I can say is, "Come. Come home with me."

He opens his eyes and turns to look at me for a long, quiet minute. Then, "*Yalla*," he says. "Let's go."

⇌

An American friend, Mark, invites me to go to Bethlehem with him for the day. He is an Aikido teacher in Jerusalem who wants to start an Aikido program in one of Bethlehem's orphanages. Aikido Without Borders. We'll go for the afternoon, do a demonstration, teach the kids a bit, come home.

My Israeli friends, even the most liberal, cringe when I tell them I am going to the West Bank. "It's not safe," they tell me. Everyone knows a story about a Jew who was kidnapped or attacked with stones; everyone wants to tell me about the Jewish people in the West Bank settlements, who have to carry guns everywhere they go.

Besides Alon, none of the Israelis I know have ever had a conversation with someone from Palestine. Alon is also the only person who understands why I want to go.

"You can't live in Israel and not visit there," he texts from Japan. "You'll be fine. I love you."

⇌

It is late afternoon when we arrive to Bethlehem—me, Mark, and one of his Arab-Israeli Aikido students, Amir, who drives us in his black SUV. Amir insists that Mark and I must first go visit the birthplace of Jesus. "For culture," he explains.

He drops us at the church and goes to park the car. Mark and I line up at the door behind a group of American Christians in khaki pants and pastel polo shirts. We inch our way into the church and then down into an underground grotto where there is a rock surrounded by flowers and candles. The Americans are taking turns kissing the star embedded in the stone. "Ooh, I got the candles in that shot," says a satisfied woman beside me, peering into her camera and cracking her gum.

The air is hot and wreaks of frankincense. I look up at the wooden beams of the ceiling, feeling dizzy. "So many religions in one place," Mark whispers. "If only Jesus had been born in Ohio." I swallow my laugh. When it is our turn, we touch the star dutifully and whisper our prayers, to all the gods, for peace.

When we emerge back into the square, the sun feels like a slap. A stooped Palestinian man is selling postcards out of a suitcase. A young boy beside him holds packages of bottled water over his head. "One euro, one bottle!" he shouts toward a crew of German tourists exiting the church.

The main street of the town climbs from the church's doorstep, straight uphill, and is lined with the typical Arab tourist shops. *Keffiyas* and *nargilahs*, bedouin rugs and—special for Bethlehem—cheap metal Christs on crosses. Quick-eyed, nervous-fingered men watch the street from the doorsteps.

"Yes, hello, hello, come in, American baby," they call as we pass. I hold my pant legs up out of the black water that drains down the hill, through the stones of the street, and try not to think about my bare shoulders. When Amir emerges from a hummus shop and rejoins us, the men stop calling.

⇌

The kids at the orphanage don't speak English beyond "Hello! Hello! Your name is?" but they lean into me as soon as I arrive, readily accepting me and the strange sounds that come out of my mouth. I can recognize only a few Arabic words from their rapid sentences, and have to restrain my impulse to answer their questions in Hebrew.

As Mark gets ready for the demonstration, I find a seat in a green plastic chair beside a middle-aged woman in a leopard-print headscarf. I smile at her, and she smiles back. "Where do you live?" she asks in thickly accented English.

"Tel Aviv," I answer, then involuntarily brace myself, expecting her anger. Since Palestinian people are not granted their right to return home, many do not take kindly to other people, from other countries, being given this right, which is entirely understandable to me. The woman only smiles though and nods her head slowly.

"Tel Aviv. Nice city," she says.

"You've been there?"

"No." She smiles again quickly and then looks down. "But I hear it is nice."

My heart grips with shame to have asked, and sadness. Tel Aviv is only a little over an hour's drive from where we are, but it might as well be the other side of the world for this woman.

The mats have all been laid out in the cement yard the orphans use as a play area, and Mark and his students begin demonstrating a series of slow Aikido moves for the excited children. Two young girls lean into my legs, sharing a bag of Doritos. "You want to go try it?" I ask them, when Mark invites volunteers up and a crowd of boys storm the mats. The girls understand my gestures and shake their heads.

"I would like to try it," the woman beside me says and laughs. She motions toward one of Mark's students, a Japanese woman who lives here in the West Bank, who is at this moment teaching the kids how to count in Japanese as they face off against an invisible opponent. "But I can't be like her. Women here can't do this. We can't be so . . . strong."

"What do you do here, at the orphanage?" I ask.

She laughs again. "I cook and clean and look after one hundred and twenty children." About fifty of these children are rolling around on the mats at our feet yelling "*Arraygatooooo! Ichi! Ni! San!*" as they nose-dive into each other.

"Sounds like you're pretty strong," I say.

⇌

Driving back to Jerusalem, we pass the wall that Israel is building to separate the Palestinians from the Israelis: towering thick concrete, topped with a rolling coil of barbed wire. The bus bombings in Israel, once a frequent horror for Israelis, have stopped since the building of the wall. It also cuts through Palestinian land like a tumor. My stomach hurts immediately at first glimpse of it, like a visceral thought: *that is no prayer for peace.*

At the checkpoint, a young soldier peers through each

window of our car, holding his gun at his side. Because Amir is Israeli-Arab, he has an Israeli passport, and unlike the Palestinians, is allowed to travel back and forth without a travel permit. Still, we all stop breathing until the soldier lets us through.

And then we are through and suddenly back in Israel—the quiet sorrow of the West Bank, in a matter of minutes, feathering away into Jerusalem's dark pulse. The blue-and-white Jewish flag flies high over the soccer stadium. Stooped orthodox Jews in black and white wait at the crosswalks. And far away, in the heart of the city, the Dome of the Rock and the Western Wall stand side by side, gleaming under the half-moon.

⇌

I sleep on Mark's sofa and wake early the next morning to don a black, rayon suit for a weekend of work at the presidential conference. It is the first job that I've accepted from the temp agency I'm registered at. The handful of various things I do for work—babysitting, art modeling, bodywork—has been enough to get me by, but this particular job sounded too interesting to pass up. It was a chance to get close to the men in charge and hear what they had to say about this complicated country.

I am posted as a door woman at the back of the auditorium and instructed to smile at everyone who passes. Shimon Peres, the president of Israel; then Ehud Olmert, the prime minister of Israel; then George W. Bush, the president of the United States—each go onstage to say what great men and what great leaders the others are. They show a video about

Israel and America's long history of friendship, working together for peace in the Middle East. They acknowledge all the times the United States came to Israel's aid in times of war—swooping in to help terminate all those who "threatened the modern civilizations."

I watch Barbara Bush smile graciously at her husband and pat his knee. Everyone claps in the right places and stands up in the right places, and the whole room is mostly full of dead people.

I manage to stay for an hour before I have to push open the double doors and escape, sweaty and angry. All the workers, like me, are lounging at their posts with their sleeves rolled up, laughing low together. They are better than I am at this—directing each suit and tie with pretty smiles and sugar in the mouth. But all I can think is, *It is because of the decisions of these men and the men before them, that an uncountable number of people have suffered and continue to suffer.* These men have all the power, and their bodies are heartless tin cans. *No one's telling the truth!* I rage. *How can they live like that?*

Then I go and lie to my boss that I have a headache and escape out the back door to go home.

Knowing that I too am also guilty.

⇌

I meet Shai at the Hoodna, but I can't settle. I keep scratching at my nose until Shai tells me I'm acting like I snorted lines. "You're not finished with something," he says. Sharon is behind the bar doing shots of arak with two men, one who seems to be wearing a blanket. Shai's neighbor Oren is on my right, fighting with his girlfriend about whether or not she should have the baby she just discovered is growing in her womb. Oren shovels bites of hummus and pita into his mouth between long, adamant sentences. He wants the baby. She does not. I jiggle my leg and feel attached to what I am saying about politics and war but keep getting interrupted because women are stopping to talk to Shai, and every time, I wonder if she is someone he's slept with or wants to sleep with.

"Yes, I'm unsettled about something," I finally admit, and he nods.

"You should go home and take a shower. You were just surrounded by some really, really dirty people."

I think about all those businessmen and politicians with stooped shoulders and fat bellies. How they will tell their friends, "We were just in Israel for the presidential conference," perhaps with pride, with self-importance. Meanwhile, they have no idea what's really happening here. They have never lived here, talked to people here. They don't care about the woman in the leopard-print headscarf, who likely will never be allowed to visit this "nice city"—just one out of a multitude of injustices she is forced to live with every day. They don't care about the majority of people, Palestinian and Israeli both, who just want peace. They care about what serves them only, and they will continue to get it, at the expense of everyone else.

I go home and take a shower, but it doesn't help. I fall asleep shaking in my bed alone and wake in the night, drenched with sweat.

⇌

In the morning, Shai texts to ask if I want anything from the Far East. Alon will return from Japan the day after Shai will leave for a work trip to China. A decision about who I want to be with must be made before then. "Green tea," I tell Shai and then cringe. Alon had asked me the same thing last night, and that had been my answer. I wonder at the symbolism of one boyfriend going back and forth to Japan, the other to China. When they ask me what I want, I say green tea. Because one can never get enough green tea. Or love, apparently.

In the late afternoon, I am crying on Shai's couch. He asks me again and again, "Who do you choose?"

"Alon," I finally manage, and he nods, his eyes sharp and angry on my face.

"I just wanted to hear you say it."

But then at sunset, we are hugging each other goodbye, and all the distance and impossibility has dissolved. We make love, and then he packs his bags and worries about things and checks the weather in Beijing while I eat cereal on the couch and tell him periodically that I love him.

And he says, "*Ken mami*" and "I love you too, *motek*," and he kisses me and tells me he'll miss me more than I can understand and that he wants to have babies with me and a garden.

I say, "But this is over" and "We can't be together when you return."

And he says he knows and that he'll write me, and will I write to him?

And I say, "I'm going to have a panic attack, because what the fuck, how do I, how do I do this. . . ?"

He smooths my hair and says, "Shh." He kisses me on the mouth. "Will you feed my fish when I'm gone?" he asks.

⇌

I go to clean Alon's house for his arrival. I put flowers on the table, and Shai texts from the plane. "I love you more than all the birds flying over the ocean."

"Maybe you need to be single," Tal says on the beach that night.

"Right. Haven't heard that one before. Maybe I should be a nun. That has also been suggested." I grab handfuls of sand and let them trickle out through my fingers. I think about regret, desire, discipline, and addiction. I think about how I'm still young enough to feel squeamish about "right action," about drinking less and focusing more. I am still young enough to want wilderness over the orderly path. Young enough to want to die in a fury—a great, sudden explosion, like my father, leaving behind a story that can be food for several generations of meaning-hungry seekers. Sometimes I gag at the words "pray" and "intend." I want to frighten people with my words. I want to say, "Hey, there's no reason to be *so* serious" and then close my eyes and sink beneath the waves.

Then I wake up and am appalled. My one self turns its nose up at my other self and taps a nervous finger against its teacup. *You did* what? *Glass fight? Slept with him again? Can't choose just one? What's* wrong *with you?*

"When I was little, my mother used to tell me that before we are born, we choose our life," I say to Tal. "We choose our parents, and together with our angel guides, we write all the things that will happen to us in this lifetime, in order to learn whatever we are needing to this time around."

"Interesting," Tal says, squinting out at the dark sea. "I like that."

I snort. "I can just picture it. Me—my soul or whatever—figuring it out with my angel friends. They'd be like, okay, your dad will leave you in this horrible way, when you are exactly at the age when it will do the most neurological damage and forever affect your ability to be in healthy relationships as an adult. And then after that, we'll just throw men at you. Lots and lots of men. You'll barely have any female friends; everyone will just be men. All the driving forces of your life will be men. Your life will be a man storm. Okay? Sound good? Great, off to a body you go now."

"Sounds as good a way to learn something as any," Tal says, laughing. "*Chuka*, maybe this story is just about love. Not the kind of love that you and I know. But the kind that we hope to know, someday."

I put my head on my friend's shoulder, and he rests his on top of mine.

I do think we're all missing something. I'm not getting it, and neither is Shai, not Alon, not even my open-minded mother, whose desire for me to marry Alon is getting as urgent and as fevered as her desire for me to eat organic vegetables and wear a helmet when I ride my bicycle. "He knows himself. He gives you space to feel your feelings. He does the *dishes*, Dayna. This is the kind of man women search for. What do you need to do to let go of Shai?" she says.

Earlier in the night, while checking my email, the instant messages flared, everyone at the same time. Shai wanted me to tell him what I think love is, while Alon typed, "Dayna, I love you," and Quin's message popped up, "Dayna, here is my love, in my hand."

Shai was in the airport in Tel Aviv. Alon was in the airport in Tokyo. Quin was at a bar in Madrid. Sharon was behind me, at the sink, talking on the phone. The pink flowering vine out the window was wilting in the streetlight. I closed my eyes and rattled with the heat in my body. A friend of Sharon's came out of the bathroom and touched the yellow flowers in the pot on the counter. "Pretty. . . ."

"From my boyfriend." A present from Alon, before he left for Japan.

"Boyfriend? I thought, you and Shai. . . ?"

"No."

"Ah. Well. You and Shai you seem very . . . passionable."

"Yes. Something like that."

⇌

I wander away from Tal and kneel at the edge of the sea. I splash salt water on my face to soothe the rash that is beginning to grow there, a burning heat rising from the center of me to my skin.

Down the beach, an Arab boy is leading his horse into the toss of the water. It is a slow process. The horse is switching back and forth between obedience and terror. The boy is switching back and forth between complete ease with the giant animal and the pounding waves, to frustration over the impossibility of the situation, as he is tugged off balance by the jerking horse, or leaps out of the way to avoid its frantic side steps.

Tal follows and stands behind me, and we watch the boy with his horse in the moonlight. "Did I tell you about the time when I lived in Chiapas with a horse tribe?" he says after a while. "We would walk for days with the horses. Going down steep cliffs with a horse in front and a horse behind. It was so muddy and so steep, that in some places the horses needed to run." He kneels beside me, his shoulder to my shoulder. "There was no time," he says. "The only thing that existed was *Where am I going to put my foot next*? I wasn't even thinking. I was finding the next place for my foot."

The water surges around our bare knees. I lean into him, and he leans into me. "And you know, it was terrifying. But it was the biggest sensation of being alive I have ever felt."

"So you're telling me nothing is wrong?" I lay my weight across his back, and he takes it easily.

"I think so," he says, standing with me draped still across his torso. "You are traveling somewhere with this, you know?" I hang upside down on his body, the sea wide and dark above the glow of the stars. He twirls me gently to place my feet on the ground again. "Just stay awake in it," he says.

⇌

Quin calls from Madrid. Says he's been locked in depression for the last month. "And that depression, I can say, was largely based entirely on you," he says, without anger or accusation. His voice is that low, sweet drawl that I love. Soon we are laughing so hard, I feel like I might shatter. "I don't even think the United States *exists* anymore," he says. "I'd get there and there'd just be a cardboard cutout of a country and behind that, a pile of sand." I want to talk to him forever. I want to run away with him, find another island, find a way for it to be Just Us. Meanwhile, the man I call my partner sleeps sweetly in the bed down the hall.

Quin describes a movie he just saw, about a woman married to a gay man. How deeply they loved each other and allowed each other in such a way that their love became something completely new—a story different from what we know love to be. Bigger, beyond definition. "I was crying, man," he says. "I could barely watch it. I miss you so much."

I close my eyes. "I miss you too," I say, my insides shaking with the cacophony of too many love stories.

⇌

The body, the body, the body, and the ground.

This I whisper to myself every day, reading letters from Shai, kissing Alon as images of my hometown rattle through my head—Washington state showing me slideshows of itself, asking, "Will you ever return here?"

The body, the body, the body, and the ground.

"I'm sorry for making your life so confusing and intense," Shai writes from China.

"It's not you," I return. "It's always like this. It hasn't stopped. I don't know how to stop it."

⇌

Alon leaves the contact jam with sharp anger and sad shoulders. I leave the man I am dancing with and run out after him, into the windy night. He has tears in his eyes. "Dayna. This is not going to work between us."

This, after a long dance together with him coaching me on my technique. "Your center is strong, but you won't let it all the way out—the movement stops. You have so much movement potential, but I can't track it. You will go wherever I go, but where do *you* want to go?"

He had challenged me to lead him, to make decisions about what I wanted. Just the suggestion made me feel panicked and frozen.

"Say no. Say yes. Lead," he said.

I retreated from Alon's feedback, and within minutes, another man stepped in to dance with me. This was when Alon took his things and left.

"You are like this beautiful flower in the garden," he says when I catch up to him outside, the stars blazing over the sea behind him. "And all the *par-pareem* want to land on you, to drink that juice that you have inside of you. And the moment one leaves, bam, another one lands. And you like it—you need it. But when are you going to realize that you only need one? When are you going to say, 'I want *this* one' and make space for me to come and stay with you?"

The wind is whipping up from the sea, and it chills the sweat on my forehead. Alon takes my hands, and his eyes soften.

"You're not ready for me. You're not ready for what I have to offer you. For what *we* have together. Because you still want your life to have no responsibility—"

I start to protest but realize in my gut that he's completely right.

"So I'm letting you go, to make your own decision, with no pressure from me. You are free now. We are not together. And if you will decide that you are ready, then I am here."

I feel close to throwing up. I can't all the way look at him.

He says, "You're twenty-six. You're not ready." And I know it is true. I am scared to even *be* ready for him, even as I know that to let go of this man is unbelievably stupid.

The waves beyond us push to shore and then out again.

Shai has just gotten back from China. I know he is waiting for me tonight, if I want him.

"Dayna, we can go anywhere together, and you know that. Maybe one day we will go to Greece. We will be completely wild. Lose everything, our minds, and it will be together."

I know that he can do this, go fully into the darkness of himself and do it with the candle still safely lit within him. He knows how to hold the light and carry it into the swamps. I have clung to him for this, needing him to teach me how to do it.

"I am afraid," I cry. "What if I will never be ready?"

"Be easy on yourself. You are twenty-six. I have ten years on you. There are things I understand that you do not yet. It's only time. You'll get there.

"Listen," he says. "I'm going home now. And I will leave it to you to decide. If you do not come home to me tonight, then it is over. You have to make the decision that is right for you. You are free to make the decision. But you have to *make* it."

His strength, his clarity, is everything that I want. And yet the thought of being free of him is wildly relieving, and I know it is true—I am not ready for him.

⇌

I knock on Shai's door at midnight, and he lets me in without a word. I sit on his kitchen counter. He leans against the opposite wall, his eyes sleepy and patient. "What is it?" he asks.

"I want to be with you."

He doesn't say anything for a moment. Then he walks toward me slowly. "Emotionally, spiritually, sexually, metaphysically?"

"All of it. All of it. Yes."

He grips my waist and lifts me onto his body. I wrap my arms around his neck, and we kiss hard and hungry as he carries me back to the bedroom.

⇌

I don't know what wakes me. The clock glows 4:00 a.m. Something has yanked me from sleep, and I begin to dress, don't even think about it. Shai wakes too and watches me from the bed. Finally, he says, "If you leave right now, I don't ever want to see you or talk to you again."

I nod. Can't say anything except "I know."

⇌

Alon is awake in bed when I get there. "Does this still count as me coming home tonight?" I ask.

He doesn't answer, just pulls me into his arms. "I didn't know what decision you would make."

I don't want to speak, don't want to think, just want to curl into the quiet of him. "I didn't, either."

ISRAEL

2009

II.

Arya, the soon-to-be doctor, is waiting for me with his hands in his pockets beside a cluster of old Arab women, their wares spread out before them on an olive-green blanket. There are stacks of grape leaves, eggplants, boxes of oranges. The narrow, dark passageways of the Old City behind him are packed with afternoon shoppers. He hugs me. "Welcome to Jerusalem," he says.

At the security checkpoint for the Western Wall, the guard waves me through but stops Arya. The soldier is young, no older than nineteen, with a set jaw and a chest that looks like he is holding his breath. "Where are you from?" he asks Arya.

Usually Arya says Iran, for this is where both of his parents come from, and he likes to see the shock in the Israeli faces when he says it. But this time he knows to be careful, and he hands the soldier his Austrian passport. "Austria."

The boy flips through it with quick, restless fingers. He asks Arya to empty his bag. Studies his face. Looks again at the passport. "Can you say something in the language you speak here?" he finally says. "Can you say something in . . . Austrian?"

Arya's eyes soften. "We speak German." He pauses and then leans close to the boy, as though he might put a hand on his shoulder. In a quiet voice, he says something that neither I or the boy understand. Then he translates: "I said, it must be hard, this job."

For a second, the boy looks like he is going to be angry. Then something drops from his eyes. He takes a breath. "It's really hard." And he waves us through, briskly, his face apologetic and sad.

At the Western Wall, I reach my hand over the top of a young girl who is sobbing into the stones and I touch the stones too, looking up at the branches of a tree that has sprouted from the cracks. Beyond it the sky is a fierce, wild blue. With my other hand, I hold the thin white scarf that I bought for this purpose tight around my bare shoulders, feeling the scrutiny of the religious women who stand in clumps to the sides, chewing their mouths and squinting. Most everyone else here is crying and rocking. I search my heart, my body, for something to say, something to whisper to the god that is living in this ancient wall. I lean into the center of my chest to see what is there and find it is only a deep prayer, as I have prayed every day in this country, for peace.

Every day for the last two weeks, Israel has been dropping bombs on Gaza. I had emerged from an intensive week of dancing in the contact festival in the North when I heard that Israel had launched a full-fledged attack. My first year, at the same festival, I was asking a lot of questions of the Israelis I met. *What do you think, what do you feel, what is it like to live in eternal conflict?* I spent that year writing and studying and thinking about it, until the next festival came. I didn't ask any questions at that one, because I no longer knew what to ask. This year, my third festival, I was on the other side of the table—being questioned carefully by the foreigners who wanted to know what I thought, what I felt, how and if I could justify it, my choice to live in a country that was guilty of such atrocities. I surprised myself by answering in the same manner that the Israelis had once answered me— gently, vaguely. *Oh, you know, it is just a hard thing, what do you say, this is life, same as everywhere else, every country has done horrible things. . . .*

Then I went home to Alon's and my apartment, and I confronted the news. I watched hordes of people, in countries only miles away from where I lived, shout for the death of Israel, shout for the death of every Jewish man, woman, and child. It was like watching a live streaming video of each of your neighbors swearing to kill you. For the first time in my life, I understood what it means to be desired dead simply for the blood in my veins. "If you've got enough in you to be killed for it, you're Jewish," Tal had said.

⇌

Arya and I leave the Western Wall and wander toward East Jerusalem, arm in arm. Arya tells me about his recent trip to the West Bank's village of Hebron, about the Palestinians who aren't allowed to walk in the streets of their own town. "I'm quite tired of it, Dayna, that's what I feel," he says. "I am glad my school is over, because I am ready to go back to Vienna. Of course, there is craziness everywhere. But this. It is too much, really." He has taken to wearing a kippah to ward off the consistent racism he has faced here because of his dark skin, his Persian eyes. He touches it with his fingertips now. "You know that I wasn't allowed into a temple because I have an Arab last name? 'Is your father Muslim?' they asked me. 'Yes. But I am not Muslim,' I said. 'It doesn't matter,' they said. 'You cannot come in.'

"But the Christians," he says, shaking his head. "They let the Christians into the temple. And I wanted to say, do you know that the Christians killed six million of your people? But I didn't. I felt very sad and walked away."

Arya's eyes are curved up and always smiling, even when he talks of such things. He is sad, but calm—the racism, the violence, it is all nothing new to him. He has been reconciling his whole life with what I am only just now encountering. I rest my head against him, feeling large and white and awkward, slipping on the slick stones in the Arab quarter as the dark-haired men sitting on the stoops of their shops call out to me in the language they know is mine: "Hey, girl. Hey, lady. What you want? Hello."

⇌

"Can you imagine what it is like, to wake up in the middle of the night and someone is there in your room to take you?" Alon says to me that night as he is cooking dinner. He is telling me the story of when he was sent to Syria to kidnap a Hezbollah leader. Alon and his special ops team took him from his bed in the middle of the night.

I have no stomach for the *betzim im tiras* he sets down in front of me. I scribble in my journal, "Talking about kidnapping over dinner," and try not to cry again.

I try not to cry all the time now. Try just to keep it quiet, the terrible grieving that is building in my body for all this suffering. For realizing that 90 percent of my Israeli friends here have killed someone or seen someone killed, or a lot of someones. That every single one of them also can tell you exactly where their family was during the Holocaust, each one a uniquely weighted story of how their particular family members survived, why they themselves are alive today. And now they live in a place where considering the death of your children is a necessary practice for family planning. That you wouldn't have just two kids, because then what would the one do, if the other died, in a war, from a bus bomb, from a terrorist with a gun? That the shape and layout of the kibbutz is based on what is safest if a rocket hits. The children are in the middle, their kindergarten and their playgrounds wrapped by what they hope is the barrier of their houses.

I listen to everyone arguing. Facebook blows up. *We stand with Israel. We stand with Palestine.* Everyone wants to be in the fray of blame and outrage. There are two sides of the coin, and everyone wants to point to one side carefully and clearly and declare it right for this reason and that reason, as though a thousand people haven't already done that a thousand times before them. But why do such a thing anymore? I feel like screaming. Can we not point to the place in the air where the coin is flipping? To say look, look, look, how this two-sided thing becomes a sphere—can we think like that, can we move like that, can we be like that? *Whole.*

⇌

I start spending a lot of time on rooftops. I sit where I can see only the endings of structures, and the sky, which goes on forever. I sit where I can see the sea. I think about how my life is nothing like these big things. I am a small spot on a rooftop. I am watching the clouds shuffle in. And I think,

Okay, maybe I will never do anything, be anything, save anything. Maybe everyone will just keep killing each other, and I will just keep not knowing what to do about it. Meanwhile, the world goes on.

My mother begs me to leave. She offers me a plane ticket home. I tell her I'm not in danger, other than emotional implosion. She says, "That is danger enough."

I write to everyone I know:

It is ridiculous to ask a person who is living in fear every day to calm themselves or act sanely. I find I can ask very little change of anyone living here in Israel and Palestine, including myself. But I do not find it ridiculous to ask those who are sitting at home by the fireside, reading the news, to take the time to search their hearts for a kind of compassion that will be strong enough to travel over water and across land, a kind of light to remind all who, in their fear, have forgotten the feeling of neutrality. Remind us that here it is, here is love, everyone deserves it, and this is the only way out of the darkness. Don't pick a side. Hold us all, with hope.

Some people write back, but it's only to debate with me. They want to point out the atrocious acts of the Israeli army, or the Palestinian bus bombings in the last intifada. I say, "Can we talk about this in a different way?" But no one knows how to.

Including me.

⇌

Q,

   Thank you for your email. It means more than I can say.

   I just cried for an hour, and there might be no end to it. I'm really confused and really tired. I don't like war at all. There's absolutely no way to live a normal life when seven hundred people have died next door to you. My stomach hurts every morning when I wake up. There's no place to go where I can forget about this suffering now. I'm too sensitive. When I tell people here that the war is bothering me, they look at me like I just said, "You know, the monkey," like there's no context to the sentence.

   I don't know how to be tough like them, to just go on with things like nothing. I feel like I am floating away. I miss you. I'm sorry for everything.

Dayna,

   Come to Madrid, baby. You can stay with me as long as you like. It might be really good for you, considering all you're going through, not to mention there are less bombs here. We do have ETA, but they're little puppies compared to Hamas. I should be around for most of the day today. Call. Come to me.

   Love, Q

I go to a dance performance in my neighborhood and sit for two hours watching talented dancers flounce across the stage, calling out vapid things to each other like, "Yair is a nice name. I also like the name Shlomit."

Three times, I almost stand up in the middle of the show

to yell, "Your country is *destroying* itself; why don't you say something about that?" but I drink glasses and glasses of wine instead and chew my fingernails off.

I yell at Alon later, furious in our kitchen. "I stayed in Israel to learn about the heart of a very intense, very powerful conflict. I thought that for sure, in such an environment, there would be nothing to say *but* the truth. But no one here talks about it. No one makes art about it. And while everyone's being silent, this elephant is breaking everything inside the room!"

Alon just looks at me with sad eyes. There is so much broken between us too. No longer do we go sailing through light fields together. Our sexual intimacy is as I once feared it would become—obligatory, habitual. The calm and ordered life I have wrestled myself into holds me now and does not let go. I have found a dance school in Jerusalem that I like, and I now have a set schedule of training weekly with a group. My Hebrew is getting better. I have friends, and I go to the beach and take trips with Alon to visit his family. But I'm distracted, can't stop thinking about Shai, and Alon knows it. We talk about it. We talk and talk and talk and talk. Talks are good, rich, honest. We can get through anything, everything—that's how good we are at talking. And it scares the shit out of me. We will keep going. We will keep going like this forever.

There are so many dead children in Gaza; the news blares it every day. I'm crying all the time, watching, reading. Israeli friends roll their eyes at me. "It's your first war here?" they say. "You'll get used to it."

But I don't want to get used to it, don't want to stop being horrified. Because it is *horrifying,* what's happening. I start going out by myself, drinking too much, angry at everyone.

One weekend, Alon goes to his parents' house near the Syrian border and leaves me on my own. It's Friday, and the sun's just rising. I'm drunk coming back from a club, and I can't quite get myself home. I stand in front of Shai's door, staring at the wood paneling. It's been uncountable months since I've seen him, the street white and silent.

Don't knock, don't knock, don't knock, don't knock.

Two soldiers, young, barely twenty perhaps, are the only ones out on the street. They ask me what I'm doing.

"I'm about to do something stupid."

"Don't do that."

They walk me home instead. When we get there, I invite them in. We all three lie down together on the futon in the living room. They curl around me and kiss my face and tell me how beautiful I am. They're so young. *These are the boys the world is yelling about.* One boy goes and finds massage oil in the bathroom, tells the other to massage my neck while he does my feet. It's bright white morning, and they're tireless. It's all sweet—so, so kind and sweet. I cry a little, and they rock me in their young, strong arms. Finally, I tell them they need to leave. No, I say, they can't have my number. They keep thanking me. The best night of their life, they say.

When Alon gets home later in the day, I tell him everything. He says he's just relieved I didn't go back to Shai. "Sounds like a good night," he says. But I know. I know I have cracked open the door to everything I have caged, and it will now destroy us.

⇌

A few nights after the soldiers.

Alon and I are having a beer at the Hoodna. When Alon is outside talking to a friend, I slip out the back alley and, as though drugged, find myself again at Shai's.

I knock once. He opens the door immediately, like he is waiting for me, his sweatshirt hood pulled over his head. I try to say something but realize I can't. He lets me in, and then we are embracing. I close my eyes. He leads me backward, toward the bedroom. I open my eyes to see him, see his house, the inside of his life again—that painting on his wall of the monster embracing the angel. I grip his hair and look at him, his long, deep stare, his heart racing beneath my hand. Then we are kissing, our mouths together like we could become each other; he presses me into the wall, I wrap my legs around his waist. My shirt is off, his shirt is off, we tumble to the bed. My phone is ringing—Alon, trying to find me.

I snap back into consciousness. *What the fuck, what the fuck, what the fuck?* I'm not drunk, but it's like a blackout. I have no idea how I got here. I can't find my shirt. I turn the light on. "Shit, I have to go. I have to go. What am I doing? Where the fuck is my shirt?"

He stares up at me from the bed. Furious eyes. I find my shirt under the pillow and pull it on, fumble with the keys in the door, and slip outside. Alon is leaning against the building across the street, his arms crossed, his cell phone in his hand. Not mad. Not even mad. "Darling," he says. "Darling. What are we going to do?"

I sink to the curb with my head in my hands, and Alon walks past me and into Shai's house. Then they're drinking whiskey at his kitchen table. I lift my head to see them through Shai's open door. "Okay, you guys take it from here,"

I mumble and try to walk away. Shai chases me down the street and brings me back by the arm without a word.

We all three sit on Shai's tired brown leather couch. "It's clear that you two love each other very much," Alon says looking back and forth between us. I can tell Shai is angry, but he's hiding it. He pours Alon more whiskey. Alon can drink all night; he never gets drunk, the same as he can go days without sleep and not be tired, the same as he can sit with his girlfriend's lover and not be angry. "I work my emotions the same as I work my body," he said to me on our first date, and the same thing I thought then is still true: *this man is stronger than me.* Stronger than all of us. Shai's matching him drink for drink and looks close to a blackout. I realize that I'm absurdly happy. That all I wanted was to be with both of them. I couldn't choose one, because I didn't want one without the other. They are the two halves of my split self.

After a while, Alon says he's going home and he'll be waiting for me whenever I'm ready. "You two need to work this out," he says. He shakes Shai's hand and leaves. I'm in love with Alon's strength, his sanity, his confidence, the freedom he is able to give me. And I'm deliriously happy to be left alone with Shai. I've missed him desperately.

Except he's drunk. He walks slanted to close the door behind Alon and locks it. It's the kind of door that can't be opened without a key. He takes the key and goes into the kitchen and when he comes back his eyes are black, dead, a stranger's. I reach for my phone and see that it's out of battery. My senses suddenly narrow, honed.

"Are you okay?" I ask, but he can't hear me. He comes at me, grabbing me around the shoulders, wrestling me to his room, and throws me on the bed. It is the same pathway we took an hour earlier, but this time everything is different. He pins my arms with one hand and tries to rip my pants off with the other. I fight him, trying to shake him out of it. "Come back; this isn't you. This isn't you!" I yell, but he keeps going, tearing at my shirt, slamming my shoulders against the wall above his bed. He gets me on my back and puts his forearm across my throat. I try to find him in his blank stare. When I do find him—a scared child crouching at the back of his eyes—I keep my voice dead calm, speak directly to him: "Shai. Do you really want to do this?"

He blinks and lets me go.

We sit in silence for a minute. I whisper, "Are you back? Are you here?" I start to stand. "Where is the light? I need to see you." But before I can find it, he launches himself at me.

"Shut up and suck my dick," he says in a voice I've never heard from him. He tries to turn me around and rip off my pants with one arm, the other locked around my neck.

It goes on like this for a long time.

An hour. More. I keep thinking I should be scared, but I'm not. I just keep moving. Don't let him pin me. Breathing. Looking for him.

Finally, he slumps, exhausted, and I'm able to slip from his grip. There are bruises blooming on my arms and shoulders. "Where's the key? Tell me where the key is?" He won't speak, just stares at the wall in front of him.

I'm oddly starving. I go to the kitchen and eat a banana. When I tell Quin the story later, he says, after he is done being furious, "When life gives you rape, eat a banana." Behind the bananas is the key, and I leave immediately, the neighborhood streets empty, the sunrise white-hot. A block before I get back to Alon's apartment, I start shaking so hard, I have to sit down. All I can think about is the images on the news, the furious, grief-stricken Palestinian fathers holding up their dead, legless children in front of the cameras—in Gaza, a short drive from me. I choke and then vomit cloudy banana sludge into the filthy gutter.

⇄

Two weeks later, I pack my things and leave all of it.

"One love doesn't diminish the weight of another love," Alon tells me as he hugs me in the airport. "You are right when you say that. It never does; it can't. But in love, there's also a wild beast. That's why we have rules about how we're supposed to be in partnerships. Not everyone can or wants to dance with him."

I nod with my face pressed to his collarbone. Knowing I won't stop and don't know how to stop—dancing with the beast unbridled.

Aside from Quin, I only talked to three people about what happened with Shai. "Who's to blame in this situation?" I kept asking, suspecting with sick guilt that it was me, not him. Couldn't I have helped him earlier, recognized the signs, made him go to therapy? It was me who pushed him over the edge; if I had only been clearer, less selfish. If I had only chosen him.

The first person I told was Alon, who got sad and said probably none of us or all of us were to blame. He held me and said he was sorry and that he didn't know what else to say.

The second friend, Oren, Shai's neighbor, called to say

that after hearing Shai's side of the story, he had concluded that I am self-centered, selfish, and a manipulative bitch. I told him I think all of those things are also true, and thank you for reminding me. Then I hung up the phone and cried.

The third friend I told was Tal, who got livid, spitting mad, and yelled, "For Christ's sake, Dayna, enough of this left-wing compassion bullshit, you have *bruises* on your arms! If you see him again *break his knees.*" He went on to lament long and hard about the grievous opinions of peace-loving liberals: "If the Palestinians could, they would kill us, all of us, and yet what do you guys say? 'Oh, give them more land, give them more freedom; maybe then they will stop coming over here and *murdering* us.'"

His voice was admittedly refreshing, waking me enough to realize that in understanding Shai's side, I'd forgotten to understand my own side. I'd forgotten that the two could, and *needed to* exist simultaneously in order for the conflict to move and transform. One side is not right, the other wrong. There are not only two sides to the coin, and picking one side and sticking with it does nothing but lock the conflict into immoveable halves. Israel has taught me this. *Point to the place in the air where the coin is flipping. Think like this, be like this: whole.*

I thought of Jesus, who cursed his killers in the minutes before he died. Then he said, "Forgive them, Father, for they know not what they do."

Enough of this banging on the wall, demanding that we be sinless, and flawlessly good to each other. Let's all just be quiet for a while, in one room, together.

⇌

"You *do* know that you don't need to fall in love with every-one, right?" Tal also said, standing with his bike on the street in front of Alon's apartment to say goodbye.

"Well, no," I said after some thought. "No. I guess I do not know that."

How *does* one not fall in love with everything? I came to Israel to study dance, and maybe I did learn how to dance, but more than that, I started living and breathing and sweat-ing and dreaming the story of this place. My body has carried the weather patterns of the city, the heat and the relentless wind, the mood of the sea and the habits of the people. For wherever you live, I have come to understand, wherever you live, the land will fold you into it. When you eat the food and breathe the air and stand on the earth under the sun there, the place in you that is that land will get louder, will rise up and become all of you.

And then the only thing to do is leave. Strip it off. Be-come naked again, as bones.

4.

SPAIN

2009

First days in Madrid:

The crowded market, the vendors selling plastic fans, white cotton skirts, rubber bands. The streets laid out like ribbons thrown from a hand—they curl, turn back into themselves, tangle, straighten out again. Fountains on every corner hurry in the sunshine, and the cars gleam past them, washed by the thin air they speed through. Light blooms in the new leaves, children skip in school uniforms, navy blue. Mothers hurry, carrying plastic bags of artichokes, canned fish, olives, long loaves of bread. The syllables of Spanish, like fine jewels that are juggled in the mouth and then rolled out rapidly— polished, cut sounds.

A man selling John Grisham novels and pirated DVDs sleeps beside his wares, his shirt off, his mouth open in the late afternoon when I am wandering, a little bit hungry, shivering in my thin sweatshirt, feeling alone.

First days in Madrid.

And I will never know this place so well again. The more familiar it becomes, the less I will see it, the less I will be empty enough to really feel it. So I try to let myself feel it— all the unknowing of a place, the unknowing of how I fit within it. My life distilled again down to one backpack, a few books, two pairs of pants. My life distilled into one stretching sensation, as though falling, a long dive from cliff to a groundless unknown.

People keep asking me what my plans are for Spain. "Why Spain? What will you do there?"

"I don't know," I usually say, which isn't true. But saying, "I want to dance and see and write and talk and experience and love," sounds too long-winded and new age. Such an answer does not hold up under fire, especially when that fire is from your own self, when you are alone in yet another foreign country, attempting to put structure to your wild, unstructured passions.

The day is chilly and lit with birdsong. I sit down to write in a park on a hillside of grass down the street from Quin's apartment. Just up from me, a group of tourists drink white wine out of the bottle. I too am a tourist again, and I don't like it. I feel small in my body, timid and quiet. This, I know, will change soon enough—as Spanish rolls easier out of my mouth, as the streets of the city unfold into recognizable turns.

A dark-eyed Spanish man with a kite and a dog stops to ask me if I am writing or drawing.

"*Escribiendo*," I say, caught off guard.

"*Que haces aqui? Estudias? O vacciones?*" The dog is eager to go, and the man holds it tight to him, the red leash wrapped around his fist.

I don't know how to answer him. What am I doing here? Studying, or vacation? What is the difference in my life anymore? I shrug. "*No sé.*"

His eyes are confused, but then he laughs. "*Que bueno,*" he says, letting the dog now pull him down the hill and away. "*Disfruta,*" he calls over his shoulder. Enjoy.

Enjoy. This feeling of having days and days in front of me, and days and days after that. Ample opportunity to feel completely and totally alone as I try to blaze the trail of my utterly unpaved life. Trying to create days where I dance enough. Write enough. Meditate enough. Love others enough. Laugh enough. Meanwhile somehow making enough money to survive.

The truth is, I realize, I have lost my nerve. I want that safe life, that husband everyone has been suggesting I find. That home I dreamed of as a child but didn't have, with big kitchen windows and thick, wooden counters and blue pottery plates and bowls. That long, overgrown backyard full of raspberries and fruit trees. I want barefoot children playing outside and no greater tasks in my life than to wash the dishes and cook them all dinner.

And yet there's still this wild need—to collect stories, dance on all the continents, learn all the languages, wrap my body in the mud and the grit of the world.

"I don't know how to do this," I tell Quin later when he comes home from work and finds me frantically making lists in his bed. "I need a plan. I need some kind of plan."

"But, Dayna, you're in *Madrid!*" he says, plopping down next to me. "You're spending time with *me.*"

"Yeah, but that's not productive."

He snatches the paper out of my hand. "Let the city come to you," he says. "Don't try to run out and swallow it."

I nod. "Okay. You're right. You're right."

Quin has changed since I saw him last. His long days of sipping frappés and the leisurely wine dinners with Jack beside the Aegean Sea are gone, and I can see that he's been working hard at surviving. There is something stiffer but stronger in his body and his eyes. His arms are still everything familiar though, and when he pulls me into them, I feel a rush of visceral memory so intense I can't think or breathe: all those moments we spent together in the secret room of a Greek island, becoming nationality-less together, drinking cold white wine while he cooked dinner in our basement apartment. The smell of garlic and eggplant. Dancing in the kitchen. Coming home at sunrise, sweating, the way his body, in sleep, would bend to fit around mine.

He gets out his laptop and shows me his favorite Louis C. K. clips to cheer me up, until we are doing what we do best, laughing till crying, laughing till sleep—twin orphans together in a bed in another foreign city, my head tucked under his.

⇄

But when I wake in darkness, hours later, all I feel is alone, Quin's shoulders gently rising and falling against mine. I am planless; I am anchorless. The world is too big. Alarms pulse through my adrenals, and my chest chokes. I can't breathe. I grip at my throat. I can't breathe. My body tells me it is dying. I recognize the sensations. It hasn't happened since I was a child, but I know what it is. *Just a panic attack, not real, just a panic attack, not real*, I assure myself over and over and over, pulling my knees up to my chest, sucking in slow, painful breath. Quin sleeps on, snoring gently. The room is the size of a closet, no windows. The completeness of the darkness is suffocating. *Just a panic attack, not real, just a panic attack, not real.*

This goes on and on, until the sun rises.

⇋

First days in Madrid, and I decide that I hate Madrid.

I pass not one, but two dead bodies in the street. The first is a homeless man with pale bare feet. A drunk with wild hair is taking his pulse and shouting incomprehensible sentences in what sounds like Russian. A Spanish man in a business suit four feet away stands with his back to the scene, getting money out of the cash machine. "Does anyone have a phone?" Quin shouts to the people who are passing. No one looks at us.

The second dead man is stretched out on the corner, his arm above his head, a half-lit cigarette burning down in his fingertips. He is wearing red shoes. A waiter from the nearby café leans over him and announces that he is not breathing. The people in their black jackets and cream dresses pick their way around them both, and I feel like doing that also. Like letting death in the middle of the street be nothing I look twice at, nothing I notice or am afraid of.

⇋

On the third night of panic attacks, the "not real, just a panic attack" theory dissolves into the very real feeling of not being able to breathe as I realize it *is* true, the world *is* terrifying, and the lack of external structure in my life *is* going to turn me into a drunk, dead on the street. And while I panic about this, I might as well accept that all the people who I love will also suffer horrible fates, namely Quin, who was supposed to be home three hours ago. And oh God, humanity is doomed to be devoured by its own shadow, and I rush out of the tiny coffin of Quin's bedroom onto the balcony where the night is stale with leftover day heat, and the streets are teeming with Saturday-night Spaniards belting out ballads and throwing bottles, which splinter and scatter out into this city of towering rose-and-yellow architecture, the polished sculptures white as bone.

Quin comes home from the clubs at six in the morning, and I am waiting for him like a mother, hands jittering; I haven't slept in days. "I thought you were dead," I moan.

"Nah. But I did see a guy roaming the streets and threatening people with a kitchen knife."

Quin loves it. The noise from the night in his body, the pulse of the people in the thin streets. He says he finds it comforting, the man who comes regularly to beat his fists to a pulp against the garbage bins beneath the living room window, cursing until dawn. "This must be his Anger Spot," we whispered the other night when we heard the man's screams. "Some people punch pillows," Quin said. "Others have their favorite garbage can."

"Madrid is like living in a lion's mouth," Quin says. Because it's not a secret here, and you can't forget that it is an ever-present, terrifying thing, being human. The darkness that stalks us is incredible, and so there it is, so what.

Just a panic attack, not real.

The next night, Quin takes me to dinner with some friends he plays music with—a French couple and their manager, an amicable, feisty Venezuelan named Poni. They smoke cigarettes and drink beer and talk about music for hours—about taking one note and stretching it, dipping it, scratching it, and what that might do to a crowd who is there to watch you, wanting you to take them. And how do you take them, how do you adjust your volumes, your frequencies of each separate sound enough to make the bass bump in just that exact way to send every person in the club into an eyes-closed, head-back, up-your-body scream? How to make them forget all the rest, just the thrill of their own aliveness, connected to every person who is also alive, connected to the great big alive earth and the soul and the streaming-down stars.

I sit back on the couch, exhausted, but listening, thinking about Madrid, the sound of it. The hum of the people with their cigarettes and *cañas* and tapas and tight pants, the buildings painted custard, salmon, daffodil yellow, all humming, the fountains a persistent percussion in this old city where even history hums—ghost noises underneath all of it. The long-ago hangings of the Inquisition in the rose-colored square of Plaza Mayor, the Civil War, Franco—all of it you hear, the same as you hear the night knocking in the streets of the day.

I listen to the DJs talk and know that I can't stay here forever, but maybe, maybe I don't really hate it. Knowing that it can't be my life—or not all of my life—to sit here in this smoky room and talk and drink, and talk and drink, for hours and hours. I'm not that kind of artist really, and it's not what I'm looking for. It can't be my life—or not all of my life —even to dance and dance in the mouth of this music, in some dark, deep city club with the heart of the crowd pulsing there, with you, into the morning. I know their path is not my path—that maybe I've strayed far from my own work just by being here—but for the moment, it finally doesn't matter. For the moment, I no longer care if I don't know how to answer when people ask me what I'm doing here. What I'm doing is all around me anyway, humming, waiting for those spacious moments when I finally just listen.

⇌

We can only find one bar still open, barely lit on the corner of a dark street. Inside, there are a handful of people crowded in the corner, and the rest of the place is empty. Quin and I order two glasses of red wine from the stoop-shouldered bartender, who brings them to us with a plate of fried potatoes and bread with soft goat cheese. The group in the corner laughs a lot. A man and a woman kiss. The room is dark, and the light from the streetlamp behind them haloes their bodies as they embrace. There is a suspended pause in which we all watch them, including the bartender, who stands with a half-finished bottle of red wine in his hand and a tender smile on his tired face. When the kiss has broken, I can't help it—I begin to clap, and the others join me with enthusiasm, some of them whooping. The bartender refills our empty glasses. "On the house," he says.

"When do you close?" Quin asks him.

The bartender shrugs and gestures at the group down from us. "Whenever we want," he says and winks.

I think about the way the American bartenders back home scream for everyone to "get the fuck out" when the clock hits 2:00 a.m. "There is so much missing in our country," I whisper to Quin. "Where did grace and beauty go? How was it lost?"

Quin kisses my hand. "Thank God we never have to go back."

Now it is two men who are kissing, a little off to the side from the group. They pause and grin into each other's eyes. All the shadows are soft, the streets outside quiet. It's 4:00 a.m. Quin and I sit knee to knee. Tonight, we are finally having the conversation we've been avoiding—the one about "us."

"I'm not proposing anything," he says, tucking my hair

behind my ears. "But what if I could change? Become less of a goldfish. Stop partying so much. What if I could learn how to be there for you, be dependable, take care of you?"

I shake my head. "That would have to be something you decide on your own is important and do it, not because of me. I don't want to be your partner but wish for you to change. That's not fair. I wouldn't be loving you for you."

"All right. So what if we're not lovers—we're friends? Find a place to live together in Madrid for the next couple months, and use this as our base to explore Spain until we find where we want to move to," he says. "But we can't live together forever, of course," he concedes. "I can't go through that again, I don't think. You being with others." He pulls his hand from mine and takes a drink of his wine. I stare at the scar on the inside of his forearm, an angry red furrow down his pale skin. I can still feel the glass in my hand.

The conversation circles, makes no headway, and we finally just leave it, hanging in the air like a question mark. We are exhausted and a little drunk when we finally get back to his apartment, the sun just beginning to tip the streets with light. When I come into the bedroom after a shower, he closes his laptop screen quickly, though not before I see that he's in midsentence of an email to a woman.

"What are you trying to hide?" I ask, irritated.

He flares at me. "You're not so pure and honest yourself. I'm sure you were with someone else and you just haven't told me about it."

"You do know that I was living with my boyfriend for the last year," I snap back. "So yeah, I was with him, you're right."

"Exactly. So why the hell do you care about me and another girl?"

"I don't care. I care that you're trying to hide it."

"All right then." He opens his computer again, but just stares at the screen, his back to me.

I sit on the bed, the silence between us throbbing. "What the hell are we doing, arguing about being with other people?" I say finally, my voice quiet.

"I don't know." He doesn't turn. "I don't know, man. We might be headed for a bad place."

The sentence makes me nauseous. I can't lose him. I can lose everyone else, but I can't lose him. I start to shake. I go to the bathroom and throw up, from the wine or the fight, I don't know, and when I come back, it is over. He curls into me in the bed and falls asleep, tucked deep into my arms. I listen to his even breath as he dreams, and to whatever god who holds our fate, I pray, *Please make our love be enough.*

⇌

The pain rips me from sleep at 6:00 a.m., and I spend two hours crouched on Quin's tiny bedroom floor as I wait for each one of his three Spanish roommates to cycle through their morning bathroom activities and leave so that I can then go pee hot, red blood from my shredded urethra for hours into the morning. It's been a while, but here it is, another pain attack.

In a yoga class in Tel Aviv, the teacher had us hold each pose for twenty-four breaths. As we all sweat and inwardly cursed him, he said, "What if this was your lot in life? What if this was the one pose you had to hold for the rest of your life?"

While others groaned at this suggestion, I felt sudden, deep relief. Maybe nothing was ever going to get easier. But could I find some way to be at peace with that? With my arms aching and my breath heaving, nausea building and muscles quaking, could I, this self inside the body, rest? *It won't be forever*, I'd thought. *Eventually I'll collapse. Eventually I'll die. There's no escaping that.*

This pose is the only pose for the rest of your life.

Remembering that yoga class from my C curl on Quin's bathroom floor, I decide to let go of my usual in-pain thoughts, the *How long will this last?* and *What's wrong with me?* thoughts. As I slowly relax and accept the state I am in, without judgement or opposition, a surprising, quiet peace comes over my body, despite the pain. And then, a little while after that, the pain just slips away.

But no sooner have I made friends with one kind of pain, when another one hits, harder.

When Quin gets drunk that night and I don't, we go out to roam the streets, settling eventually in a smoky jazz bar with three huge, dreadlocked men spinning notes and catching my eyes like it is part of the music. I want Quin to be with me, but he is glassy-eyed and clumsy in his body. I want him to be strong, stable, dependable, solid ground for me to land on. He is none of these things and has never been, and I hate myself for needing it from him.

Quin says, "Where are you? Are you still in pain?"

"Yes. But different." The panic is back, wringing at my lungs. "I can't live this kind of life anymore," I say. "I can't drink and stay up all night like in Greece. My body can't handle it and neither can my mind. I want to be working on something, building something. I want to have kids or at least feel like I'm headed toward that."

He nods, but I can see in his face that he doesn't feel the

same way—Quin, who can't stay in at night, who wanders the streets of Madrid till 5:00 a.m. chatting with the beggars and the sex workers. "I can't *feel* anymore, Dayna," he told me last night. "It's like I need things to be more and more dark, more and more disturbing, in order to feel anything."

Being with Quin helps me see myself the way Alon saw me, watching the one you love disappear in his eyes. Can't sit quiet, looking all around, and you know that what he's thinking about is the night streets, the dark roads to get lost on, wanting to numb out, wanting to die for a little while. And you, who loves him, watches him with great sadness, understanding that some siren sings to him louder than you ever can, and what is there to do but kiss him and let go?

Alon has done this with me, kissed me and let me go. Assuming perhaps that I, like I assume for Quin, will never find quiet. That the nights will never cease to gnaw at me, that I will never stop seeking out my own destruction.

My poor mother. The way she'd wring her hands, reading this, wanting only for me a safe life, a bright life, an inspired life. I want that too and want it for Quin, but feel helpless about how to find it for either of us. I know I will never be better or bigger or stronger than the pull of his addictions. I'm not sure I'm bigger or stronger than my own. I think of Israel, like a lover whose dark side, at last, emerged in all its filth and danger. And the same as I feel for Shai, I still find her secrets lovable, her actions understandable, her horrors forgivable. But I also finally realize that understanding and loving does not mean I have to live there too.

"I don't think I can stay here, Q," I say. The jazz musicians are taking a break, and they lean on the bar beside us, their cups of red wine small in their huge hands.

"Where will you go?" His eyes are dulled from drinking, but I can still see the pain in them. My bladder starts to throb again.

"A friend of mine from Israel is in Ibiza; there's a dance community there. Maybe I'll go check it out." Dance, my home, what has always saved me.

A Pakistani man stops at our table, selling roses. I shake my head, but Quin says, "Hold up, man," and reaches for his wallet.

"Q . . . don't. . . ."

He ignores me. He hands the man a euro and selects a flower from the bunch. The man says nothing, just nods thank you with a little sad smile and shuffles on. Quin presents the slightly wilted red rose to me across the table. "Baby, I love you. We can do this. I just need you to tell me you love me too."

My eyes burn. "Of course. I love you. More than anything." And it's true. I have always loved him, fierce and wordless. I will always love him.

He nods, his eyes also damp. "So we'll just figure it out. Okay?"

I take his hands across the table. "Okay. I'll stay. We'll figure it out." Over his head, the saxophone player is staring at me with a gaze like one long note, held. It's all I can do to not look back at him. Instead, I grip the hands of the person who I adore, pushing away the terrible truth in the back of my body: that for either of us to survive, we both need something much sturdier to hold on to than each other.

⇁

It only takes one night for everything to change. Finally it rains, and Madrid's streets smell like flowers with names like daphne and gladiola. I walk to the metro station early, my backpack heavy on my shoulders. Though I know I look it, I am not courageous, independent, or strong. Kissing, yet again, in some bedroom, some guy. Poor Quin, poor Quin, who looked at me with cold, hard eyes when I finally came home, who told me it's all worthless and impossible between us, that we're better off in different countries, he can't stand me anymore, he can't stand it. Self-hatred so vile, like shit in my mouth.

"Forever," he swore. "Forever, Dayna. I'm done with you." He held my phone in his hand to show the text I just received: "The connection we had, was it just me, I've never felt that in my life. . . ." A new man, old words. I am sickened by my horrific choices and the unstoppable fierceness of this pattern.

I had woken in late morning in a rooftop apartment, wild green plants tangling out of the window boxes. A French man, long and lean, wrapped around my body. He stirred when I stirred, whispered he'd miss me when I'm gone.

He was one of Quin's closest friends. "No, I'm not Q's girlfriend," I'd told him at the club where Quin was DJ'ing, downing my third shot, intent on destroying all things that bound me. *I'm nobody's girlfriend; I belong to no one.* A sentence that would make me sick for years to come.

Beyond the edges of the Frenchman's balcony, the city spilled, green mountains and russet rooftops. I drank the fresh orange juice he brought me in bed and tried to remember how to stand, my balance gone, my bladder screaming, peeing blood again.

⇌

The next thing I know, I am holding hands with sixty naked hippies in a wax-floored gymnasium on the island of Ibiza while a small, round man wearing nothing but a clown nose is instructing us on the art of playing with imaginary buses full of Japanese tourists.

I am naked also. I am staring at flaccid, uncircumcised penises gently swaying to and fro, brown breasts with nipples like raspberries.

Someone says, "It's so wonderful. When you're naked, you can't hide anything."

This is supposedly a festival of improvisation. I came here to dance. What I found instead was a parking lot in the middle of the city transformed into a small hippy sanctuary, complete with tepee, yurt, communal kitchen, and an abundance of red foam clown noses, which indeed were functioning as the smallest mask in the world. For it was impossible to connect with anyone unless I pasted on a smile, put on a nose, and acted like I was also flawlessly happy in a parking lot turned hippy haven in the middle of a city where everyone honked and cursed and cried on the outskirts of our bubble world. Nobody knew my name. They called me Dina, Dona, Danya, Diana, and I did not correct them. When you're naked, you can still hide absolutely everything.

It has been a month since I left Madrid. My plane to Ibiza had been delayed for three hours, and I sat in that steel-colored airport with my hands pressed between my knees, hovering and indecisive, planning and unplanning, standing to leave and then coming back as the clock lumbered its way in circles around and around again. Only one thing was clear. My time in Madrid had been a disaster: raging pelvic pain, nightly panic attacks, and the ruins of a hopeless love.

But still, I hovered in that airport. The security guards eyed me as I paced back and forth. The clock slugged around and around. I paced in that airport and tried to logic my way through an illogical question, which was, "Should I or should I not run this time?" Knowing full well that running itself was merely a figment of my imagination, and that everything miserable was, along with my trusty backpack, coming with me.

Finally, I just stopped. Stopped and stared at what had caught my eye—a man sitting in a corner alone, his hands in his lap, his eyes closed. Eckhart Tolle's *The Power of Now* poked from the top of his backpack. I stifled a groan.

I hate the book.

It has never failed at making me feel guilty. Because I fight the present moment with my teeth and claws. Then fight myself for doing this. Then fight the people who are reading *The Power of Now*. Yet suddenly, there was this man. It was not a sexual attraction, but something deeper, something like being drawn to sit at the edge of a very still sea. It pulled me toward him, as though perhaps I could absorb some of that peace emanating from his bearded, long-haired, I-eat-only-raw-food body. I wanted, with my whole being, to sit beside him. But instead he stood. And boarded the plane, which had finally decided to come after three lubb-dupp circles of the clock. And in a daze, I followed him, laughing out loud when I saw that our seat assignments were right beside each other.

He turned to me as I sat down and smiled a green-lettuce smile. "Hello," he said. "My name is Now."

"Your name is *Now?*" I repeated, incredulous.

He just smiled and pressed his palms together in front of his heart.

This is not a joke. This was the moment in which Eckhart Tolle started to stalk me.

⇌

It was an hour-and-a-half flight to Ibiza. Tal met me at the airport with a grin and a hug and drove me to the place where he was now living, an old finca with a small community of people who, on this particular Sunday afternoon, were having a diksha ceremony for a young pregnant woman whose baby was due to come the following week.

I did not know what a diksha ceremony was, but when I got there I could deduce a few things about it, like that it came from India, due to the statue of the goddess Kali on the altar, and the Indian chanting played loud from the speakers. And apparently you were supposed to sit in a circle while people went around and put their hands on your head for a certain amount of time. This looked fine and good to me, because I was exhausted and still in substantial physical pain, and everyone was sitting and being quiet under an almond tree on a terrace of wildflowers in the late-afternoon sunshine. I sat in the gentle chanting, bird-trilling, flowerful afternoon. I let people come and put their hands on my head. I thought about Madrid, about Quin, and Alon. I thought about my habit of always leaving the people who I love. I thought about sadness, and the way it was pouring through my body, like thick, dark water. I thought *Where will I go next, after Ibiza? Where will I run next?* when suddenly I became aware of someone next to me, speaking Spanish too fast for me to understand, and what I heard was this: Spanish, Spanish, Spanish, "Eckhart Tolle," Spanish, Spanish, Spanish.

At breakfast the next morning, I was pouring a cup of coffee when I heard the conversation at the table behind me: Spanish, Spanish, Spanish, "Eckhart Tolle," Spanish. The following night, at a performance in a small bar in the middle of a rainstorm, a long-legged musician bounded up to me and said, German, German, German, "Eckhart Tolle," German, German.

So I thought, *Fine, Tolle. You win.*

What else was I going to do? There was nowhere to go, and I was withered with exhaustion. "Welcome to Ibiza," Tal had said when he met me at the airport. "This island either chooses you or doesn't. If you are quiet with her, she will come to you."

I had nothing left in me other than quiet. From now on, I decided, I will think only about the present moment. I'm here now, and here is going to have to be home.

So home became a terrace of land above the sea, shared by a small community of one builder, two musicians, three dancers, one pregnant woman, a yoga teacher, and an anarchist doctor. I thought, *Okay, I've spent enough time in my life rubbing elbows with hippies. Maybe I can fit here. Maybe I can be a hippy too.* I knew the standard requirements. I held eyes for the two and a half minutes expected upon greeting— honoring the other's light, and so on. I filled my mouth with words like, "Mmm, exactly, yes, thank you, universe, mmm." We talked about using human shit for compost. We talked about drinking your own pee for nutritional benefits. We talked about eating the placenta after the baby was born. They all hugged each other a lot. They kneaded each other's shoulders and said, "That is so mmm, yes, exactly, thank you, universe, mmm."

And the next thing I know, I am standing in a wax-floored gymnasium at a festival of improvisation, and we are all naked. And the naked clown has finished his talk about eating miniature imaginary Japanese tourists, and the next improvisational suggestion is that we have a big, openhearted, love-filled group "sharing." There is a discussion about the way to proceed. The Germans want to organize the guidelines and the time limits. The Spanish immediately complain that structures imposed kill the authenticity of the moment. The Spanish say, "Why can't we just feel and just be and receive?" The Germans say, "Yes, let's just feel and be and receive for three and a half minutes each, then a five-minute break for tea, then a second round of two minutes each."

I stand there in the circle, trying to be very quiet and very tranquil and also trying not to look at everyone's penis, vagina, and so on. I am sure everyone sooner or later is going to know that I am an impostor. The only people in my life who think I am a hippy are my right-wing conservative friends. Everyone else knows that I shave my armpits and wear clothes from sweatshops and do not use nonviolent communication. Ever. I am a wolf. My nakedness now is my sheepskin.

The Germans and the Spanish start to argue, very gently. Someone says, "This discussion is making me feel a lot of opening and some closing, and a lot of receiving, and light from the universe coming down."

An Argentinian pulls out his cup of maté and suggests that perhaps there has been a loss of passion and truth.

An Italian man proposes that we do our sharing in the yurt, without words and with massage oil.

My mind says, *All that conflict in Israel . . . still happening. . . . All that heartbreak, still hurting. . . . All that panic about the future . . . still panicking.* I look around at the circle of hippies, and they are so happy. They are so tranquil, they are so glowing, they are so *now.* The wolf in me starts growling. The wolf in me wants to run out into the middle of the circle with Gaza in my hands, all of its broken houses and desperation, and set it down like a poisonous flower in the center.

A thick ache starts in my wrists and pushes up into my shoulders. I press my shaking hands between my knees and clench my jaw to keep my limbs still. They long to flail wildly, knock my palms against the walls of this bubble world. Every night, I have dreamt of Quin. I am begging, begging, begging, but he turns away with flat eyes. This morning, my sister emailed, blaming me for a fight I unwittingly instigated between her and her boyfriend with a comment on Facebook. "You were the one who brought up the sensitive subject—which you have such a knack for," she wrote. Her words slapped. *Yes, I do this.* Pull everything up, in myself and others, like a writhing fish from a black swamp. Hold it up like a shout. Hating myself for doing it, but wanting to know the answer even more. *Here it is. The thing we're not talking about. Is this or is this not the antidote to love?*

What I thought was unbreakable between Quin and me has at last been shattered. The destructiveness in me is too great to be close to, and Quin has shuddered away from it. And I realize that even if I wanted to, I cannot tuck it back into hiding again. It throbs on the surface of me now, and I blaze like a wild animal, the women drawing back with suspicious eyes as the men lean forward, as though hypnotized by fire.

⇌

Despite staying home, not drinking, and saying very little, it happened anyway. Within one day of arriving to Ibiza, in a tiny house on a tiny island, two men materialized and began to pull hard on me. Falk is a tall, blond German with kind, blue eyes and a strong, unshaven jaw. After breakfast one morning, he asked if he could show me the terrace where he was going to build a dance floor on the land where we lived, and I followed him up, knowing full well what he really wanted. On the terrace, in the rain mist, with Queen Anne's lace and pink cups of wildflowers all around us like a song, he caught my arm without words and pulled me into an embrace, my cheek on his shoulder as I looked out at the terraces upon terraces of white-green almond trees. He smelled like clean, freshly cut wood.

With my cheek on the shoulder of a stranger, I thought, *Maybe this is just one more way to practice nowness.* Not to ask *why* or *what for,* just to let these moments with men sit in my hand the way toddlers will bring you things, a toy or a stick or a blueberry. Here it is. Then here it is, taken away again.

Falk invited me to his favorite beach that afternoon, then his favorite sunset spot. Soon we were spending whole days together. I started to know him and love him. Falk—forty-one, he wore old Diesel jeans and flip-flops every day, his blond hair long around his face, and he pushed it back behind his ears with strong, sun-dark hands. He built things with those hands—furniture and houses and dance floors. He drove a huge, rumbling Jeep full of tools and wood and solvents. After a week together, he took me to dinner at an Italian place with five things on the chalkboard menu, and we got giddy off of one glass of wine, grinning at each other over our plates of fresh salad from the garden outside. We talked about what we wanted, our dreams. He said, "I'm ready to have kids. Right now. I'm sick of waiting."

We locked eyes. I didn't know who he thought I was, and I didn't know who I was anymore, anyway. He said, "You want your house and garden, and I'm foolish enough to put myself in your picture." We laughed. I watched his face, lit with the late sunset light, the way his eyes adored me. "I love you," he said, so clean and quiet and quick that I thought I imagined it. *Is it habit? Projection? Or true, this feeling?* I realized that I didn't care anymore—just wanted to be *now*. Now, with the fucked up, illogical feelings. Now, now, now.

⇌

The doctor who has come to stay with us to help with the upcoming birth is Swedish, blond, and wiry and speaks seven languages. He speaks English with a flawless American accent or British accent, depending on how he is feeling. A few days after arriving from Madrid, I went to him for help in the late morning when my bladder pain was so sharp I could only walk doubled over. "Is it bad, that I'm peeing blood?" I whispered to him where he sat on the couch working on his laptop.

His eyebrows crinkled with concern. "Let's see what we can do," he said. He took me up to the flat, whitewashed roof of the finca and thumped on my kidneys, which thankfully didn't hurt.

He said, "Do you trust your body to work this through?"

"Yes," I said, "but the pain. . . ." He had me lie down on

the roof in the sun while he gently, with much quiet and deep listening, massaged my abdomen. Slowly the pain drained away, and my body softened with relief under his hands. He kissed my forehead.

"I love touching you," he whispered in my ear. "Has Falk claimed you for his, or. . . ?"

He smelled like fresh grass and skin hot from the sun. In one swift movement, he pulled his pants off and lay naked on the roof beside me. I closed my eyes and tilted my face to the sky, my cheek against his arm, his fingertips resting in my belly button. Besides being a doctor, he was also one of the organizers of a sex festival in Europe, complete with work-shops on BDSM and oiled, naked dance orgies.

I told him, "Something in me is relieved to know that there is nothing in me that would horrify you. You, who see people cut and needled and whipped and slapped."

He rested his blond head on his folded arm. "It's true. You are free to be whoever you are with me."

"But I don't want to let myself be free." I closed my eyes again. "Not the wild parts. I want children, stability, a garden."

He stroked my shoulder down to the elbow. "Well, if you're looking for a family, Falk is your man," he said. "He's got a huge heart. So grounded, organized, supportive. . . ." His voice dropped to a whisper, and he put his lips to my ear. "And me. I will be your forbidden fruit."

I laughed. "I can't believe you actually said that."

He had already invited me to come visit him at his house in northern Spain, where he lived with no running water or electricity and ate only raw food straight from the garden. And I knew that he would probably make love to me in ways that would terrify me, and the thought was not tempting at all, not tempting at all, not tempting at all, except for the moments when it was.

⇌

As the hippies are beginning their naked sharing time, I slip away and put my clothes on. I go to the beach where the water is metal colored and flat, and I sit on the rocks as the rain drops down on my hands. I stare at the sea and think of Quin and cry. He will not answer my texts or phone calls. I write and write and write, and he does not respond. From deep in the center of my heart, I begin to pray to him. *Please, Q, talk to me.* I am interrupted by a man calling out to me in Spanish. Balancing on the rocks, he shouts, "Why are you crying? I am sorry. I am so sorry."

I stare at him with blurry eyes. He is a skinny man in nylon jogging pants. "Can I come sit next to you?" he asks, gesturing.

I feel like screaming. *Why all the goddamn men?* I sit alone on the rocks, and I cry, and they fucking come. They keep coming. Why is it that I seem to be absolutely worthless at doing anything except losing the ones I love and pulling new ones to me like a siren? More than love, I realize what I want the most is to be invisible, to blend seamlessly into a crowd. To belong.

I glare at the man and gather my things to leave. "Wait, señorita, maybe I can make it better. . . ." he calls after me, and I turn and scream, "Don't *fucking* come near me!" and he blinks in surprise, holding out his hands.

That night, I drink to destroy myself.

I get raging drunk on Hierbas Ibicencas and play chase games with the children for hours in the crowded city plaza while the hippies perform on a stage in the center of it all. I do not join them; I do not know how to join them. Falk carries me home over his shoulder, tense with worry and rage. "All you do is sit on the outskirts. You make yourself separate; you make yourself alone."

"I know," I say. "I know."

⇌

In the morning, the Swedish doctor hugs me. "Was that the wild side you're so afraid of?"

I cannot meet his eye, the shame suffocating. "I wish someone had stopped me."

He shrugs. "You wanted to destroy yourself. Sometimes we need to do that. So I let you."

I want to crawl inside of him—he is suddenly that comforting. He keeps smiling, and with kindness he says, "That's nothing, Dayna. I don't mind it. I'll take it."

⇌

In the late afternoon, I hike down to the small beach near the finca. I stand naked in the fresh, hot sunshine as the waves whip in over the rocks and seize my hips, white and demanding. Out beyond the cliffs, the strong shoulder of a small island juts from the sea. It is Es Vedrà, the rock that is said to have housed the sirens. I imagine their luminous bodies lounging on the dips and crevices of the stone, singing the men to their terrible doom.

I wonder about them—the sirens, what they were singing for. I wonder what dangerous song radiates from my own body. The way I long for intimacy—to feel the one thread, the one sustaining connective tie between human beings, and to feel it always, unbreakable. The way I crave it toward me, aching to banish the loneliness from my body. And yet every closeness, I break.

Last night, I Skyped with Alon on the roof of the finca. The connection was bad, and his face froze and then moved and then froze again on the screen. He asked me twice if I was seeing someone. I told him I loved him, which felt to be the most important thing. "Dayna, I need to know if you are moving on," he said, leaning forward, and his face froze in that serious, painful stare. I knew that it didn't matter to him if I slept with other people. He wanted to know where my heart was. And as usual, I couldn't tell him.

The doctor caught me crying quietly in the kitchen after the conversation, and he locked his arms around me. He'd overheard us talking. "You are a good person," he said into my hair. "People only hurt themselves. All you can do is be honest with yourself."

I wondered if I was being honest. Most days I felt flighty and on the run. I told Falk I could only be friends, and he accepted it graciously. "I see your need for intimacy, and others' need for your attention. And I want to allow it. Allow you. Allow everything," he said. He took my hands and told me earnestly, "I just want you to have my children. Can we just do that?"

I closed my eyes. "I don't know. Sure. Yes. No. I don't know."

He laughed at me.

"How does one go about knowing anything?" I asked him, really wanting an answer. He just kissed my forehead and smiled.

I have spent every day with him since I met him, and our connection is easy and deep. He invited me to share his caravan on an upper terrace of the finca's land, and we now sleep every night together in his bed with platonic, childlike love. I like his practicality, his gentleness, his play. He says he feels he has returned to the age in which he was his purest, happiest self—seven. And he is. He skipped and giggled when we hurried up the hill to catch the last of the sunset over the sea. "Let's find a way to just be with each other," he said. "Beyond personality, title, or expectation."

"Perfect," I said, as though I hadn't heard or said the sentence a hundred times before. "How do we do that?"

"I don't know!" he shouted gleefully and bear-hugged me in the orange light. "I don't know, I don't know, I don't know!"

⇌

Meanwhile, the men keep coming at a rate that would be humorous if it didn't make my stomach cut into itself with panic. I was feeling constantly responsible, constantly on a cliff edge of plunging myself and others into terrific pain. In contact class this morning, the Spanish painter, Azul, came crawling up to be my partner. But halfway through the exercise, he stopped and confessed that he wanted to make love to me. He said it in Spanish, and I hoped that I'd misunderstood him, but then he said it again. "Really. Really. I want to make love to you."

"Awesome," I sighed.

He looked confused, then understood my sarcasm and grinned. He was small, with strong feet and a bushy, black beard, sharp eyes. He said, "I'm sorry for saying it to you like that, but I just had to say it. I'm sorry. It's very strong, what I feel. The way you move, the way you listen. . . ."

I stayed silent. His body beside me looked thin and breakable and starving for something. I wanted to take him in my arms and rock him. But I kept my throbbing hands gripped tight in my lap.

Later, the doctor said, "I've fallen for you" and crept up behind me in the dimly lit dance jam to play with my shadow on the wall. He touched the outline of my hands and stroked the length of my legs, standing two feet behind me. He did not touch my physical body, and I did not turn around.

⇌

My phone dings now with a text, and I leave the sea to check it. It is Alon. "Don't worry about our conversation, I'm fine," he writes. "Be good to yourself. You're just wrestling with some things. It's a process."

"How are you such a good man?" I respond.

"I've worked to get here, darling. It takes work to learn how to love."

I sit quietly with his words for a long time, feeling my breath push back and forth from my body like the waves to the land.

It is night by the time I make my way back to the finca. I walk the winding island road, through the dark forest and then out again, into the light of the deep stars. The rocks cut into my feet on the path to the front door. The kitchen is full—everyone who lives in the finca is there, whispering together around the table. Falk meets me and embraces me. "The baby was born."

The placenta sits, like a veined, red fish, on the cutting board. They are grinding parsley and garlic in a wooden bowl. The mother rests naked with a blanket, her baby at her breast. The room smells of flesh and dark blood, and there is a living, breathing, round circle of human light, forty-five minutes old, sprung from the inside body, now among us.

This is how we all came here. This is how we all came here. There is no one here who did not come like this.

I lie beside the new mama, my cheek against her shoulder. The hippies eat the placenta with garlic and parsley. They pass around a bottle of champagne. I say yes to champagne, no to placenta. It doesn't matter if I do it like them, or they do it like me, I realize. Because in that moment, suddenly, I am so sure about *us*, all us souls in these bodies, who swam through the same tunnel to get here, who know the same home as I do, who know the same god as I do, who are pieces of the same stuff that I am. Whether I feel it or not, we are always, all of us, together.

I lie there and stare at the tiny, squished, sleeping face of the newborn child. And it feels like a memory, watching her.

After all the work I did in Israel, I am slowly more willing to tell people about the bodywork I do—though each time I say it, I feel shy and wonder what it means, what it is, if I should be doing it at all. I still shake, hard, every day. Falk catches me outside the caravan we share one night, convulsing quietly under the stars. He says, "You're not a bodyworker. I saw people shaking and moving like you in Nepal. And Africa. They were called shamans."

I cringe at the word. One more way to mark me as an outsider from normal society. "Shaman for what?" I say as my shoulders continue their involuntary shudder. "Men? The men lunge for me, and the rest of the world doesn't want anything to do with me."

Falk sits on the mattress beside the caravan and watches me with calm, curious eyes. After a while he says, "Yes. Why not for men? We certainly need it."

Later that night, I am wrenched from sleep and lie jangling with electricity beside Falk until he feels it and wakes too. He reaches to touch my hand and then pulls back quickly as though touching a live wire. "How long have you been shaking like that?" he whispers. "What do you feel?"

Outside the open window, the clouds have settled on the hills, low and heavy, the night shimmering with moisture and heat. I am aware that in my sleep, guides had been instructing me, urgent words that now resonate with movement like shapes of meaning.

Falk says, "You have to get up and dance."

"I don't want to. I want to sleep." My body is jerking and shuddering.

Falk tries to touch me again and again pulls back. "You have to let that energy out. Come on. I'll go with you, I'll watch you."

I go stand bleary-eyed in the wet field and let my body rip open. *It's time to walk your tiger.* Huge arms, jagging torso, bent at the waist, I am instantly afraid at the bigness of it, the thick white night, the sense of witches. But Falk's presence on the mattress is an anchor, and I hold on to the rope of his attention as I dance with all the wild things.

⇌

A week later, Falk complains of a stomachache as we are falling asleep. I feel him tossing beside me and reach a lazy hand out to work on him but am sucked back into sticky half dreams after a minute of touching him. The pain in him builds louder, and he moans. When he goes outside, those same guides speak to me, patiently and urgently through my dreams: "Wake up, Dayna, wake up." My body feels full of sludge, heavy, too-thick water, and I toss, trying to escape the voices, the sensation, but it persists. "What you just touched in him will kill him. Wake up." I wrestle myself into consciousness and go to find him on his hands and knees in the wet grass, retching.

Without thought, I kneel beside him and begin to work, the stars cold and fierce above us. At my touch, he writhes and screams. I hold on, hunting for it until I find it, the center of his pain. It is something like a starving animal, huddled in the back of a cave. I pull it from him, and he cries out again, hot white sensation ripping through my hands and into him, blasting us both. And I cry out too, holding on to his body as we shake. He grips my head and shouts, his torso bucking, and he looks for my eyes and says my name, and I say, "It's okay, it's okay, it's okay."

Then it is over.

The silence tremendous. Sweating and trembling in the field that now vibrates palpably around us, he presses his face to my shoulder. "That pain has been with me since my mother's death," he whispers. "Whenever I feel it, I vomit, and the vomit is black, like something terribly sick coming out of my body. I could never get it out. I would vomit and vomit, and it would just stay in me—my organs like they were being strangled. But tonight, I felt you pull it from my body. It's gone." He holds me against him, his cheek pressing tight into me. "That was my mother's," he says finally. "That was my mother's pain."

I am shaking, just barely, in his arms. Breathing slow, feeling the stars boil above us.

"Dayna, you need to stop pretending that you are not this. This is your work, and you do not need to be alone in it. There are others out there who are doing this. If you do it too, they will find you."

I close my eyes. "I am afraid of it," I say. And then, "I don't know why I'm afraid."

"I understand." He kisses the top of my head and grips me. "I understand."

With my face pressed to his chest, it comes to me suddenly why this talk of mindful nowness has felt so empty. Because there is something else more fascinating than simply witnessing with the mind. It is to step *into*, rather than away. Step *into* the moment with full, alive, awake attention and let the body direct you, move you, show you what it always knows: I *am* that sky, the body shouts, that wildflower, that wind, that sun, that rain. I move according to everything, and everything moves according to me. Don't watch it, *feel it.*

⇄

In the morning, Falk takes me back to the beach of Es Vedrà, the home of the sirens. "You need to dance," he tells me. "That's how you move all the things you feel. That's how the world can move through you."

I stare out at the thick blue of the sea, the rock that thrusts from the water. I begin to shake, and I let the shaking smooth into movement. The curves of story that spool from the shapes, colors, sounds of where I stand enter me and move me. Then my body is no longer my own, my impulses belonging to something larger—some force that lives in the throb of what is unseen. My voice is taken too, and I begin to speak, while Falk watches through the lens of his video camera. I feel the glistening, pearl bodies of the sirens, the hot rock beneath them, the fierce urgency of their story. The words tumble from my mouth, quick, foreign, repetitive. Not mine.

⇋

Later I watch the video with Falk and transcribe the story, he and I both shaky and amazed and a little scared. "Of course! The story of the sirens was only ever told by men," he says. "But now, this is *their* story. Why didn't anyone think to tell their story, from their side?"

I listen to the words over and over again, something luminous blooming through me. "No one told their story, because no one could hear their story," I say.

"Until now," Falk says. "You can tell it now."

⇋

Sirene

We came slowly, out of the earth.
We came slowly, we weren't called women yet, how do I say, we came slowly, like . . . bowls of light rising from the bottom of the earth.

The water opened, and then we came out. That was how we started. We were so quiet. We were just here. Nobody knew we were here yet, not even the birds. We were just here, it was so quiet. It was so quiet. We were just here.

We came up from the bottom of the earth, we came up backward, bowls of light, the sea, she made way for us, and then we were here. Here, nobody knew where we were, not even the birds knew where we were. That was how we started.

And then we started singing.

Slowly. Just. One day we started singing.
And light transformed into song, it was quiet, it was just a color that turned into sound, and it went up into the sky.

This was how we started.

We came up as bowls of light, rising up from the bottom of the sea, and we started singing.

The light turned into sound, and we were heard.

People started coming, slowly. Just coming, slowly toward us. They said, "What is that singing?" and they came toward us. We didn't mean for anyone to come toward us, we came up from the bottom of the sea, bowls of light, the light turned into sound, people started coming.

They wanted what we were.
They wanted what we were.
They wanted what we were.
They came toward us.

Then we were women.

Then we were known as women. These bowls of light
that came up from the bottom of the sea, then we
were known as women.

People started coming.

We didn't know how to say, we didn't know how to
say we are these bowls of light, we didn't know how
to say anything other than sing and people started
coming.
They wanted what we were.

What do we do from now?
What do we do from now
to be something that somebody wants?
What do we do from now?
There's just. . . .
What do we do from now
if your song is. . . .
What do we do from now, if the singing. . . .
What do we do from now?
We stopped singing.
What do we do from now?
We went back down
into the sea

so you hear us now when you
float on her.
You hear us now when the sun goes down
into where we are.
We came from this bottom land where the sun comes
into.
We are still there.
We are singing

and we hope that nobody will get to us.

We hope that nobody will get to us.

because
there's no place in your world
for us.

⇌

I decide that we need to make a home for all of us—the sirens and the dance and the artists who need to create, who need somewhere to land like me and put roots down. I need to make a place for myself, to do this work. And I think of Quin. Maybe if I build it—the strong thing to hold on to—he will come.

⇌

As soon as I decide to, I find it.
The House.
An old finca, newly renovated, it sits like a patient wisewoman on a sea-facing hillside, backed up against a

mountain of pines. Falk and I see the FOR RENT sign and stop to look at it, knowing full well that we can't afford the seven-room giantess. Still, we wander through the almond trees, dip our toes in the pool, lie on our backs on the stone patio, stare up at the grapevines.

We start dreaming. We see a retreat center where we could host creative workshops, dance residencies, performances. Falk finds a flat place under trees. "We can build the dance floor here." Falk, German and practical in the best sense of the word, immediately starts budgeting. I say, "Yeah, but how? We have no money. . . ."

He says, "Maybe we should *think big*. As an experiment. Let's see what happens if we think like we can do anything."

He calls the real estate agent. "We want this house."

I dance on the white flat roof, the big sea below. *Here goes, let's try it one more time*, I think. Diving toward the dream.

⇌

All we need is money. A lot of it. Which is possible to obtain, of course it is, if we simply think big enough, we tell ourselves. Ibiza, the island who was once, for me, only innocent soft forests and quiet blue coves, starts slinking up her dress. And behind that fabric, I see a whole new side to her. Skinny girls in silk dresses, Prada bag here, diamonds all over there, designer sunglasses, Maseratis, and look, there's the Cirque du Soleil guy, he just spent twenty-five million on a trip to outer space, how could we get *him* to help us. . . .

And the next thing I know, I'm going to parties with girls in Gucci everything. Trying to blend in, though I look more like the hippies the millionaires hire to entertain them. They're at all the parties too—the hippies—on platforms, juggling fire or dancing contact or playing the handpan, their hair and their clothes unmistakable evidence that they sleep on the dirt floor of tepees and oceanside caves, while the guests watch them with cocktails perched in their manicured hands.

At today's party, I'm wearing pants that are made from bamboo that an Israeli friend handed down to me; they are heavily soiled from days of straight usage, and my hooded sweatshirt is also heavily soiled. As I walk past one of the tables in the club, a man stops me and says, "Are you in a fashion show? How much are these pants? Can you walk by again?" He is drinking champagne; the bottle rests in a bucket of ice at his elbow. I consider selling him the pants directly off my body.

But then Falk calls, right on schedule, to remind me: "Don't panic."

Beyond the open balconies, on the crowded tourist streets, a man is playing a gambling game with three boxes and a pea. He's scamming people sideways out of their cash, and every day someone is yelling at him. "You're a disgrace to your country!" a blond English woman is screaming now.

He shouts back, "Blah, blah, blah. Give me your money!"

And they do.

Beside him, a man is doing a neon painting of the planets with spray paint. Down the avenue, there are three more men painting the exact same painting. People are selling cheap clocks, cheap bracelets, cheap portraits—real artists, slouched in their chairs, smoking cigarettes, drawing smiling tourists perched on stools across from them.

Falk and I have two weeks to come up with a whole lot of money, more money than I've ever needed to have in my life. Then after that, we need to keep having money, a whole lot of money, before everything can be launched and sailing smoothly. It's an edgy line to walk, but we have decided to be fierce believers in the story that any dream can be realized by hard work, good organization, and *big thoughts*. We are the writers of our own story, and we are boldly building our path through the darkness. We are *making it happen*, and this part, this part of the story is where maybe *I make it all happen* by selling my own pants.

But then Falk calls, says, "Don't panic. We have a solution." A rock star wants to sublet our house. He'll give us half a year's payment on the house in exchange for us subletting it to him for two months and not telling anyone that he's there. Fine, good, great. But how much does he want to pay? No, no, that's not enough. He's a rock star! Let's ask him for another thousand, maybe two.

Below me, the man with the boxes and the pea is still shouting, "Give me your money!"

Am I in the tourist business now? I think suddenly. How quickly I moved from "creating a home for the artists" to "party-home rentals for rock stars." My mind flashes hard to several people I have met recently who rent their houses out for big money, each one of them looking like the situation is as kind to their health and well-being as a run-in with a chainsaw.

"I'm not sure I want to do it like this," I say, and now Falk starts to panic.

"But what else can we do?"

Around and around we go for a while on the telephone as

the sun sets and the tourists take pictures. Eventually we understand what has happened. Where we once thought we could do this project alone, now we are suddenly convinced that we absolutely cannot do it without rock stars, seeing as *he* is a big person with *big money*, and we are only *small people, can't-succeed-at-anything people.*

We declare it a "big thinking" crisis. We call for immediate "mind stretches." We meet on the rocks by the sea. I bring my books—the big-thinking books. The ones that are supposed to help you dissolve all your self-blockages and be big and be free and be happy. We work on our self-judgments. We both make lists, sweating. "These could go on forever," he says, two pages deep, looking up with wide eyes.

I'm four pages in, stabbing each self-judgment down on paper as I find it. Aha! And here's another one! When we are finished, we each pick one to work with. He chooses "I don't love myself." I choose "I can't succeed at anything."

I say, "Maybe we could just stop here. . . ."

He says, "Big thinking, Dayna, biiiiig thinking."

We follow the steps of the exercise through to the end. He cries about his mother. I cry about my father. The real estate agent calls—the rock star has reneged. "Can you still do it?" she asks.

We take deep breaths. We're at our last option, which is both of us borrowing the money and going into major debt, believing enough in ourselves and our dream that we'll pull ourselves out of that later. We lock our teary eyes and smile.

"Yes," we say. "We can do it."

This is when I think I know the ending of this particular story. This is when I start to write the story, but get all muddled halfway through, like the puzzle has warped and the pieces don't fit. I'm sitting with this story all confused in my hands, when we bravely finish it—the contract signed, the keys in my pocket—and suddenly I realize why the whole thing was such a headache. I had been trying to write the story when the story was already written. I was planning the arc, the climax, the solution. I had two possible planned outcomes: one tragic, one sweepingly inspirational. I would either be a *success* or a *failure*. This is when I realize that my life is going to be exceedingly boring if I keep "big thinking" it into place. My outcomes trapped in the genre of cheap, inspirational made-for-TV movies. When I tell my mother about it, she laughs and says her big thinkings never quite manage to make it out of an ongoing sitcom from the fifties. This is when I ask myself, how do we *really* think big? How do we make way for what is coming, for what we ourselves have not even thought of?

The house ends up being poisoned.

It's plastered with chemicals from a now-illegal solvent on the wooden beams of the ceiling. On the day we plan to move in, Falk and I both get so sick after an hour of breathing the air that our stomachs cramp and our heads spin. It takes hours in the open wind and several glasses of milk to clear our bodies of the poison. It is at this point that we begin to laugh. We laugh and we laugh because it's the only thing we can do.

How do we think big enough to make way for what is coming, for what we, ourselves have not even thought of? It is to let go of our outcomes—not to write our own story but to *read* our own story, as it arrives, one word at a time. To be willing to follow it to wherever surprise place it takes you, with deep breaths and open eyes.

As our blistering poison headaches ease, Falk and I hug each other on a cliff above the sea. The waves below are wild, unhurried, free—God's big thinking.

"What do we do now?" I ask him.

And with complete surrender in his voice he says, "Who knows?"

⇌

Two days later, we de-sign the house contract. The landlord is a thickset, chain-smoking Ibicencan woman. She, the real estate agent oddly confided in us, was sure to be sympathetic to our case "because she is a lesbian."

She pushes €1000 across the table at us and refuses to give the rest of the money back that we have paid her for the house we never lived in. She barely conceals her scowl when we make our plea for the twentieth time: "This paint on the ceiling is illegal in Spain, Maria. You cannot rent your house with this stuff. Everyone will get sick."

"*Lo siento*," she says around the cigarette in her teeth. The woman smokes a pack before breakfast. Chemical poisoning is not exactly her biggest concern.

We decide to leave quietly. It is not worth it nor can we afford to bring the issue to the Spanish courts. Maybe Maria will take the money and go on a vacation. Maybe that will be nice for her. Maybe she will buy medicine for her dying father. I find I cannot care too much about the lost money, eclipsed as I am by a much bigger concern, which is that most of my twenties is starting to feel like a process of painstaking bridge building—attempting to construct a connection from this island that is me, out to the land that is the world—only to watch each bridge, shortly before the last board is laid, burn. Just burn, and there I am watching, like an exhausted castaway.

That night, Tal and Falk and I go to a movie showing on the beach. I lie flat on my back under the stars, *in which I disappear into another island.* Surrounded by rich women in white dresses and glittering bracelets, holding fat babies, eating grilled fish off of earthenware platters beside the hippies who are all juice fasting right now—they sit cross-legged, squeezing lemons into glass bottles as they discuss a homemade sunscreen that one of them has made from pine needles and almonds. "Can you eat it?" one of the hippies asks. I imagine the ideal beauty product for a hippy—all-natural, homemade, *and* you can have it for dinner.

Oh, the hippies. I laugh at them so much, I think only because I know that I *am* one. That I have also decidedly turned my back on the so-called normal life, in favor of, well, yes, peace and love, or at least just plain and simple happiness. And where does it get me? I'm the driver of my own life, but that just means I end up again and again stuck in the car with my hands on the wheel saying, "Shit, where am I *going* again?"

The movie screen billows in the wind at the far end of the beach, flashing images of oil-soaked seas and cities of skyscrapers. The narrator is pleasantly listing offense after offense that humans have committed against the planet, from the gross waste of Dubai, to the starvation of sea lions due to commercial fishing. I lie on my back in the middle of all this, staring up at the stars, and hold my own conversation—good hippy that I am—with the earth. "Listen, I *want* to do something, I want to *help*, I *do*," I pray to her. I had big plans for that house. It was going to be a retreat center, a cook pot for art, a meeting center for the creative and unconventional. We were going to host workshops, I invited teachers—hours and hours of focused work washed away because of Spain's lackadaisical poison laws. And now chain-smoking Maria is going on vacation with my last pennies. "I'm trying to do something here, world, but *you* apparently don't want me."

This is no new accusation. I keep arriving back to it. It has become a convincing argument to justify staying in bed all day. But the world, for her sake, always retorts, sending someone, always, eventually, to kick me in the ribs and say, "Dayna, you are" and "I want" and "Do, please."

This time, it is my boss. My middle-aged Dutch boss from my one-day-a-week job, the only thing that I have left going for me on Ibiza—working at the market on Saturdays where I help sell baskets of dusty, African merchandise to hordes of European tourists. It is not a hard job, and I have the distinct sensation every week that my university degree could probably be more aptly used somewhere else, but what the hell. We drink cold Estrellas at 11:00 a.m. and talk about Love, capital *L*, while Germans and Italians and the Swiss line up to buy glass beads from Ghana and camel-bone bracelets and soapstone hearts dyed dark rose.

"Bought a million of these," my boss tells me, holding a heart up to the sun early on Saturday morning. "I was in love. I bought so many fucking hearts." He turns to me. "Dayna, are you happy?" he asks. His quiet, Dutch-accented voice lilts like a frog, something green moving from rock to rock.

"Am I happy?" I answer. "Now? Yes." We are sitting in the sun, drinking cold beer, talking about my favorite subject, and I am getting paid for this. I hold a heart in my hand. It is cold and fills the whole of my palm.

"And what about yesterday?" he persists.

I think about lying on my back at the outdoor movie, arguing in the darkness with the world at large. "Yesterday? Not so much."

He nods. "No. Me either." He is in the middle of a messy divorce—his business, his family falling apart in his hands.

I ask him if he still trusts this funny concept of falling in love.

He takes a drink of his beer and winks at me. "Falling in love? It's just nature's trick to get you to make babies. But it's also, for that reason, the most important energy in the world, because it's about creation. I try to fall in love as often as possible."

A sunburnt German standing at my elbow holds up a soapstone heart and asks the price. "It's free," my boss says, laughing. "Yes, it's like this," and he rolls his eyes at the German's confused expression. He hates Germans. His ex-wife is a German.

He turns back to me, the more important task at hand. "Dayna, seriously, what are you *doing* here? Go fall in love. It's the only thing worth doing."

"I can't just *run*," I protest. "All I've been doing is running. I started a project here; it failed, but that doesn't mean I should *run*. I'm twenty-seven. I have to *commit* to *something*."

He laughs again. "Since when did you marry Spain?" An Italian woman who is next in line buys two wooden elephants and a beaded necklace from Kenya. I count out her change while my boss leans close to me, his white-blue eyes digging into the side of my face, his white-blond hair sticking up from his head in windblown tufts. "Listen, Dayna, don't commit to the wrong thing. I traveled all over the fucking world barefoot, and when I got to Jamaica, they wouldn't let me in unless I put my shoes on. I wouldn't put my shoes on. So I didn't get to go to Jamaica. Even though I was *right there.* That's commitment to the wrong thing, my dear. Be committed, yes. But *know* what you're committing to."

And so here it is again. One of those *moments. Directions to a sacred place.*

As a fairly young woman, far from my country and wandering as I do, people tend to get three ideas about me. One is that I'm "lost," two is that I'm "confused," and three is "therefore, I need advice." In Greece the advice was that work is something to be suffered, not enjoyed, and also to stop eating because I am looking fat and will soon not be able to find a good husband. In Israel the advice was to stop feeling basic human emotions like grief and terror about war "for the sake of your ordinary life." And from the States, people write me wherever I am to tell me that I should *find* an ordinary life, any kind of ordinary something, please, so that we can all stop worrying about you, and hey, by the way, we also think you should get married.

Most of the time, I just stop listening. But then there are these *moments.* Like those rare nights when you're swimming in the sea and the phosphorescence lights up around your body, when the lights follow your body in the darkness; every now and then there is this moment of pure illumination in which someone tells you what to do, and they are right, they are right, they are right.

So I go home from work that afternoon and I pack everything into my ragged backpack. I say, "Falk, you feel like getting off of this island?"

He says, "Hell yes." And then, with a grin, "Big thinking!"

We do not say goodbye to anyone, except for my boss, who I call as we are getting on the ferry to Barcelona. "You're going to have to find someone new to work for you on Saturdays," I say.

"Very good, Dayna!" he says, laughing. "This is how it should go, no? Good luck. Good luck to you."

And then I am leaving.

Plowing through blue sea into sunset, shrugging off Spain like a coat that got too heavy on my shoulders. Shrugging off, with it, the disdain of my own inner critic, who hisses, "That's right, Dayna, always running."

I smile to myself in Falk's Jeep as the city of Barcelona peels away into dark hillsides, as I think, *Ah, but why not run? Run, full speed toward love, just run and run and keep running.* In this case, it's toward a dance school in Germany where there is an audition in two days. Run toward love, for it is the movement, not the result, that matters. It is the movement, again and again, toward what I love, that is the only bridge worth building.

5.

GERMANY

2009

We cross the Spanish border into France early on Sunday morning. Falk is telling me stories of his last days with his mother and her cancer as the dark lines of Spain, all that salted pork, those oil-soaked tortillas, rinse slowly away into France's white-green vineyards. We leave the radio on, scraps of music catching us and then abandoning us again as we weave between hills: Celine Dion, something Flamenco, then a European club hit from five years ago, the rhythm mindlessly coming back to me. I hum and tap the beat with my knuckles against the window. It starts to rain.

"She wanted ice cream, so I bringed it to her. Vanilla and chocolate," he says. "She eated it like a child. I knew it was her last meal, when I watched her."

"Brought it to her," I correct. "Ate." He has asked me to help him with his English, though he only makes mistakes when he talks about his mother.

"I brought it to her," he repeats dutifully. "She ate it. Like a child."

Beyond his window, the green hillsides go streaming by. I put my hand on his elbow.

⇌

Southern France is full of cheese the way Spain was full of pig. The waitress asks us after our meal of macaroni with cream and sausages if we would each like a plate of cheese. I think maybe I haven't understood her right. I say, "Dessert?"

She says, "Cheese."

I say, "Okay," picturing cheesecake, mascarpone, blintzes. She comes back with plates of blue cheese, chevre, gruyere. And spoons. Bon appétit.

We are in a village called Besse, nestled in a narrow valley among mountains crowned white like kings, jagged big, swimming green. The French woman who owns the guesthouse where we stay is always smiling and humming, and once I even see her skip, her chestnut curls bouncing around her shoulders. When I praise her for her sweet cheerfulness, she says, "Well, sometimes I'm not happy. But I close the door when I cry." She has three young children and skin the color of milk. I wonder what is more, the happiness or the sadness, living as she does, so far from the wreck and the tumble of humanity. So close to the upward thrust of mountains, these heights that steal the words, the me as I know myself, out into wind.

⇌

CLOSED FOR FIVE MINUTES reads the sign that hangs on the rough wooden door of the bakery at the end of the lane. They are relighting the fires. We wait outside among the peaks of the mountains, gleaming in the late-afternoon light. When the baker lets us in, she is holding a broom, and without greeting, she returns to sweeping flour into a corner beneath the twin burning ovens. We buy bread, salami, two kinds of goat cheese and eat on the grass outside, the bread burning our fingers as we tear big chunks from the newly baked loaf.

"Marry me," Falk says, putting his hand on my knee. "Marry me. People have done it. People have done it in less time than this."

"Like who? Celebrities?" I say, spreading cheese onto a piece of bread for him. I know that my answer could easily be yes. I need a European passport, and we love each other. Why not marry a friend? Raise children with a friend? I have tried being in love, and it ruins me.

Falk shakes my knee a little, so I set down the bread and look at him. At his clear, deep eyes, his kind hands. We have not been apart for longer than a few hours since we met. He has become like my right lung, breathing me, breathing with me, always together. My old path has broken and a new one now begins. I feel wildly relieved and deeply sad, both, as I watch myself again let go of what I had, who I loved, in order to love wholly what is directly before me.

I put my hand on his hand. "Okay," I say. "Yes. When we get to Germany, let's do it."

"Yes?!" His face lights with his smile. "Ho-ho!" he shouts to the mountains, and his voice ricochets against the snow fields, the emerald pastures and soars off into the tremendous blue of the sky.

⇄

So now I live in Germany.

In a little city tucked up against the Black Forest, with cobblestone streets and bike lanes, bustling Saturday markets. Everywhere you go, you can hear the church bells ring—a gentle, melodic thunder that rolls through the smoke-colored evening air on the walk home, the path through the trees, the smell of autumn like some long-awaited hug, a scent you might find in the curve of someone's neck who you love. Who I love, now, is my own body, walking (miraculous—walking!) with pain in every muscle, finger joint, eye socket. And it is a good pain, this pain of use, of activity, of working hard for something important, which is the unpeeling of layers and layers of miscellaneous junk that has separated me from feeling myself.

I spend six hours a day, five days a week at school, foraging deeper into my body, attempting to figure out this turn, that jump, how to use this muscle, relax that muscle. In class one day, we take four hours to try and understand the spine. How does the spine feel, really? How does it move? The discs between the vertebras are little packages of fluid, which means each bone rests on water, which means each bone is a boat. And the spine, it's a series of boats, balancing, one stacked on top of the other, and when I feel this, when I really *feel* this, I began to cry, in speechless awe.

Falk and I found a house to rent on the outskirts of town, in a valley called Hexental—Witch Valley. With the last shreds of our money, we bought an Ikea mattress, pillows, a down comforter, and a wok. Every day he meets me after class and we wander through the city, drinking in our new home: The jungle of pansies in the wooden window boxes. The foot rivers that trickle through stone troughs at the side of the streets. Boys playing ping-pong in the park. Red rose gardens. Picnickers in overgrown grass fields. Old men playing boccie. An independent movie theater. Everyone on bikes. And sitting at cafés, eating cake, forks dipping into bright jellied raspberries. Playgrounds built with recycled wood, by children, for children. Yards wild with nasturtiums.

"So these are the Germans," I keep telling myself, never having been so fully surrounded by them. Tall, strong-shouldered people, looking cheerful and tired and slightly awkward in summer clothes as they buy organic muesli at the health food stores.

Germany being my third new country in the last three years, I have finally gotten good and fast at assembling my checklist of to-dos in order to create a life that I am happy with in my new home. Number one is always, where can I dance? Number two, what is my transportation to dance? Number three, where will I write? Number four, how do I make money? Number five, where do I live? After all of these have been taken care of, number six comes trailing in: "Language?" she says, to which I agree with more and more foot-dragging, especially when I'm in a country where all the words sound like the dentist has just numbed your tongue to a sack of turnips. "*Darf ich dich kussen?*" one might ask here, which means "Can I kiss you?"

"Let's be honest," I say to Falk, "it's just not all that sexy."

Number seven comes wandering around shortly after six has been checked off. She lights a cigarette and leans against the doorframe, when I'm washing the dishes and feeling happy alone. "So, Dayna," she says. "What are the men like here?"

"Hush," I told her this time around. "I'm here to dance. I'm focusing."

"Sure," she says. "That's cool," she says. Then she waits till Friday night to say, "But you know . . . it doesn't hurt to just look. . . ."

So one night, Falk and I go looking. Just . . . looking, we

say. Beer in hand, we settle onto a bench in the middle of the main square and wait to see what the city will produce. Middle-aged couples in sensible khakis and brown suede jackets mingle among young college students with coiffed hair and ill-fitting jeans. Bands of teenagers march around in packs of twelve, trailing the scent of cheap hair gel and drugstore cologne.

"Anything?" I ask Falk.

"Wellll . . . maybe that girl over there by the bakery. . . ."

"The blond one?"

"Yep."

"I think she's sixteen."

"Yeah . . . well, then I have nothing."

Despite how cozy and settled I feel in this new town, my last years have been lived in countries with narrow streets that end in sea, hanging candles in the lime trees, sea-salty skin, and thin cotton dresses. Now there is real worry in my heart to see that I must switch over to wool hats and snowflake mittens, sensible khaki pants, and, from the looks of things, no romance for two years.

But I have dance, I tell myself. *Who needs romance? And I have Falk.*

Falk and I have set a date for our marriage this fall. His sister agreed to be our witness, and my mother has sent the necessary papers. Our marriage will provide me with German citizenship, and at a certain point, we have agreed to have the children both of us are fiercely impatient for. "Since when did you know you would get married not for love?" Falk asked me once.

"This *is* love," I answered. "Just a different kind than I thought I wanted." The disaster of Quin is still loud in my body and also the memory of Alon and Mirav's wedding album, the one I looked at despite Alon's gentle advice not to—his hand in her hand, that white dress, her smile. Even after seventeen years, despite the depth of their compatibility, even *they* could not last forever. *No one can say forever,* I remember realizing with a black thud and had to rush out to the beach and breathe thick, long breaths, understanding that everything we love, we are guaranteed to lose.

Now Falk and I live as though we are one body, passing in and out of our various moods together—bliss, panic, boredom, irritation, bliss again. We are together in a way I have longed to be together with a man—a connection that is steady and strong. We sleep like children, his face pressed to my shoulder. And yet there are nights when we toss beside each other, burning with a need the other cannot quench. Tonight we stare with dejection at the sexless streets of Freiburg. I link my arm into Falk's arm. "It might be a very long winter," I tell him.

"Dayna," he says. "You and me could. . . ."

I laugh, then realize he's serious. I look at his intent blue eyes and resist the urge to pull my arm away. Fear like black water is blooming through me.

"Let's not fuck with a good thing," I say.

"Maybe our good thing could just get better."

"No. That's not how these things work."

He stands abruptly and turns away from me, his shoulders stiff in the black leather of his jacket. I reach for his arm again. "Hey. . . ."

He turns back to me, the emotion wrestled back from his face. "Hey. I'm sorry," he says, squeezing my wrist.

"Me too." But all I can think is, *They always say it's okay in the beginning.*

⇄

We spend too much time together, I decide. We just need space, other friends. I stop meeting him after class and go out on the weekends by myself. He starts leaving town, traveling to visit his family and friends in other parts of Germany.

The first friends I find in Freiburg are all doctors. Every one of them, and it starts to get a little humorous—being out at the bar and chatting with a few new people, they ask me what I do, I ask them what they do, and they tell me cardiologist, neurologist, radiologist, dentist. There's every kind of doctor in every bar I go to. I scan the city for wider social circles and end up meeting an ear, nose, and throat surgeon, and nurses. The girl who moves in downstairs from us is a med student. They are all about my age, with baby faces and kind eyes, who work twelve hours a day prodding and poking and cutting into bodies. Then they meet me for a beer and listen, quizzical and polite, as if the English I am speaking is a language they do not know, as I talk about dance, about saddle joints and synovial fluid, about learning how to move from your blood.

One Saturday afternoon at a new friend's house, we take out his stethoscope and he lets me listen to his heart. It is the first time I have ever done this. I have heard the heart, sure, my ear pressed to someone's chest, but never have I gotten past the insulation of muscle and bone, into the inside, directly next to the pumping organ and let that beat pour into my ears. The sound is like a coded whisper from a musical god— information that every one of my cells wrestles forward to try and understand. *What is this music?* It brings tears to my closed eyes.

My new friend, Peter, an ER surgeon, watches my face as I do what he does a hundred times a day. Watches me as I dissolve into a sappy mess over the bump-bump of what to him is a piece of meat among other pieces of meat in the big meat that is him, and he laughs for a long time. "Who *are* you, and where did you come from?" he says. He shakes his head. "I think you are so many things, Dayna. But the one thing you are not is superficial."

I wipe at my eyes and laugh, loving the ease of this friendship with a new person—the ease of my life these days, in this new country that is now my home.

It is early September. The vineyards are harvesting the grapes, and from Peter's open windows, we can see the farmers selling new wine in plastic jugs at the market, the children crouched beside the stalls, building worlds in the mud with their shovels and pails. I think about September in Israel. Those piss-stained streets of Tel Aviv, packed with dogs and rabbis, beggars and beautiful women, the heat like a filthy wet towel against my skin. I remember walking in the North next to Lebanon, with Alon's brother, who pointed it out to me, that country we can see over the hills but never touch. He said, "It was a clean war, the last one"—clean for him, as a pilot, whose only job was to drop bombs with no fear of fire from the air because the Lebanese have no planes.

"Clean?" I repeated back to him, and my sarcasm was not lost on him, though he had been defending himself and his country for too long to look ashamed.

He answered with the standard answer I'd heard from many Israeli men: "When you see someone trying to kill your family and destroy your home, you do not think twice about trying to destroy him."

I knew him to be a sensitive man, gentle with his children, and good, quiet company; he made delicate clay mugs painted pale blue and fed me the entire contents of his refrigerator every time Alon and I came to visit. But I knew also that despite his intelligence and kindness, he strictly adhered to a common belief of Israelis: that his family, his country, and his race will be destroyed if Israel does not apply fast, hard violence to all threat.

"But how do you *feel?*" I asked him, walking in those quiet evening apple orchards. "How do you *feel* when you drop the bombs, when you push the button?"

He smiled barely, like a grimace. "We try not to feel," he said.

⇌

Peter bakes garlic bread with feta and sets out a bowl of fresh salad greens from the market below us. He lights a long tapered candle, and we sit at his small table to eat, my shoulder pressed against a bookshelf. Every book on it, I notice, is devoted to Hitler and to the Second World War. "Wow. I can see you are as interested in the Holocaust as I am," I say.

Peter smiles. He is a short man with pale freckles and ruddy brown hair. He pushes his black-rimmed glasses up on his nose and takes a bite of bread. Around his mouthful, he says, "It's my time period. I was almost a history teacher instead of a doctor."

"Why did you choose to be a doctor instead?"

He shrugs. "Because history has no worth, and medicine is practical."

"Where were your grandparents, during the war?" I ask.

He flinches, takes a few rapid bites of his salad, then stops, his fork poised over his plate. "Listen, Dayna, your questions are too much sometimes. This is private."

"Oh. Sorry." For the hundredth time I feel incredibly naive, a stupid American tourist, fumbling around in other people's cultures with no grace or sensitivity.

We eat in silence for a while. He stuffs bites into his mouth while I pick at the cheese on my plate. He downs half of his apple juice and then says, "Look, Dayna. I'll tell you something because you're Jewish. Just because you're Jewish. My grandfather was a doctor. And he criticized what was happening—they were killing all the mentally ill people, and he didn't like it. So the head of the medical board called him to Berlin for questioning. He could have been sent to a concentration camp, but he still spoke out. My father was a young child, but he remembers it. We don't talk about this, but I tell you now because you're Jewish. We did nothing wrong, my family, in the war."

I realize with a start that there is shame in his voice. He is shifting in his chair and avoiding my eyes.

"Do you think I *blame* you?" I ask.

"Of course!" he bursts out. "You're Jewish, you come to Germany, you ask all these questions. . . ."

"Every mind is a world," Quin said, the night before I lost him. Me, I go poking around in them as if they were merely a bathroom cabinet.

"Look, Peter, I am a white, American middle-class woman who grew up—in comparison to so many others—with incredible privilege. No one has done me wrong, and I have no complaints against anybody. But when I was a child, my father did some really terrible things, and his is the story I carry with me everywhere. My father was a good man. But what he did was . . . *not* good. So I am fascinated with Israel, with Germany, with Hitler, with this time period of yours where humans did a very *bad* thing, and very bad things are still happening as a result of that time. People are complicated, so bad and good at the same time, and I just want to understand why we do the things we do. You say history has no worth. I say history is one of the most valuable things we have, because it is a story about our own selves, here for us to try as hard as we can to understand. In order to love better. To grow."

He listens. He stops fidgeting and listens, sitting very straight in his chair, the candlelight flickering on his black-rimmed glasses. "Okay," he says, when I have finished, nodding slightly, relief evident in the drop of his once-rigid chest. "Okay."

After dinner, I put my hand on his neck where he tells me it is hurting him, and his body seizes slightly. He is one of those who is sensitive to the electricity in my fingertips. This seems to be the way I find my friends—they are the ones who hear loudly the language of touch. He closes his eyes and says, "What *is* that?" and again I am with someone in that place that is not sexual but so deeply intimate, strangers who know nothing about each other and yet our bodies know everything. They greet each other as long-lost family, cells soaring into embrace, merging in wild relief, as we witness, as we let them.

With my hands on his neck, I think about my home in Israel and now my home in Germany. The juxtaposition of Israel's filth and disharmony beside Germany's idyllic, hobbit-land villages. The Israelis sexy and defiant, terrified that any-

one will see them as weak, the Germans pale and polite, terrified that anyone will see them as too strong, each feeding each
other's present moments and memories. Though I do not
know how to tell it, I feel the story in my blood, pulsing, and
I think about the stethoscope pressed to Peter's chest. The
sound of his breathing body inside of my breathing body. That
sound, I realize, is the only sound that can tell the story—not
these words, only this body, till we get to the place where not
feeling is no longer an option. Till we cannot escape the sound
of each other's hearts inside our own.

⇌

Peter walks me out, and in the darkening evening, in the
stone courtyard beneath the trees, he grabs me awkwardly
and presses his cheek to my cheek. "Dayna, I hope you keep
dancing. I think that's all you have to do. Just dance. Because
I see how important it is, what you learn from it."

I hug him back, and for a long time, neither of us lets go.
He says, "I want you to know"—he pushes me to arm's length
and grips me by the shoulders so he can look me in the eye—
"I want you to know I am your friend, and I won't ask for
more than that. I promise I will never leave you out in the rain."

And true to his word, he never does.

⇌

It only takes one night for everything to change.

Falk is waiting for me when I get home. He's been gone
for the week, visiting his father in the North. I sit in the
doorway, taking off my shoes. "Did you see your sister?" I

ask him. "Is she still okay with being our witness?" Next week we are scheduled to get married.

"Dayna," he says. He is holding my red knit hat, the one I wore every day in Ibiza. I realize his eyes look like he's been crying. He turns the hat around and around in his hands. My whole body suddenly feels very cold.

"Listen, I can't do it, Dayna. I'm in love with you. I can't even live with you. I have to go."

I feel like I'm choking, and I don't know what to say, so I just walk back out into the silent midnight streets, barefoot and furious. I walk the two miles toward town, then turn around and walk all the way back and past our house out toward the black hills until I'm too cold and don't know where to go and then turn around again. I burst back into the apartment and scream at him in the kitchen. "You promised! You promised me! Were you lying this whole time?"

"Dayna, I have nothing here!" he shouts, tears cutting down his cheeks. "I can't find work. I sit all day and wait for you to be done with school. I want to be with friends. I want to create things. I want to fall in love with someone who loves me back."

"But *you* said this was what you wanted!" I shout. "*You* said you could do it, it was *your* idea. I believed you, and I trusted you, and now you're just another weak man, wanting me to be yours."

His face hardens, and for a second, he looks like he might scream back at me, but instead he stands abruptly and leaves, the door slamming behind him.

I call Alon, whose sleepy voice sharpens and wakes instantly at the sound of my voice. "What's wrong?"

I try to catch my breath, speak coherently, but my heartbeat is crashing in my throat. "We had a plan, a deal, we were a team, and now he's going to leave. He said it was okay, he promised. He said it was what he wanted, how we were together. He said it was okay, he's my best friend. Why can't he just be my *friend*? I can't do this. I can't do this again."

Alon is patient on the other side of the phone, listening. Finally he says, "Darling, give me his number. I'll talk to him. Let me help. Let me try to help."

I hear Falk answer on the second ring. He is sitting outside, beneath the open kitchen window. Falk says, "Of course I know who you are. Yes. Yes." I listen to his side of the conversation for a while. "I know," he says. "That's true, Alon. I thought things could change. She would change, or I would change. But I can't do it."

Finally my fury breaks apart and I just cry. I climb to the uppermost part of our apartment, to the loft where I lie under the skylight. It begins to rain. I cry, sleep, wake, and cry again. I dream of Quin: Quin sitting beside me. Quin with his head in my lap. Quin walking with me in the Van Gogh Museum we always talked about visiting. He is happy; he tells me in my ear what he likes about each painting. An old school R & B song is playing: "Myy-yyy love, do you ever dream of candy-coated raindrops. . . ?"

And he says, "Seriously, that's such a *specific* question," and we collapse into each other, laughing.

I wake and Falk is there, watching me in the rainy half-light. He says, "I'm so sorry. I feel dead inside. Really, I feel dead." And he cries hard for a moment, hunched over and gasping. "I can feel time pushing on me. I can't sit here and wait for you to love me too. I have to go."

"But I do," I cry. "I do love you."

"What are you talking about when you say 'love'?" he says, looking up, and it is with anger, his eyes cutting at me.

"I don't know. I don't know anything about this anymore."

⇌

He climbs down the ladder of the loft, and after a moment, I follow him. I see that he has packed all of his things, and they sit neatly in a pile by the door. He is standing beside them, his blond hair messy around his tear-streaked face. He says, "I was thinking. Maybe Quin is a part of us all. Maybe we need him—Alon, me—in order to have a relationship to you. Maybe you need him to have a relationship to us." I picture all three of them sitting together at our kitchen table, the way I might cook for them as they talk and laugh. They would all love each other, I realize, and for a moment, relief surges through my body, as though just the thought of that love could knit me back together.

But the moment passes and too quickly. "The truth is, you don't want a lover, a partner, even a friend," Falk says. "You want a father. You want a man to stand by your side and support you unconditionally and do it without any romantic or sexual interest in you. But no one's ever going to do that for you, Dayna. I'm sorry. Your dad left you, and it's not any-one else's job to do what he couldn't." He hoists up his bags, and a sob catches in his throat. "This will be the last time I see you, Dayna. Goodbye."

I sink to the floor and cry ugly, gasping tears as he closes the door behind him, hard and final. The love I long for does not exist. Not here. Not anywhere.

⇌

Winter slams in, early and terrible. Every day, the temperature drops another ten degrees. The snow seems infinite, white cold crowding down from the sky, white cold crowding up from the ground. I duck my head and move in the small space between, trudging to school, trudging home again. I move in and around the Germans, and we do not touch. A man on a bicycle yells at me for walking on the bike path. A woman with groceries yells at me for biking on the walking path. Everyone's hair is very neat, even when they take their hats off and shake their hands at me. I smile tight and apologize as I continue forward, and they are swept away from me as the snow is swept into the wind.

February has been disastrous.

A depression, like cold, won't leave my chest. Drink coffee to avoid it, then the cold slams in harder. Can't breathe. Drink whiskey to quiet that pain. Huddle in the doorway downtown, suck in icy lungfuls of air, snowflakes blurry, trying to sober myself before I walk into the restaurant to meet Peter. He is with two doctor friends; one of them notices the scar above my eye, asks about it. I tell him he could never guess the story in a million years, and I snap that a little bit, so that his polite eyes flicker shock and he looks away. I talk too much like I'm happy, then fight with Peter in the bathroom about why he won't give me a key to his apartment.

"I can't ride my bike in this snow, it takes me an hour to walk back home, in the middle of the night, alone. . . ."

"I just don't want you to take a man there," he says. "That would be weird for me."

"Why won't you just *trust* me?" I hiss as I waver on my feet.

I leave him in a rage and stumble around in the cold streets for a while before he finds me and makes me come home with him. "Dayna, Dayna," he says. "I told you I would never leave you out in the rain."

"I don't know how to love, I don't know how to love, Peter," I say over and over again, raving and wild-eyed, and he takes me into his arms in the darkest part of the early morning and grips me until finally I just cry. For a long time, I cry, my forehead pressed to his shoulder, my whole body shaking, and he does not try to stop me; he puts his hands on my hips and anchors me close against him until, in the width of his patience, I am soothed.

⇌

In the morning, he gives me a key to his apartment. "I'll be at the hospital tonight, you can sleep here if you don't want to walk all the way home. I'm sorry I said I didn't trust you. Please, just don't fight me like that."

We eat muesli at his kitchen table and watch the blue sky burn steadily through the wash of clouds. I decide that I will stay steady. I have to find a way to stay steady.

Since Falk left, I have been intent on destroying everything. "Darling, shall we try to meet somewhere?" Alon would say to me through the Skype screen, as I stared away into space, feeling nothing and hating myself for it.

For no reason that I can remember, one morning I told him I couldn't talk to him anymore. "Why keep doing this? Why keep talking? We are holding on to nothing." A strange pain started in my kidneys as I said it. Within seconds, I was dizzy and then close to passing out, my head between my knees in a cold sweat, Alon's eyes impassive as he watched me. The end of us took all of ten minutes.

He said, "Goodbye, Dayna." And I nodded, sucking in slow breath, somehow grateful for the sudden kidney pain—a welcome distraction from the panicked voice deep in my rigid heart, begging me not to do what I was doing.

Later that day, in our first major feedback session of the year, my teachers informed me that while my dancing showed great promise, my chronic back injury would likely cause many problems in my career, due to my spine's inability to handle the long length of my own arms and legs—a flaw in my design, which maybe I would never be able to do anything about. In one sentence, they summed up my greatest fear: you have great potential, but maybe not the strength or capability of doing anything with that potential. They said, "Two years of an intense dance education might be a waste of time for you with your injury. Do you really want to study dance, with all of its consequences?"

It was a strange translation, from German to English. "What do you mean, all of its consequences?" I asked.

My teacher checked his dictionary. I checked my dictionary. There was some fumbling and some extra words used that didn't help. The time for the meeting ran out, and we ended obediently. I walked out of the office feeling like Orpheus deciding if he could or should go down to get his love out of Hades. *With all of its consequences?*

It has been over two years since I watched a dance performance in a decrepit studio in Jerusalem and decided with some full-body, heart-blown sureness that from thereon out I would give myself to dance, to the work and training of it, to the irrationality of it, to the joy. Since that moment, I have had to make that same decision for myself again and again and again—bursting into whatever I've gotten distracted with to haul myself out by the ear and send me on my way again down the dark road innocuously labeled, "Dance and All of Its Consequences."

But suddenly I don't know anymore if I want to say yes. In this mucky, unending, German winter, with the snow heaving itself down from the sky, I don't remember anymore what I love about dance—what I love about anything.

⇌

After Peter is called in to the hospital, I walk the entire city, trudging through snow. I watch black birds fill the sky, like night coming. I look for the streets I don't know and run down them, trying to exhaust myself, trying to break the ice between my heart and my gut. I bump into a classmate and his visiting Italian friend near the Deutsche Bank. After some convincing, I agree to go get dinner with them. After enough wine, I take the Italian back with me to my bed.

February has been disastrous.

The Italian's kiss was everything I was craving: His lips and his tongue. His deep, quiet eyes. The easy affection. Smiling nose to nose. Waking together inside that wave of wanting. In love for one night.

And then it is over.

He has a girlfriend back in Rome, who he confesses about in the morning. He walks away through the fists of snow fall-ing, and I never see him again. Another goodbye, the pain so familiar now. It's difficult to breathe or speak. Don't know why it matters, any of it. Being attractive. Being flawed. There are men who want me, and men who don't care about me at all. Men who have left me, and men who can't let me go. And none of it matters, nor is it enough. Whatever it is that hurts inside of me just keeps hurting. *Everything you love, you'll lose.*

⇌

For our midwinter break, I go to Vienna to visit Arya, my Iranian doctor friend who I met in Israel. We walk the streets of the city as though carving slowly through an elaborate wedding cake, through the curls and silver-frosted architecture of long-ago days when style and beauty and magnificence and decadence still meant something in cities, when people went to balls and orchestra concerts, operas, and lavish coffee shops with felt-covered booths and waiters in tuxedos. We walk with linked arms as we talk about Iran, about love, about Germany, about home. I catch sight of myself in the window, my orange sweater from a German flea market buttoned to the neck, my eggplant-colored peacoat from Spain, my fraying Israeli haircut, and I wonder, *who is that person?* A collage of countries.

We meet Arya's father for lunch and eat sausage with stewed cabbage and potatoes, his father a short, fierce-eyed man of seventy-seven whose answer to my question about the situation in Iran is, "Oh it's very, very good. We have an incredibly intelligent president. A thriving economy. The people are so happy and healthy and educated. This last election, well, we are very lucky . . . all went exactly as it should."

He saws off a chunk of his wurst and pops it into his mouth, his sarcasm impeccable.

"People go up on their roofs every night and scream, 'Death to the dictator,'" Arya tells me. "Because if you walk in the streets holding two fingers aloft—a silent plea for peace—you *will* be shot. No question. So under the cover of darkness, you scream."

Last year at this time, Israel started dropping a whole lot of bombs on Gaza, and thus commenced the beginning of a month-long killing spree in which legless, dead children were regular images on the news every night. The whole world started roaring about right and wrong and punishment and blame. I left Israel in utter defeat, panicking for humanity, and I have not yet stopped panicking—the feeling like a door gouged into my body, left open to the wind and rain. But I am also beginning to understand that it is through this door that I can best feel the world. The darkness in me peeks out at the darkness of humanity, and there is an echo, a resonance. I am more and more willing to witness, just witness all of it, for it seems that our only hope to transcend the shadow in ourselves is to be relentlessly honest about everything that we are and, again and again, forgiving.

⇌

Later, while Arya is at work at the health clinic, I watch *Legends of the Fall* in his bed, his blanket wrapped around my knees. I have seen the movie several times, but somehow this time it shakes me, and tears course down my face as I helplessly identify with every character, especially Susannah, the "water that freezes inside a rock," who then splits the rock into pieces. "It was no more her fault than it is the fault of the water when the rock shatters," the narrator says. I am still crying when Arya comes home and joins me on the bed. When the shot flashes to Susannah, he says cheerfully, "Oh, this girl. She's a whore."

I stare at him.

"What?" He widens his dark eyes. "She is."

I think about men's creation of the word "whore" and my own emotional adoption of it—to be a woman whose sexuality wields power, and to live in a slow, continuous terror that you might abuse this power, lose this power, or be ostracized and killed for this power. It is not a beautiful woman, but a *sexual* woman, I realize. That is the thing that everyone is terrified of.

⇌

With polite German timeliness, spring erupts on the first day of March.

There is a round blue sky, thick sunshine. Flowers of which I did not ever see their buds have suddenly burst, pale lavender globes shimmering in the grass and pink languid blossoms on the thin branches of the cherry trees. Everyone takes their jackets off and sits on the lawn by the university. I see bare arms for the first time in months. I am happy to have survived the winter, the loss of Quin, the loss of Falk, the loss of Alon, and to have made it this far in Germany on my own. I work hard all day until my muscles cling taut to my bones and hold me upright, an indescribable comfort in that embrace. Perhaps an ancient fear is finally quelled just knowing that I could run fast and kick hard if I needed to, bike uphill through snow, sleep five minutes and then dance all day. It is not happiness that holds my hand now, but fierce determination. I will survive.

⇌

I meet a student from Berlin, who is passing through town, at a party one night—Johannes. He has messy dark curls and blue eyes that flash shards of rust, gold, green. We spend three straight days together. I try to remember what it's like to fall in love, start a new relationship, "know." I realize there is nothing real left for me in this game. I hold his hand in the lobby of the theater before a dance performance. My whole school is there. "Is that your boyfriend?" a classmate asks.

"No," I say, and she looks confused, eyeing my hand locked into Johannes's hand. My friends back home can't keep up with who I'm with, their foreign names, the shifting faces they meet over Skype. Ruby nicknames them—the Surfer, the Jewelry Guy, the One Who Can Dance. She's often at least three behind: "How are things going with the Mustache?" she'll write, and it will take me a minute to figure out who she's talking about.

Part of me just wants to say it: I'm a girl who likes to have someone by my side, men as decorative ornaments. Men have trophies; why can't women? I like men, I use men, so what? But also I feel immeasurable shame. Something, somewhere, has taught me that I'm not supposed to do this, that while it's okay for men to be promiscuous, women should not. Women should be careful and discerning of who we are with, and if we are not, then there is something wrong with us, we are damaged, a whore. Women should be careful, also, of men's hearts and their egos; we should never use them and cast them aside as they do to us. No one had to sit me down and teach me this—my mother certainly never would have. And yet I *know* it, in the water of my cells. The world in so many ways has imbedded this understanding into me, and all the women I encounter know it too—they look at me, what I do, and their eyes leak hatred and disgust. *Keep your son and your brother and your best friend away from her*—that's what they've been saying about me for as long as I can remember. Once, in high school, on a first date with a boy, he confessed, "I had to lie about who I was with tonight because my mom said I'm not allowed to date you." I had never even met his mother, but she had been warned about me from another mother. It hurt and it shocked and it mystified me, for I was so *good* then. I was an athlete, a virgin, a straight *A* student. I did not party; I did not cheat. And yet the mothers saw something dangerous anyway, some blazing wild witch, waiting to be unleashed. And they were right, and here she is, and this is who I am now. Terrified and unstoppable and bitterly ashamed, with a heart so dead, nothing, not even the spring, this frenzy of blossoms, can open it.

⇌

The performance tonight is a retelling of a myth about Artemis, the Greek goddess of the moon. I know the story by heart—it is one of my favorites from when I was a child. Fiercely independent, the goddess refused to marry and spent her nights hunting alone. One night, while bathing in a forest pool, the hunter, Acteon, stumbled upon her with his dogs. The goddess was so enraged to be seen naked by the eyes of a mortal man that she instantly turned him into a stag and watched him die at the jaws of his own dogs.

The male dancer recites the story, and though I already know it, he holds me captive with his dramatic, exaggerated relaying of events. Speaking rapidly in French, he shows us with his body the hunter's proud stance, the eagerness of the dogs, then back to the bravery and strength of the hunter, the beauty and heft of his massive spear. His female partner stands to the side, letting him have the stage. Laughing. Appreciating. Sometimes gently telling him to hurry it up a little. Finally, with much bravado and show, he dies, mimicking in grisly detail the dogs ripping him to shreds. When he finishes the last of his death throes, he sits up and says brightly, "You understand the story? Good. Now, she will tell you another one."

The stage darkens. The woman, who had been only a laughing, appreciating bystander to the man, now becomes someone I can't tear my eyes from. She stands in her same corner, but her body has completely changed. Upright and cold-eyed, she watches as Acteon dances and dances and once again dies. Then it is only her, alone in this grotto of the forest. And she dances. Her movement is full of fluid, commanding sexuality, interspersed with sudden, startling witch-like contortions of her pelvis and rib cage. I watch with held breath as she dances her power, as she dances her rage, as she dances her beauty and her ugliness and her sorrow, and— most poignant of all—her utter and complete loneliness.

When the performance is over, I feel so silent inside I cannot even clap. I don't want anyone to speak to me. I just want to walk out of that theater and touch nothing, have nothing touch me, lest I lose the deep understanding of myself, the liberation and *permission* that woman's dance has just given me.

I leave Johannes at the after-party and bike home in the gathering darkness, the crows above me calling to each other in the cold sky. Their sound is not the cry of the heart but the rattle of the rib cage, like wind against a loose glass pane. *That shaking. That rage. That wanting.* I stop on the forest bike path to listen to them, as something deep within my body contorts, cracks open. I am alone in Witch Valley, and for the first time, for one brief moment, I feel what it's like to be as that female dancer was: willing to be everything, willing to be all of me.

⇌

With the help of a good chiropractor, my back injury has slowly gotten better. But my school has gotten worse. We dance six hours every day, and I miss . . . dancing. Classes feel strained, and my classmates look deathly bored, sluggish, distracted. Everyone starts injuring their knees. In the breaks, we all turn into ravenous, bloodthirsty sugar addicts. If someone puts a bar of chocolate down on the table, there are seventeen people instantly upon it like those flesh-eating jungle ants that eat entire cows in minutes.

The feeling in my belly is impossible to ignore: *we're missing something.*

Some sensuality, some soul-deep satisfaction—the thing I had normally always found in dance.

I argue with my teacher on the Friday before our break, a continuation of a steady rift that has been growing between us for weeks. "I don't want to learn how to put a mask on when I go on stage," I say. "I don't want to be only pretty, graceful, pleasing to the eye. I want to train how to be honest. That's the harder thing, isn't it? That's a whole life training. But *that* is what is truly beautiful."

My teacher, a small German woman who makes us do choreography that feels like it should be executed in neon stretch pants and eighties hair scrunchies, argues back that the body is not beautiful to watch unless it is controlled. I want to say that there is nothing beautiful in everyone learning how to move like everyone else. I want to say how the breaking down into pieces, the sanitization of what they are teaching, is killing the whole wild, magic art of dance. But I say nothing. My classmates stare at me like I've just crawled out of a sewage drain. No one agrees with me; in fact, I have the growing sensation that most of them despise me.

I start running every day after school to counter my restlessness. I run through the trees. Through the fields, under the yellow sun, across the river, through the city, the bustling streets. I run through rainstorms and spring rattling its way into summer, the heat like a wall you didn't see and slam full power into. I run into the wall of summer. I run to the hills, I run to the grocery store, I run to mow the lawn—I man that old, rusting mower, feeling like a soldier, the grass to my knees, the ground rutted from winter snow melt. I dive in and out of the cherry branches, and soon I am yelling, deep scratches on my arms, bruises on my legs as I charge back and forth across the overgrown field.

When I drop the mower off at my blind landlord's house, he is struggling to hang a German flag on the side of the house. "Bet you didn't even know what a German flag looked like," he says to me when I offer to help him. "Not many people will hang a flag in Germany." I agree that they are indeed hard to come by, which makes this time now so much more dramatic and startling.

It's World Cup time. And the word "patriotism," which usually hides in the corner here with words like "national socialism" and "six million Jews," has been dug up from the back basement box and hung up—flags on cars and window boxes, flags on rearview mirrors, side mirrors, bathroom mirrors. Flags the entire length of small houses. On Germany's game days, every beer garden, café, or quickie mart with a TV is full of yelling, slightly drunk, bullhorn-blowing fans. Screens the size of, again, small houses are erected in the streets, and at each goal scored, you can hear the whole of Germany roaring as one voice, together. They tell me that the last World Cup, which was held in Germany, was even crazier. Not only did the Germans plaster the country with their own flag they—get this—rode in cars *without seatbelts* in front of *the police*.

And no one even died or got arrested. Can you imagine?

After living in a country for a certain amount of time, I always reach this point where I *hate* that country. It always has to do with me feeling frustrated and sad and homesick, and then I start alienating and offending all of my German friends by doing god-awful things like cheering for the other team in the World Cup matches. I nearly got myself jumped in a beer garden when, while sitting in the middle of a hundred yelling German fans, I inadvertently let out a small "Yeah, go!" as a Ghanaian made a sprint for the goal.

I run the clean cobblestone streets every day, feeling like a predator, past the little German restaurants with little windows and little wooden benches, full of big Germans in tweed suit jackets and too-tight jeans eating schnitzel and *maltaschen* and spaetzle with cheese.

In my German language class, we talk about stereotypes. "What are the stereotypes for a typical German?"

"On time," says an Italian.

"No style," says a Spanish girl.

"Organized," volunteers a Greek.

"The men are passive-aggressive, ball-less dicks," says a French woman, and everyone howls with laughter, including the German teacher. Our teacher tells us that for this class, she interviewed some Germans on the street and asked them the same question. "They all said the exact same thing as you."

"Including the ball-less dicks part?"

"Well, not exactly those words but . . . yes."

⇌

Spurred by some soul-deep boredom, one evening I agree to go on a real date with a German man. He meets me at Bertoldsbrunnen in trekking pants with his hair meticulously mussed, two beers clinking in a plastic bag. He suggests a walk up the hill, through the forest, to a lookout spot over the city. He is an economist. When I ask him why, he says he doesn't know, he had wanted to be an architect. His laugh is forced and goes on for too long. "Where are you from, again?" he asks me for the third time. The boy needs a lot of alcohol, fast, and probably so do I, but we stay with it, puttering through the subjects—hobbies, friends, the difficulties of apartment hunting in Freiburg.

We pass small golden plaques as we walk, embedded into the sidewalk and inscribed with the names of the Jews who once lived in these houses, who were taken and now gone. From the books I've been reading on Hitler, I've learned more about how he did it—got ahold of the German people like that. Before Hitler, German artists were known for their incredible emotion: Wagner, Beethoven. And what Hitler did was appeal to the German people's emotions, used songs, art, rhetoric to bring a vision to a broken-down country. An inspired dream. Now, in the wake of that dream's horror, Germans have eschewed emotion to collectively embrace rationality instead. And me, I ridiculously walk around, wanting to rip them all open again. As though I could be the one to remind them: *It's safe to feel. It's safe to feel everything.*

We go back to his house later to watch a movie and I choose *The Pianist*, thinking, *If this doesn't deepen our conversation right now, nothing will.*

We watch two and a half hours of Nazis shooting Jews in the head. He sits on the other end of the couch with his hands gripped over his belly. A Nazi pushes an old man out of a top-story window. *Smack*, in the snow. The boy looks like he might throw up. Later when we say goodbye, he whispers, "I'm sorry."

The Germans have the lowest birth rate of any people in the world, my books also tell me—high infertility and hysterectomies.

⇌

For our break from school, I decide to just keep moving.

I catch a ride to Würzburg with a young punk. We drink cappuccino, listen to Metallica, talk about car races. He leaves me in front of a closed public swimming pool. Across the street, in the parking lot, motorcyclists are running drills, someone shouting orders from a bullhorn. There are a lot of slow-rolling, direction-change maneuvers through and around each other, like drugged ants. It reminds me of my school. I sit, face tilted to the sun, until Johannes comes, also on break from school in Berlin. His pant legs are rolled up, and he holds a nervous dog at the end of a red leash.

It's Friday, early evening, birds singing full, like color in the air. "They sound like they are saying great things about love and poetry," Johannes, who is studying ornithology, says as we walk the path to his parents' house. "But really, they're just arguing about whose branch is whose, and then there's a lot of fights about fucking." The sun is still high enough to be hot, floating above the hills. Dog walkers stroll through the fields, pearl green and gleaming. I think about how nothing, in the end, is really as beautiful as it sounds.

⇌

Prague: Sunny and empty but for the knot of tourists moving in one lump of shadow through the old town, over the bridge, eddying around the tourist blips—caricature artists, city oil paintings, marionette puppets, portraits of Kafka. The buildings are sternly graceful, crowned with the leer of gargoyles. All the restaurants on the street boast goulash. Goulash in bread bowls. Goulash with potatoes. Goulash and pork knuckle. I sit on a castle wall while Johannes smokes a cigarette. I gaze out into the valley below us, where there is a farmhouse, green fields, apple trees.

I buy a fistful of Mucha postcards at the museum gift shop. Quin would like them. So would Falk. I think about Alon—how quickly I left him. An act done out of spite toward the first two. *Look how quickly I can also leave.*

Now I wander new streets with a new boy. He crosses his arms over his solar plexus like he always hurts there. We fight later, beside the river as the sky turns black and then it rains. I sit with my forehead to my knees. "If you tell me to go, I will go," he says, so I say, "Go," and he walks away.

The rain. The hovering night. Alone in a foreign city. I tell myself to panic if I need to. But what I really want is to never get up again. My school has started back now, but I'm not there. No one has called to inquire about why, and I don't call to tell them. Tears rise in my eyes and blend with the rain that cuts down across my face. Johannes comes back, hair dripping; he puts his cold, wet hands on my hands and draws me, a lopsided ball, to his chest. "I can't leave you. I'm sorry. I'm sorry, Dayna."

"Next time you will," I tell him. "Next time you will be able to."

⇌

Leipzig: A drunk woman is screaming in the sunshine of a park. She says she'll give €50 to anyone who can get those men down. She points across the street at construction workers resting on a half-finished roof. She wobbles as she points, her breasts tremendous and pouring from her T-shirt, a mostly empty beer in her hand. Everyone in the park does their best to ignore her, except for a dog the size of a small horse, who aims his body at her, rigid with anticipation. The dog's owner reaches to hook his fingers into the dog's collar but does not look up from his conversation with a beautiful woman who sits beside him on the blanket.

I lose everything that night, shake myself down into the

broken glass of the city, the grimed bathrooms, the street benches at dawn. Is there a place where utter disgrace is okay? Shame and failure? Throwing your body like it is an animal you cannot love, you cannot keep. Shoving yourself forward, nothing good, nothing classy, nothing pretty. Kissing women in the club while their boyfriends look on. Remembering, later, nothing but some soft cheek in your hand. *I am one of those people who destroys everything. I am one of those people who destroys everything.*

⇌

Berlin: On the radio today, Hitler. I sit in someone's kitchen, watching the city beyond the windows, the long gray of it. Hitler's voice is familiar, bringing back the once crowds, the flags, the inferno of burning books. (In that square now, there is a memorial: a hole in the ground, a window. Looking down through it, you see an empty room, empty white bookshelves—a tribute to loss.) Hitler's speech is eventually interrupted by the modern-day radio man, his voice cooling, gentle, apologetic for this biting history reminder. And yet it must be done, he says, lest we forget, lest history repeat itself—that age-old adage. Across the alley, on someone's window flower box, hangs the sign NAZIS AUS, written in bold, green letters.

Berlin is a city of straight gray lines and surprising pops of beauty—a blood orange door, a cornflower blue balcony. The flats have old wooden floors, ceilings with crown molding. Everyone speaks a different accent of English.

In a crimson-painted wine bar, a British man offers to buy me a drink and introduces himself with a strong outstretched hand. "I'm Tom," he says.

"Tom." I'm drunk enough to not think—dreamy, detached, as I play with the ruby rose petals that have fallen from the vase of flowers on the bar. "That's the name of the man my father killed." His hand withdraws quickly. There's an excuse to leave. "That is the fucking *best* way to get rid of a come-on I've ever seen," says the bartender admiringly.

⇌

All night and all day I wander, from one end of the city to another, on foot and on trains. Underground on the metro and then emerging like a rat into the city again, into the violence of graffiti, plastic bags in trees, rows of apples outside the Turkish shops, bloodred. There is a time just before sunrise when the entire city seems to have no noise, only color. A boy sits beside me on a bench when the new sun is just beginning to bleach the streets, in the silence of early. We don't speak. He offers me a bag. The white powder matches the white of the sky. I stand to leave but can't help but touch him, his cheek to my hand. Our eyes rest together for a moment, birds above our heads streaking quiet across the morning.

⇌

I search for escape from Johannes, who annoys me—his simpleness, his bullheaded pride, his silly youth. I pull his bookshelf down from his wall in a rage, and he sits in the wreckage of his broken things—the tumble of books and papers and boards—and cries like a small child, his lower lip jutted and trembling, the sound wailing up from his belly. And though I don't, I want to leave him like that.

I sleep deep and short next to other bodies. "Can I see you again? Do you promise?" they say.

"Why would you want to?" I laugh, hard and mean. "Really, why would you want to?"

Sooner or later, they all leave me. I leave myself. Split whatever happiness I find, like soft fruit thrown down.

⇌

In every woman, there is a witch, but we are not supposed to talk about it.

When I was a young girl, I used to kick the heads off all the dandelions in the fields with focused, violent rage until I was breathless and then terrified because I had no idea what I was so angry about. Sometimes I'd take my Cabbage Patch dolls by their soft cloth legs and smash their faces into the cement sidewalk outside my house repeatedly until their painted smiles cracked off. Then I'd feel sick with shame. I knew I wasn't supposed to be so angry. I excelled at sports like football and soccer because we could tackle and push. My best friends were boys because we wrestled and called each other *jerks*, and if I did that with the girls, they cried and I felt terrible and mystified and then angrier. When I hit puberty, the boys wanted more than friendship, so then I became a girlfriend. The attention I got from boys made the girls hate me; they whispered about me in the hallways and didn't invite me to their sleepovers. In middle school, sitting alone at lunch felt like the social equivalent to being naked in public, so I spent lunches crying in the bathroom until I figured out that if I always had a boyfriend, I would always have someone to sit with; I would never have to feel so horribly alone. The habit stuck. I became a girl who always had a boyfriend.

I made a few female friends as I grew up, not many. To be a liked woman, I learned, one must deprecate the self, play small. She should never talk about the cold goddess within—those cruel, manipulative, destructive drives. Don't talk about *her*—the shadow of the feminine, the one who despises the weaknesses of men. Despises their dumb-dog stupidity. Despises the way the urge for sex can drive them to their own doom, the way they seek to control it by controlling women, by raping us and shaming us and creating a culture where women are too afraid to be violent, to be cruel, to be cold, to destroy like men do.

We know the shadow of the masculine, the violence and killing and raping. The senseless wars. The emotion men are taught to repress compounds in the basement rooms of their body and becomes their dangerous, bloodthirsty *shadow*. The Greek god for men's shadow was Aries, the god of war. He was ego driven and cowardly; he loved to start wars and yet abandoned them and howled without end if he was injured. His twin sister, Eris, was the goddess of discord. She sowed chaos wherever she went. It was her malice that sparked the Trojan War, when she, furious that she had not been invited to a party, tossed a golden apple at the feet of the three most powerful goddesses and decreed that it should go to the most beautiful of them. The three goddesses fought, and their vanity led to destruction for everyone. Eris wreaked havoc, was unrelenting in her rage. She was the goddess of the dark feminine, the counterpart to her brother's dark masculine. But while her brother was revered in all his vanity and war lust, the same as the masculine shadow is revered in our bloody movies and war stories, Eris was banished from view, rarely spoken of, never included.

⇋

In every woman there is a witch, and I want to talk about it.

It is early evening in Dresden, the gothic buildings across the river Elbe gray green in the fading light, and the air smells like sun on the rose blossoms. I sit by the water, thinking about Eris, what she's teaching me. I have finally grown too tired to try to be likeable anymore, to anyone. "I would rather be whole than good," Carl Jung said, and now I understand. I can't hide her, the witch within me; the only thing left to do is allow her. Let her teem through me like wild roses, let myself be that intoxicating beauty, that power thick with thorns.

In every woman there is a witch, and I want to talk about it.

About the ways we control men for our own gain. The ways we misuse our sexuality. The ways we are violent or want to be violent. The ways we cheat, and lie, and manipulate. The way we sometimes feel horrible shame about these things and other times just fiercely alive with the cold and glittering power.

It was the dark masculine that imploded my father—all the things he wasn't allowed to feel or talk about. I finally know now that I won't go his way, that I am incapable of locking anything into hiding—there will never be a repressed shadow that grows monstrous in the pit of me, to eclipse my life suddenly and gruesomely as it did his. The more I talk about Eris, the more I look at her, the more I write about her, the more I dance her, the safer I am with her. But it also means no one wants me at their party anymore.

And so I sit alone by the river, feeling the echo of the siren's story, sung for all the women who are not allowed to be whole.

⇌

Peter is waiting for me outside of the hospital in Freiburg, his white doctor's coat rumpled, exhaustion heavy on his normally cheerful freckled face. His voice was taut yesterday when he called. "Something bad happened. Really bad, Dayna," he said. His cousin, Stefan, had contracted meningitis and fallen into a coma. "It all was so fast," Peter had said, trying to keep the tears out of his voice. "I don't know what's happening."

I got the first ride back south to Freiburg that I could find, and now I stand in front of him with no idea what to do in the face of this sudden, shocking tragedy. He pushes his black-rimmed glasses up his nose, and I give him a tight, fierce hug.

"How is he?" I ask into the side of his head.

"The same."

He takes my hand and leads me through the narrow white passageways of the hospital to his cousin's room. Stefan's wife sits with her forehead pressed to her partner's forehead. Her eyes are closed, her fingertips at the back of his neck. Their heads like that, together, are the shape of a heart.

I realize I am utterly unprepared. Unprepared to see this man who I know only as the lanky, shy pharmacist who had once or twice stopped by Peter's apartment when I was there, who stayed for one beer and smiled more than he talked, now naked and covered only with a thin white sheet, stained yellow with urine and streaked with blood. His pale chest is covered in a rash, and from his gaping mouth, his tongue bulges, a spool of drool spinning down to his chest. The intimacy of seeing him like this shocks me and then shocks me that it shocks me, for it is rare that I ever feel uncomfortable anymore with what the body does.

Stefan's wife opens her eyes and smiles weakly at us. She smooths her dark hair and says something in German about going to get some food, and then she wanders out the door. I collect myself with a breath and take Stefan's hot, swollen hand in mine.

And am shocked again.

The hand is hot, but dead. Lifeless. As I feel into his body, I become increasingly light-headed. I am unable to find him— that surging life force that will leap up to meet me the second I touch someone, that movement of cells and breath and blood circulating. In this man, I can find nothing, as though there is wood between my hands and his body.

"I can't . . . feel him," I whisper to Peter, who stands at the opposite side of the bed, holding his cousin's other hand.

Peter nods, his eyes on Stefan's face. "He is on a lot of medicine," he says. "Machines are creating his body rhythms because they cannot happen naturally. It is like his body is just one big mush now, with no ability to respond to anything."

I close my eyes and try and listen deeper. Indeed, Stefan's body feels like dull mush. And the dull mush, I realize, the longer I listen, is familiar. It is a state I often have to shake my own body out of.

As I am starting to think that I should admit defeat, suddenly, I find him. That hum we call "life force," the thing we sense immediately in another, that tells us if a body is alive or dead. There it is; my hands find it. But how *deep* it is, and how hard it is to stay with it—to not slip back to the outer layers of his body that are numb and dull and undifferentiated. I keep losing him. It takes all of my concentration and focus to look for the pulsing rhythm underneath the pacemaker in his heart, for the breath underneath the mechanical inflation and deflation of his lungs.

But when I find it—that current of light in the secret room behind the rooms of this man's body—when it courses through me, just for a moment, I suddenly know something that I have never known before.

This is what we are made of—unerring power.

The word "unerring" pours through me, and I shudder and shake and lift my hands.

And just like that, the knowing is gone. I am back in the low-ceilinged hospital room, with the clicking machines and the wheeze of the ventilator, the plastic tubes of various liquids entering and exiting his body, the vague smell of feces and disinfectant.

But with the memory of this man, the inner hum of him, still rushing through my body like a secret, like love.

⇌

Everything is more real when I walk outside. The low, tumbling clouds. The German bikers and the smell of the summer rain, the smudged hills of trees. My heart, open for the first time in a long time, is a sound in my chest like a low-hummed song.

At the old train station, my classmates are performing for

their summer show, and I wind my way into the small crowd to watch them. The pieces are largely uninspired, as they have always been, and yet the dancers' efforts are nevertheless made poignant this night by the setting—the growing darkness, the misting rain; the red trains pushing into the station and then lumbering off again; the performers in pink, white, lavender, dripping wet, their bodies luminous in front of the dark, green trees.

Squeezed tight between the spectators, shoulder to shoulder with strangers, I think, *There's the time in every country when I hate everything. And then there is the time when the rage just drops away.* It's when I become weary of the rigid structures I have built around my heart—the angles of which cut and groan as my heart continues to grow, regardless of them. Weary of the rules the protectors in me have made about who can and cannot enter, who is safe, who is unsafe, and the endless fury that storms up from my belly at the injustice of not being loved, of being abandoned, feeling afraid, of the fallibility of humans, of the fallibility of myself. Suddenly it happens: the work of keeping myself separate becomes too great. And I fall back into love. Remembering as I do, *Ah, yes*—to love is the body's most natural, wild state.

It is this moment that I know without doubt that I will not rejoin my classmates at school. That, God help me, I will never go to a dance school again. But I know that my answer is still *yes.* Yes, I do take you, dance, and all of your consequences. And that doesn't just mean chronic back injury, or enduring mucky, freezing winters, or trying to survive as an emotional foreigner in a Hitler-scarred culture. It also means being willing to encounter my own self, in my own body, when I dive into it. Into the vast, limitless space of me, because the truth is, it is not a path at all, dancing, but rather a falling into the universe that my body is. And the more I dance, the less I can avoid the consequences of that falling, that eye-to-eye meeting of every place I never wanted to know, or feel, or look at inside of myself.

But when I look at it—when I really, *really* look at it—I suddenly understand that it is not disgusting at all, what I did not want to see. It is simply one more doorway leading me deeper and deeper into a place of living and feeling and loving where even the fear—even the fear!—is so achingly, heart-wrenchingly, give-thanks-to-God beautiful.

It is the body.

It is the body that I love.

And the body does not need to be taught how to dance. The body is always dancing.

The next week I catch a ride to Eifel, Germany, a small village outside of Cologne. The sun is thickly warm, the fields leaning into yellow. There are no coffee shops, no restaurants, no grocery stores. Just a few squat houses, a broken down bus from the Czech Republic in someone's front yard, and a giant, roaring golden lion on someone else's stoop. I wander the narrow lanes, hot, thirsty, lonely, exhausted. All of these things are somehow bearable; I carry them easily, like an infant in the crook of my arm.

I'm not sure what time the training starts, and when I get to the place where the class is supposed to be held, I'm not sure if I have the right building. I push through a side door and wander for a while in the dimly lit hallways. There is not a sound, and I am just about to go back outside when I turn a corner and bump into someone. She is a small woman with gray hair to her shoulders and bright, curious eyes. "I'm sorry," I say to her. "I'm not sure if I'm in the right place."

She takes my hands in both of her hands and regards me gently. Then she says, "You are definitely in the right place."

This is how I meet Bonnie Bainbridge-Cohen, the founder of Body-Mind Centering. Body-Mind Centering, or BMC, is a method of studying anatomy, and something that Falk once recommended to me. It has been talked about on the outskirts of everything I've been studying since Israel, though it is not until this moment that I have decided to actually turn my head toward it, pay attention. *No more studying dance. Now I will study the body.*

Bonnie Bainbridge-Cohen leads me back through the building and into the studio and sits me down beside her in a circle of fifty waiting students. She begins to teach.

For the next ten days, I am in love.

BMC is the work that I've been searching for. It is a way to study the body that is deeply rooted in anatomy, physiology, *and* dance. For ten days, I stay knee to knee with Bonnie, inhaling everything, as she explains the development of the muscles, the way the cells move, how to *feel* the cells move, how to feel the constant steady dance of your body supporting you, guiding you, growing you.

It quickly becomes clear to me that this training is about learning how to first and foremost follow the body. In every class session, there are almost always one or two people lying on the floor taking a nap, while the rest of the group dances or studies anatomy charts or practices hands-on exercises around them. In the world outside of this class, the body has always been something to be managed rather than followed. You are expected to make the body do what you want it to do —or more often, what others want it to do. If it is tired, you wake it up with caffeine or sugar or pills or cocaine. If it is awake and you need it to sleep, you knock it out with other substances. In the working world, you are only allowed a certain number of days per year to be sick, and in many work environments, you are expected to power through being sick and work anyway. You go to the doctor to change an undesirable physical experience, and the doctor tries to find the right pill for you to change that experience. This is the normal I have been raised with, and I never questioned it. Then my body stopped doing what I wanted it to. It started doing weird, painful, terrifying things, like shaking and feeling and hurting with tremendous intensity for inexplicable reasons, and I started to despise it. I tried to throw it away. I drank too much and let it get fucked by people I didn't care about, and in my darkest moments, I fantasized about ways to kill it completely. I tried to save myself with dance, but even at my dance school— a place where the body was our instrument and in theory should have been venerated above all else—there was no culture of care for it. If your knees hurt, you got a cortisol shot. We were expected to overbend, overextend, work beyond limits while we could, while we were young, and endure the consequences later, in old age when our instrument would no longer be beautiful to watch anymore.

But here, at this training, suddenly the only thing expected of me is to follow my body. Not train my body to do a certain thing someone wants of it, but rather *train myself to do what my body wants*. "It's called Body-Mind Centering, not Mind-Body Centering," Bonnie explained. "Because it's the body acting on the mind. Most of the time we do it the other way around. The mind tells the body what to do and how to be. But we have access to so much more information when we let the body *be* the mind—let it lead us, inform us, move us."

In a ten-day course, along with learning the names and attachments and individual movements of every muscle in the body, I also learn how to nap when I am tired, even if it is in the middle of class ("You'll learn something different if you're asleep, but you'll still learn," Bonnie said), how to eat when I am hungry, roar when I am angry, cry when I am sad. All fifty of us do it together; we are a moving, living organism of authentic impulse. And as all living organisms do, we find a natural balance together, so that when one of us cries, there are three of us who are feeling calm and strong and awake to hold her, support her and ask nothing of her. When one shakes or shouts or encounters something terrifying within herself, there are even more of us who can listen and allow it. And when our own bodies say they can't hold anymore, we take space or sleep, and there are new, fresh bodies to step forward and hold hands and feet and heads. I am cradled and rocked and touched and sang to, and I cradle and rock and sing. My pelvic pain comes back one morning, and an assistant teacher hums deep, quiet bass notes into my kidneys until I shake gently and scream and then laugh and then rejoin the class, who is dancing.

⇌

During a tea break one morning, I tell Bonnie my story of being sick for years back home and she listens with quiet eyes. Then she says, "I too had to be still for a very long time.

This is one of the ways the body helps us reclaim somatic intelligence."

And suddenly I have a name for it. No longer am I weird, crazy, or alone. *Somatic intelligence.*

"Somatic," another teacher explains to me at lunch on the last day, "means cultivating an alive, awake body. When we study somatics, we are developing the intelligence of the body." He goes on to tell me that somatic people are those who understand this intelligence inherently, without needing to be taught. "I could see right away that you are one of these people," he says. "Somatic people recognize other somatic people. We are marked by certain characteristics: long, unexplainable illness or a big injury that brings us to the brink of what we can physically handle. Heightened sensitivity to food and environment and other people. We will have a throbbing need in our hands to work on other bodies, and other bodies will always shout loud to us when they want our help, even if the inhabitant of the body does not know how to ask. Bodies will throw themselves into our hands. We fall into so many kinds of love, easily and all the time, because our bodies are open—in fact they *crave*—to connect on the deepest possible level. And we hear and understand movement like a language."

He takes a bite of his potato salad as tears course openly down my face. He doesn't need to ask why I am crying. He just keeps eating, but he puts one of his hands on mine. In a few sentences he has explained and decoded all of the mysteries of my long illness, my shaking, my strange, explosive connections with other people, my ability to see and read things in other bodies. "You make us sound like some mystical tribe," I say, wiping at my cheeks.

He shrugs his broad shoulders. "You can think of it like

that, but it can really all be explained biologically. Somatic people have heightened sensitivity in their mirror neurons. Either you're born with this, or you develop this through study."

"Mirror neurons?"

"They are the neurons that allow us to physically experience what another person experiences—everyone has them. This is why watching someone dance is so pleasurable—because when you watch what he is doing, your mirror neurons create the exact same sensation in your own body. Humans are constantly feeling what others are feeling. But some of us are more sensitive, and we feel other bodies more loudly than most."

I realize I have finally found my people and my place. The deepest part of me—that restless gnawing ache—loosens when I hear his words, and finally, finally lets go. I put my face in my hands for a second and sob, and because he is a somatic person, nothing about this frightens him. He pulls me into his body, and I feel the sound of his cells, deep and steady, humming in my ears.

"You are beginning to understand," he says, holding me. "Now just let it go. Let your understanding go, and it will come back again. Let something new and deeper find you and then find you again."

We are in the garden behind the studio, the late-afternoon sun warm on our hands. When I manage to stop crying, I ask him how to continue. The BMC programs in Europe are in Italy, France, Germany, and Slovakia. In order to catch all of the courses in the program, I would have to travel nonstop for the next year between all of these countries. As usual, I have very little money.

He says, "I suggest a backpack and the couches of a lot of friends."

I take a deep breath. "Okay. I guess. Yeah. I guess I can do that."

He is confused by the panic he sees in my eyes. "Haven't you been traveling for the last several years?"

"Yeah, but I always had a home. A place to return to."

He nods. Smiles. He rests his palm on my shoulder. From the course I have just finished, I now know that he is touching the place where my clavicle meets my scapula, a graceful confluence of bones that curve and rise like rocks shaped by water and wind.

I think of all my running, through the trees and the cities. I think about my time in Israel, all those people fighting and longing so deeply for a home, and I think about how hard I have searched for some place to rest, some ground to lay my head down on. And I realize that every moment before now has been training for this moment, teaching me to find trust in my body. Teaching me to need nothing but my breath, the lungs of me, and the feet and the muscles and the bones of me. And now I am ready. I will let my body be the place I rest in, the place I live in, my true and only home.

6.

FRANCE AND SPAIN

2010

My surfer rideshare is a bit chubby with a ponytail. He told me that he was half Russian but he had never met his Russian father. He was a baby when his father had moved away and then at some point killed himself. True to his word, he does what he promised and drives me sixteen hours to drop me directly at Alex's doorstep. The house leans down toward the ground on all sides, its green shutters hanging on one hinge over windows that are broken and repaired with yellow masking tape and old T-shirts. It is five-thirty in the morning, and the sun has just risen. Alex is standing in the doorway wearing ripped jean shorts and a red hoodie, with a brown corduroy train conductor cap pulled low over his messy blond hair. His eyes are tired, but he's grinning. He wraps me in his long arms and kisses me hello, as though we've been doing this kind of thing for years, and I have a fleeting memory of the way Alon would meet me each time I returned or he returned from somewhere far. *How quickly everything, at least on the surface, can be replaced.*

⇌

My next BMC course is in Italy in three weeks. I packed up my apartment in Freiburg, gave notice to my landlord, spent one last afternoon with Peter drinking beer on his balcony, and took a solid twenty-four hours to panic about how the hell I was going to pull it all off. My schedule is like a connect the dots game from someone else's life—a rock star or a queen. I needed to be in Rome in September, Paris in October, Milan two weeks later, then Cologne. And while this would probably be nothing but pure pleasure if I actually were a rock star, catching private jets from here to there and resting in between in penthouse suites, sipping fresh orange juice mimosas, the truth was I had not a penny to spare, which meant that there was high potential for an experience completely opposite of pleasurable.

But after training steadily for the last years in the art and practice of improvisation, I also felt determined to do this in a way that would not be stressful. This would be my new dance training, I decided. I was going to stay present in my body and let my body lead.

⇌

"We started as a vibration," Bonnie Bainbridge Cohen explained to us in my last BMC course. "You and me, each one of us, started as one vibration in the womb. And from there, we grew. Effortlessly."

Through all of these complex stages, in our mother's body, we grew. From a creature of water and light, we developed spine; we became structure, bone. Our growth was inevitable. The will to become something so utterly different from what we were—to transform ourselves into a thing we could not possibly previously know, and do it, again and again, every day —did not need to be found or created. It just *was*. There is no force to this process, no necessary extra effort, only a willingness to follow the body.

The body knows the way, I have finally come to realize. It always knows the way. All we need is to say *yes*, no matter how incomprehensible it is to the mind. *Yes* to what the body tells you. *Yes, yes, yes.*

A week before I needed to move out of my apartment, I met Alex at a bar in downtown Freiburg. We danced all night. He told me at sunrise that he was leaving for his home in the South of France the following morning. He asked if I would come visit him there. There was no magic in our connection, no love at first sight, but inexplicably my gut said yes, my heart said yes. So I said yes.

And that's how this one started.

⇌

I pay my rideshare for gas and give him a little punch on the shoulder goodbye, and he gives me one too. Alex and I go into his tired house, where he lives with four other people—a dishwasher, a psychologist, a cabinetmaker with early-onset osteoporosis, and another carpenter who isn't carpentering anymore because he had just swallowed fire with the wrong kind of petrol in his mouth and burned out half his lungs. Alex tells me all this as he carries my bag into his room, a small box off the corner of the living room, with a dingy mattress on a floor that looks slightly damp and very dirty. Alex does not apologize for the dishevelment of his house. I take this to be because he is twenty-five and probably doesn't know yet what it is like to live well, with money, in nice houses, so he doesn't know what he should apologize for. To him, it is probably just normal, for he is simply out for the adventure, and the experience of places: fuck the comfortable living situations, if I need that I'll go home to my parents. And I think, *Well, I guess that is my life too,* and then I lie down with this boy on his bed.

He had moved down to France nine months earlier, he told me when we met in Freiburg, to do an apprenticeship at a carpenter studio. After the six months of apprenticeship were over, he had been asked to join the staff because he was good, precise, and hardworking. The French people liked his German organizing mind, his plans for the shop, his suggestions for renovation that he sketched out for them and labeled in both French and German.

As the sun rises and fills the room with warm light, he traces the line of my ribs through my T-shirt and the curves of my face, one finger gently outlining the cartilage between my nostrils and the arc of the bone beneath my eyebrow. "You're here; I'm so glad you are here," he keeps saying, and I wonder who he thinks I am and what we are beginning. I remind myself not to ask; just dance, now, with what is here, the sound of the morning starting outside, his roommates in the kitchen, the neighbor shouting at her kids in French, the river across the street and the cars.

⇌

He goes to work in the mornings, and I pack a backpack for the day and just wander. Anglet is a typical small European village with a mixture of romantic old Europe, and worn-out, ugly new Europe. The narrow, curving streets are crowded with garbage; the centuries-old stone buildings with black iron balconies rub elbows with dingy McDonald's restaurants, and the tables outside the bars are green plastic like the kind you get in Walmart for $6. Laminated menus, streaky from the wet river air, sit in piles on chairs by the edge of the sidewalk. The town is getting ready for a fete, a four-day party where everyone wears red and white—Basqueland colors—and, from what Alex tells me, drinks themselves crazy. Most of the streets are blocked off, and there are roller coasters being constructed in a lot beside the river. Already the village is full with children excited for the party, wearing white pants and white shirts with red scarves belted at their waists like little pirates, running around with croissants gripped in their grubby hands while their parents trail after them drinking sangria out of flimsy white plastic cups.

On the narrow strip of spotty green grass between the river and the road, teenagers are constructing their own campsites, stringing up sheets of plastic between sticks to create shade for their old army-colored sleeping bags and their boxes of whiskey and Coca-Cola and baguettes and Brie wedges and ham.

⇌

After wandering the streets all day, I meet up with Alex when he has finished work, and we go to the beach to drink stubbies of warm French beer and watch the sunset, me leaning back on his long body, my elbows on his knees.

"Favorite color?" he asks. It's our "fast track to knowing each other" game.

"That one." I point—the blue over the sea after the sun has dropped. "Favorite food?"

"*Flamkuchen*," he says. "Favorite movie?"

"*True Romance.* Favorite smell?"

"Seriously? *True Romance?*"

"Yeah . . . why?"

"I hated that movie. Too violent."

"Life is violent. You Germans."

"Us Germans what?" He sits me up so I will look him in the eye.

"I feel like your history has made you terrified of anything aggressive or masculine. You probably sit down to pee, don't you?"

"Dayna!" He pulls me back onto his body again. "Are you always this difficult?"

I cringe. "I'm sorry. Only sometimes."

Alex is not difficult, and I like him immensely for this. I am twenty-eight now and becoming more and more concerned that I may never be able to maintain a long-term relationship. That voice in my ovaries has started to hammer at me with increasing desperation. On the sixteen-hour drive down from Germany with my rideshare, I decided to approach it the same way I organized myself each time I moved to a new country: I wrote out a checklist, a three-year checklist.

- Find a partner.
- Figure out how to tame your dark side so you can stay with that partner.

- Develop a sustainable career.
- Have a baby. (See 2. Don't fuck up the baby.)

⇌

Though I don't know Alex or how I feel about him, I take the opportunity with him to practice being the kind of partner I think I should be. With gusto, I mop his floor and wash his sheets. When he comes home at the end of the day smelling like cedar and sweat, we pull off each other's shirts immediately and I massage his smooth, strong shoulders, tanned dark as the stained wood he works. He's the type of guy that likes to bike and surf and hang glide, but he isn't one of *those* kinds of guys, he insists; he cares about other things besides sports. And one night, just to prove it, we spend two hours looking at a big book he keeps underneath his sweaters in his drawer, a carpenter's manual from the nineteenth century. He talks for a long time about the art of building staircases and how people knew how to do things then, with their hands. "Now it's just machines," he says. "And that makes me so sad."

"Were either of your parents carpenters?" I ask him. "Or your grandparents?"

He shakes his head. "Just me. I'm not anything like them." And then his eyes fill with tears. "My grandfather is dying," he explains, swiping at his cheeks. "He was a Nazi. You have no idea what it was like to grow up knowing that."

I put my arms around him, and he puts his face in my neck. I think about my Jewish grandfather and his Nazi grandfather, what they might feel to see us embrace.

He has brought home a fish from the market, and we eat it in the garden that night, drinking cold, white wine, my feet on his lap. In the house, his roommates are getting drunk, listening to reggae. The music wafts out to us, as hypnotic as the sea, an invitation to float. We toast each other. "To life!" we say, meeting eyes. For a moment, it feels like love, and it isn't until later, while Alex snores softly beside me in his separate dreams, that my fears about the future pour in, demanding answers to the formless questions. *Is this. . . ?* and *How will you. . . ?* and *What if. . . ?*

That old, familiar panic attack shudders through me. I put my hands on my chest and focus breath into my tight-knit lungs, the way BMC has taught me. I rest my mind inside of my body and listen, listen, listen to the unwinding terror until eventually it passes, and as the sun is rising, sleep comes.

⇌

I put on a white dress I've been carrying around since Greece and have never worn, and he puts on a red scarf and a white T-shirt, and we venture out to the fete.

His psychologist roommate, Valerie, is the only girl and the one out of two people in the house who speaks English. This doesn't mean that she speaks it *well,* but nevertheless, she is beginning to be a fairly good friend. She would come and sit with me in the evenings sometimes and tell me in half French and half English about her miserable boyfriend, some long-haired dude named *G*-something, who skulked around drinking beer and complaining about things. She comes running out after us as Alex and I are leaving the house in our fete gear and grabs my hand. "Be careful," she says. "It is very dangerous for women at night there."

Alex drapes his big, heavy arm around my shoulder.

"Don't worry, I got her," he says, and I smile reassuringly at Valerie. But her eyes stay worried as she looks from me to Alex to me again, and it takes her a minute to let go of my hand.

The road to the city is scattered with greasy bread bags from the bakery and red empty cola bottles and smashed beer bottles and piles of human shit decorated with long strands of pink toilet paper. Young men sit together in bunches drinking whiskey out of enormous bottles that you can buy across the border in Spain, and they all stare at me with red, hot eyes. I wish I'd worn a sheet, rather than a dress, something shapeless and full of bulk, and I wish for a drink, which always makes me fearless before it brings disaster.

All the bars have their doors open, pumping music, and all the music puddles into one big sound that flops over our heads together with all the yelling and the laughing and the fighting and the singing. We meet a few of Alex's friends, and we hold hands and arms and elbows and together push our way through the churning sea of red and white. Alex needs to be at the front of the line because he knows where we're going, so he attaches me to the arm of his friend, a tall, dark-haired, dark-eyed guy with a red scarf wrapped around his throat. I smile at him, and he smiles at me as our arm chain maneuvers its way through the crowds. He tries to talk to me at first in French, but when I shake my head, he switches to Spanish. He apologizes and says he speaks no English, tells me his name is Alejandro and that he is from Madrid, and something like he moved here for a job, or is here for some weeks for a job, and then something about the French being crazy, and what about you? I am just about to attempt to explain in my broken, terrible Spanish that I am here with his friend, when our whole hand-arm chain stops in a narrow alleyway outside of a tiny bar, where Alex and another guy go in to buy us drinks. Some kind of pressure starts to build in the crowd. We are pressed shoulder to shoulder to shoulder to both sides of the stone walls of a passageway. It seems that a group of drunk French rugby players, singing rugby songs at the top of their lungs, are trying to push their way through, plowing into people, and people are starting to stumble and then panic because there is nowhere to stumble to. A man beside me falls and catches himself hard with his arm against another man who falls and knocks someone else, who crashes into someone else. Everyone starts pushing and yelling, desperate to get out of the passageway. I lose my hand chain and fall also, forward against some small girls who get yanked up by their bigger boyfriends, and my knees hit the ground, hard. Someone steps on my calf, and another person bashes into my shoulder, and I think about the six people I read about who died by trampling yesterday at a street festival in Berlin. I'm about to panic when I feel someone's arms around me, and then I am pulled to my feet by Alejandro. I grip hold of his body and he grips hold of mine, and we go spinning and scuttering like a leaf in a torrent, together keeping our balance until we make it to the door of the bar. We burst into where there are still so many people but no more stampeding, and we look at each other and we kiss.

Later there will be so much broken because of that kiss.

Over how it happened, and why, the argument of who kissed who, and for how long. But for now, let's just stay with the kiss itself, something like two buckets of water thrown toward each other at the same time, the water meeting and crashing together in the air, weightless, for a second, the split of sound, the ground and the sky mirrored, before it drops back to the earth and disappears. We separate, grinning, stunned, and it is all I can do to not grab his face and kiss him again. I see Alex, a head taller than the crowd, pinning us with his eyes as he pushes through the bodies to get to us.

This is when the guy next to me starts to puke. It is another one of Alex's friends, a little bald man with glasses, and his glasses fall off when he throws up—all this orange-red, fruit-studded vomit that covers his glasses and the edges of his shoes. Alejandro leaps forward to pull him in the direction of the bathroom, motioning to Alex to help, and Alex, throwing one last murderous glare at me, takes his friend by his other arm. Together they half lift, half drag him to the toilet at the back of the bar.

I look down and see that my knees are bleeding—profusely, thanks to my brush with death in the alley. Blood is drying in a thick, gummy river down my shins and in between my toes, so I maneuver my way toward the women's bathroom to try and clean myself up. There are four or five other girls in line, one of them with a bottle of whiskey. When she sees my knees, she offers me a swig, which I take, gladly. And so the waiting in line goes. By the time I make it to the toilet, I am happily tipsy and a little less worried about what is going to happen when Alex and Alejandro finally come out of their bathroom on the other side of the bar.

Except that they never come out of the bathroom. Or they do, but don't care about finding me. At any rate, I am left.

The rational thing to do would be to try and find my way back to Alex's house. Or to a hotel. It is late, and the crowd, which is mostly men, is only getting drunker. Valerie's warning is echoing in my head, and my bloody knees are throbbing, but for some reason that will never be known to me I toss reason aside and do what I feel to be best for the situation—I get totally and completely drunk. I call Alex's phone some hundred times, and he doesn't answer. I cry, and at some point I also puke. I dance for a long time with a man who has no arms and then go running around the streets getting pummeled by miniature stampedes here and there. I'm searching for the high head of Alex, or one of his friends, or something, anything familiar, but the streets are all winding and packed with the same color, the same music, the same shouting, pushing, screaming. I'm pretty sure I also start to scream, with blood on my hands and sangria on my dress.

Finally, finally, I come to a road I recognize, and there I am at Alex's house. Bleeding and breathing ragged, I walk round the side and catch sight of Alex's face through the broken, T-shirt-patched window. He is sitting on his bed, reading, as peaceful as a peach, and I am flooded with an unnameable rage. I charge into the house and kick down his bedroom door, shards of wood flying, the ceramic doorknob falling to the floor and shattering. Alex is instantly on his feet, backing away from me. "You fucking asshole, how could you *leave* me?!" I am screaming. Then his roommates are there, the dishwasher, and the cabinetmaker with osteoporosis, and even the lung-burned carpenter; they are all three holding me back as I struggle and flail to get to Alex through the splintered wood and glass. A lot of French is being yelled. Alex is against the wall with his hands stretched out but not saying anything, and somewhere, roosters are crowing, and that's when I wake up.

I sit up with a start, as though to say, "Who's been driving while I was asleep?" The Eris within me eases back into the shadows, leaving me terrified to deal with the situation at hand —four angry, scared men and a whole lot of broken things as the sun spills its light through the half-shuttered windows.

⇌

The hangover lasts for days. I can't eat nor get out of bed, and eventually I realize it's not a hangover, but rather a flu. I shake with fever as the sun rises and falls, as the house beyond Valerie's bedroom door clatters to life and then drops into silence again. She brings me water and bread between her work shifts, and every day Alex climbs the stairs and sits beside me as I shiver and slide in and out of delirious dreams. One morning, I wake to a feeling of fire and realize he is cleaning the wounds on my knees. "I'm sorry, Dayna," he is saying, and I open my eyes to see that there are tears on his cheeks. "I shouldn't have left you; I should have just talked to you. I'm a stupid boy. I'm such a stupid, young boy."

"I'm sorry too. About the door."

He wraps a clean white bandage around my knee. "I'm a carpenter. Without broken doors, we'd have nothing to do."

"I'm sorry about . . . that kiss . . . I don't know what happened."

He pulls the bandage tighter. "I believe you. I am going to believe you. I have to."

"I should go. I will try to go. As soon as I can get up."

"I don't want you to." His eyes pool with new tears and two little bright spots of red come to the surface of his cheeks. "I kissed a girl that night, after I left you," he says. "It's worse. What I did."

I'm surprised by this admission and his kindness. Valerie had told me that Alex had come home that night with the story of seeing me kiss someone and that the four men had sat around for hours drinking and calling me a whore and spitting when they said my name.

He says to me now, "It's finally my holidays, and we're leaving for Spain this weekend. I want you to come with us. We're going here, Picos de Europa." He pulls a guidebook from the backpack at his feet and flips through the pages, showing me pictures of tall, rugged peaks and green alpine meadows. "Look, this waterfall is supposed to be amazing." He helps me to sit up a little so I can see it more clearly. "Come with us," he says again. "You can fly to your course in Rome from Bilbao. I'll drop you off there."

I fall back on the pillow, feeling sad and scared and alone. *Yes to the moment.* I don't know what else to do. "Okay," I say. "Yes."

⇌

The whole house is going, with the exception of Valerie, who is spending her holidays with G-something, her sulky boyfriend. She hugs me before we leave, holding me by the shoulders to look me firmly in the eyes. "I don't care for this word 'infidelity.' What idiots who think the world is black and white," she says. "I think he's too young and stupid for you. But"—she waves her hand, as if scooping up handfuls of air and then offering it to me—"every moment is giving you to the next moment, you know?" Then she kisses me warmly on the cheeks. "Goodbye, Dayna, goodbye."

And weak but feverless, I climb into a van with three men

who hate me and a boyfriend I barely know, to rattle south, back to Spain.

⇄

"They don't *hate* you; I *explained* it to them," Alex had tried to convince me when I'd expressed my doubts about a vacation starring the four of us. But Alex was given to some dubious mood swings in the days leading up to our departure, going silent for hours and ditching our evening dinners to go surfing instead, so his reassurances were none too reassuring. Granted, when the guys had seen that Alex was more or less forgiving me, they all tried to straighten up and be civil. They resumed the French "kiss you on the cheeks every time you enter or exit a room" thing, but beyond that, they did not look at or speak to me. Only Nikola, the one with early onset osteoporosis, watched me a lot with big eyes and asked me questions that I didn't understand.

"What's he saying?" I asked Alex for a translation once.

"He's just repeating the same thing over and over again: Who are you? What are you doing? Where are you going? Why don't you learn French?"

David, the carpenter with half-burned lungs, was only coming with us part of the way. After four hours of driving, we left him in a green valley at a reggae festival, where he met up with his girlfriend, a cute Spanish girl with purple dreadlocks. Before the whole "Dayna is a psychotic whore" episode, David and I had been almost friends. As in, he'd play me all the reggae music he liked and I would show polite interest: "Okay, yeah, I guess this song *does* kind of sound different from the one before." He'd draw me pictures, because he didn't speak English—a lot of drawings of staircases, so that I imagined that him and Alex must be kindred spirits, conversing often on the art of handmade wooden things. But to my surprise, Alex told me that he hated him because "he thinks of no one except himself." This was another thing on Alex's long list that was unforgiveable. Fortunately for me, being kissed by another man didn't make it onto that list. "Just so long as it was him who kissed you and not the other way around, and you better not be lying to me," he said— sternly and often.

All of this—lying, thinking of only yourself—happen to be things on *my* long list that constitute "things humans do." Of course, I didn't tell Alex that. Nor did I try to explain to him the fact that a person is never just one thing and is always its opposite. Though I did pull him into the kitchen for a second before we left the house in France in order to witness David quietly making an elaborate picnic for his girlfriend— roasting eggplants and peppers and zucchinis in the oven and then arranging them in Tupperware with slices of white goat cheese and caramelized walnuts, which he caramelized himself. "Look how thoughtful he is being for someone else," I said, but Alex just rolled his eyes and whispered that I only see people's good sides, before he stomped out of the kitchen.

⇌

For a while we do all right, the four of us. We prowl up and down the coast of Asturias and Cantabria in Alex's beat-up white van, in search of waves for the guys. When we find them, they all three race out to sea and don't return until their whole bodies sag with exhaustion. Meanwhile, I spend hours prowling through whatever village we are close to, dreaming up meals for them, inspired by David's careful salads and the art of not thinking only of oneself. One morning, I buy a couple of kilos of fresh shrimp off a fisherman. When I bring it to them with a container of aioli, the way they smile at me and close their eyes when they eat makes me think maybe I've made up for the destruction by my witch, for good. I think of a friend's wife in the States, a Japanese woman who willingly devoted herself to serving her husband, including heating a towel in the microwave and coming to wipe his face for him after dinner. I think, *I could be like that, couldn't I?*

⇌

I continue to have panic attacks every night.

I wake shouting, sometimes weeping, from dreams about a demon. One night, I dream I am at a party when I catch sight of a beautiful man watching me. From a distance, I think he is "the one." I move toward him before I see, too late, that he doesn't have a face at all. That in fact, his face is darkness, layers and layers and layers of black, terrifying darkness, and the shock of it is so deep that I scream and wake screaming. Alex hushes me, holding me. "I'm here, I'm here, I'm here," he says, but there is no comfort in his touch, so convinced am I in that moment that the darkness will win, that no matter what we do, the shadow will destroy everything.

⇌

It is just past sunset when we arrive at the Picos de Europa. We set up camp in an old, abandoned village at the base of the mountains—dramatic, sharp, gray peaks that pierce the rolling, black clouds. We string up an old sheet of plastic using two sticks and the door of the van, and the four of us huddle under it, watching the shadows of the night deepen over the ancient broken houses and then the steady, icy rain as it falls. Finally, when the silence between us is too much, and the darkness and the cold, we all go to bed, Alex and I to the van and Nikola and Lucas to their tent. In our bed, Alex stares unblinking at the ceiling until I put my hand on his chest and say, "Hey. What is going on?"

He bursts. "I don't trust you, I don't trust you, I don't trust you one little bit, not at all!" And then his whole body goes dull and flat under my hands, and he stares off like he is alone or dead, like he can't even be bothered to push me away from him.

"What . . . I mean . . . why?" I will myself to be patient, take slow breaths.

"What happened with him? Really? Tell me the truth."

"Who?"

"I'm talking about Alejandro. The fete. Did you forget?" Now he pushes me off of him. He pushes me hard, rising up on his elbow, glaring.

I cringe. "Why are you talking about this again?"

"Lucas told me that it was *you* who kissed him."

"Lucas told you. . . ?"

"Yeah, he was *there*. And it took you a long time to come home that night. Why did it take you so long? Were you looking for Ale?"

I close my eyes, suddenly so tired. "When did Lucas tell you this?"

"Last night. After you fell asleep. Is it true? I need to

know. Dayna, you come all the way down to see me, and then the second I go away, just for a minute. . . ."

I keep my eyes closed. I let my body go flat, go limp, go numb. Alex keeps talking, fast and at times incomprehensible, mumbling and then raging outward again. "Listen to me, I'm mumbling. You're making me *mumble*, you're making me mumble, and I can't breathe, and I haven't been this angry since I was a kid. I don't get angry like this. No, I don't get angry, but now I'm angry, I'm so *fucking* angry. Who the hell are you? What are you doing here? You come down here in your nice little dresses, and you make people want you, you *need* people to want you. You use it, you use your beauty, your eyes and your hair, to get people to love you. You get people to love you, and then you just leave, you just disappear, because you're addicted to it, to the power. I think you need therapy; you should go home and get some fucking therapy. . . ."

I think about that dance performance I watched in Freiburg, Artemis in the grotto. How I witnessed for the first time this part of me who I have hunted and hated, restrained and then set free. A goddess and a witch, a woman bent and twisted with uncontrolled emotion, who will also rise up into something searingly beautiful, searingly sexual. Who will seduce, who will discard if he is not enough, who will do as she pleases, and may no man tell her that such a thing is wrong.

In Witch Valley, I swore I would allow her, see her, talk about her. *I will let you teem through my body like wild roses, thick with thorns.* And yet every day since then has been an echo of the siren's story. The shadow of the feminine is abhorred by men and abhorred by women. So rather than allowing her, I have instead become two people. Day Dayna and Night Dayna. Day Dayna is reasonable, even-tempered, accommodating. Everyone seems to like her and not mind having her around. Night Dayna is unbearable for everyone.

And so it seems that the only way to sustain a relationship is to cage or tame the witch I once swore I would never forsake.

"But I can't be caged," she hisses at me as the cold rain slams into the windows of the van. "You know I can't be caged."

I wait until Alex wears himself out talking, until he turns on his side away from me and sleeps. I put my arm over my face and listen to the storm, until I finally also sleep, and dream of faceless men, glaring at me across acres and acres of darkness.

⇌

We hike through green, wet pastures, the fog down around our shoulders, so thick we can't see anything but the backs of each other, disappearing. We hike up, up, up, till the soup of fog thins into mist, through hillsides of red clover and tiny, pink star-shaped flowers—my mother would know their name, they are the ones that mark the end of summer. We pass fit, butter-colored cows grazing among the constant jostle and shout of their bells, past young sheep with wool wet and illuminated in the metallic light. Finally, one high, gray peak emerges from the mist as though a mirage. It is the point where we are climbing to. Then the sky breaks free, so blue it hurts.

I walk behind them, the two French men and a tall German whose ankles keep catching my eyes, narrow spindles from the pushed-down rumple of his white hiking socks. I walk behind them, where their French words are just sound, like the cow bells echoing up from the valley, a few words catching me when they turn on a switchback. *C'est sa, si cum sa, c'est bon, c'a c'est fe.* They snag in my mind and refuse to leave. *Poubelles* echoes in my head for hours. Trash.

I think about pacing in the Madrid airport, knowing that if I left, I would never see Quin again. Leaving anyway, following Now onto the plane, and deciding from then on to live my life in *now,* the present moment and nowhere else. And because of that decision, here I am, alone with men who hate me. But who's to say where the mistake was? Or if there was a mistake at all.

"I just want you to be happy," so many friends and family say to me, as though happiness is a destination one arrives at finally and never departs from again. Me, I know enough now that I don't just want to be happy. What I want is to trust my body to lead me where I need to go—when I succeed at this, the sensation is far bigger than happiness; there is a rightness that hums through me, a profound peace, a sensation of merging with the world's natural rhythm and flow. But I am still so untrained, unstable in this practice—my mind, consumed with future worry, fights my body's immediate state and pops me out of the rhythm, into disconnect and terror.

I think about my BMC teacher's advice in Germany. *Let your understanding go, and it will come back again. Let something new and deeper find you, and then find you again.*

With his words, I hike. I hike and I hike and I watch Alex's ankles. I watch the way stocky Lucas plods steadily with his head down. I watch long and lean Nikola, who gazes about with hooded eyes, stumbling occasionally, one hand resting on top of his flattened curls like he's just forgotten it there. No one translates for me, and I don't care.

When we finally reach the top of the mountain, we collapse on a pile of rocks, exhausted and silent as we look out across the miles and miles of gray mountains biting up into the blue sky. We tug out the food from each of our bags and pass it around—cheese, one tomato each, serrano ham—laying it all out on the cliff before us when suddenly we realize that we have only brought one baguette instead of four. The only option is to make one big sandwich and share it. With stomachs growling and mouths watering, we pile all of our ingredients onto the bread, until it is so fat we can barely fit our mouth around it. Alex takes the first bite and then passes it to me beside him. I pass it to Nikola, who passes it to Lucas, who passes it back to Alex again, and so it goes, the four of us slumped back on the rocks and silent, ravenous but patient as we sit among the towering presence of mountains.

"Life is perfect," Nikola suddenly professes in English, his mouth full of sandwich.

"Your English is perfect," Lucas replies, his mouth also full of sandwich.

"This sandwich is perfect," I say, taking a bite.

"You're perfect," Alex responds, which startles all of us, and his eyes flutter wide and his cheeks get red. Then Nikola starts laughing, and we all do, on the edge of the world, our mouths gaping open to the open blue sky.

After lunch, Alex puts his head on my lap and looks up at me with clear eyes. I'm sorry, he mouths, and I put my hand gently on his forehead.

⇌

He always forgets his apologies in the mornings. *Day Alex and Night Alex.* At sunrise he shakes me on the shoulder awake and stomps off, muttering to himself under his breath. I feel a familiar pain deep in my gut. Sure enough, when I go to pee there are a thousand angry warriors stabbing my urethra with rusty knives: pain attack. *God. Damn. It.*

Within twenty minutes, I am shuddering, pacing the gravel road beside our camp and cursing to myself as I double over with clawing pain. "Dayna, we have to go," Alex snaps, coming around the side of the van, his brow wrinkling at the sight of me doing whatever I am doing.

"I don't think I can, I'm—" Another knife of pain cuts through me, and I sink to a squat. "It's just this thing that happens to me sometimes. It goes away, but when I'm in it . . . it's the worst pain."

"I doubt that," he says. He stands with his long arms akimbo, his pack leaning against the side of the van in the gray morning light, looking around, as though embarrassed that the others might see me like this.

"I'm sorry, I probably won't be very much fun today." I attempt a smile, though it probably looks more like a grotesque grimace from where I am, crouched down in the dirt, rocking back and forth.

He stares at me with narrow eyes and then grabs up his pack with one decisive swing of his arm. "No, you won't be," he says. And without looking back, he walks off to join his friends at the top of the trailhead.

⇌

Of course he apologizes when they return that night. He crawls into the van where I've been writhing and moaning all day and holds my shivering, fevered body against the long heat of his body. "I'm sorry, I'm such a dick. It's okay, let me hold you," he whispers. Finally, just as the clouds clear, under the sharp, cold eyes of the stars, the pain slips out of me as quickly as it came. We sleep like exhausted children, our faces pressed together, our hands entwined.

In the morning, he is gone again. But the pain has shaken me back into myself, and when his angry eyes meet mine upon waking, I don't care about how he feels anymore.

⇌

The sun is setting, and Alex is sure we need to restock on food, but nobody agrees with him. "We have nothing to eat for dinner," he argues, "and what about tomorrow? It's Sunday and the stores will be closed."

Lucas and Nikola grumble about too much money being spent. "We have some bread left, a bit of cheese," I manage to understand in Lucas's French.

"I'm not just eating bread and cheese again!" Alex bursts and starts rearranging things in the back of the van. He takes his pants out of a box and then puts them back in again, takes his book and puts it on the front seat, then picks it up and puts it in the box with his pants. "And you." His eyes meet mine, where I am sitting placidly in the lawn chair, welcoming the quiet, heavy exhaustion in my body that always comes after a pain attack. We are back on the beach—no one asked me about the decision to return here, but I'm not complaining. I had had enough of those towering, cold peaks, the thick fog.

"You probably don't even want to eat with us anyway. Maybe you want to find some other guys to eat with?" he says. It is meant to be a joke, but his voice quavers a little, and no one smiles.

"What's wrong, Alex?" I say without looking up at him, examining the sand particles that are clinging to the hairs on my forearms.

Lucas, sensing my tone, snatches his book from the grass by his shoes and heads for the sea. Nikola keeps standing there, leaning against the van, watching me and Alex as though we are a foreign movie with no subtitles that he's found on TV—a bit bored, but too lazy to change the channel.

"Nothing. Nothing's wrong. I just think we should buy food." Alex tucks the strap of his surfboard tighter around his board, takes the towel off of where it is hanging on the door, and tosses it onto the seat.

I rise and climb into the front seat. "C'mon then. Let's go to the store." Now it is automatic, my inner housewife, I note, though it is not the kind generosity I had hoped to cultivate. Rather, there is violence in my compliance, in my refusal to argue.

He feels it. He gets in the car, his anger trembling in the grip of his hands as he turns the key, puts the stick shift in reverse. The sun is pink, heading down toward the water, lighting the small waves and the heads of the surfers bobbing like small, colored driftwood on the swells. Alex drives fast, up the curving roads, through the green forest, between the hills, and then out again, saying nothing, just working his jaw and changing gears with quick thrusts of his leg and grinding, direct motions of his arm. After some time, he flips on the stereo and plays something from his iPod I've never heard him listen to before, some screaming punk that rattles through the van, and I almost laugh before "the housewife" stops me. *Don't antagonize.* I fold my hands in my lap.

We pull into the parking lot of the closest supermarket, a giant, looming thing on a hill of concrete a few kilometers outside of Ribadesella. The parking lot is full, and young and old and middle-aged Spanish people are everywhere. They are sunburnt and sandy in shorts and sunglasses and bright splashy sundresses, loading bags of groceries into their vans and hatchbacks, yelling for children to come, or go, or run back into the store for another bag of something. Alex finds a corner space to park and turns off the car and just sits there, his hands on the steering wheel. I put my feet out my open window, and they turn pink in the pink light of the sunset. Below us are all these hills of trees, rolling out toward where we have come, the sea.

"You were the one who kissed Alejandro? Weren't you?"

I widen my eyes. "Seriously? Again?"

"Listen, I've been thinking about it. I wake every morning, thinking about it. You just used me to have a place to stay, because you needed somewhere to go. And now you're just trying to make it through, until you can find some other guy, and then you will just go. Won't you?"

I try to gather myself. *Inhale, exhale, don't react.* I turn toward him. I do my best to touch him without touching him, because I know that if I do—if I reach out to touch the part of his chest that is locked, I somehow know without a doubt that he will hit me. I think about his Nazi grandfather, dying slowly in a bed back in Germany. I think, *How long the path is, where we each come from.*

We sit silently, me looking at him, him not looking at me,

as the sun drops into the trees, throwing handfuls of pink light back into the sky, into our faces as it goes.

His leg starts to jiggle, and he says, "It was never anything. There was nothing special between us anyway." He says it with clenched jaw, and much to his surprise and mine, his eyes fill with tears, betraying him.

"That's not true, Alex."

"How can I trust you? You are always on the edge of leaving. I can feel it. I never know if you are going to stay or go."

I lean toward him, catching his full eyes. I want the things he says to not be true. I want to be able to love all of him, his youth, his silly rages; I want to love all of him and for him to love all of me, for surely this is what all of us deserve and need. I want to be able to promise what no one can promise: I will not leave you; I will never leave you. And maybe that desire in my eyes, it looks like what he wants, because he suddenly kisses me, full, deep, with the heat of a high fever, pulling me on my ears and the roots of my hair, pulling at my breath, before he pulls away, cheeks flushed, his chest shuddering.

He gets out of the car, quickly, and I watch him stride across the parking lot before I get out too and follow him into the store.

The lines at the checkout stands are bustling with fathers and children and mothers and surfers bagging packages of toilet paper and Coca-Cola and boxes of wine. The kids are tugging on each other's shirts and asking for candy and running toward the door and then back again and Alex is gone, somewhere in the mess of this, his tall shoulders nowhere to be found. So I just stand there, in an old, yellow flower-print dress from Israel, sand in my hair, stomachache, not sure where to go or what to do. And then, from all that noise, all that color, a figure surfaces, a man in purple swimming shorts with messy black hair. He is holding a bag of oranges, stock still at the end of the checkout, and with coal-dark eyes he is staring at me.

I turn immediately and walk out the door.

But he finds me anyway. Over at the edge of the parking lot, behind a red van with a stack of surf boards strapped to the top, my heart beating like a hummingbird on fire.

"It's *you?*" he says in his thick accent, holding two full plastic bags and leaning forward at the waist as he hurries toward me. I put my thumbnail in my mouth, bite down hard, release. Take a breath.

"Alejandro," I say. The man from the fete in France. I try to smile. "This is kind of a bad time."

His dark eyebrows pull in with confusion as he studies my lips, the same as Toothless Vaccillis used to do, as though a translation bubble might appear upon them.

"*Un tiempo malo,*" I try.

"*Que es malo?*" he laughs. "*Estamos aqui! Que coincidencia, joder!*" He keeps talking, too fast for me to catch, and anyway I am stuck repeating his words in my mind, over and over again, translating into English and then back to his Spanish: *We are here. What a coincidence, Fuck.* My heartbeat races circles around me, and the pink sunset light swoons orange down to the ground, around our feet and his brown legs, his arms, his mouth as he speaks, his big, strangely familiar smile. A car honks some feet away from us—a blond, muscular-chested guy is waving his arms at Alejandro and pointing to his watch. "I have to go," he says in Spanish. "How can I find you, do you want to—"

But I interrupt. *"Estoy aqui con Alex."* A quietness comes to his eyes, a nod, and a warmth.

"Vale. Lo siento, guapa." He switches one bag to the other hand, and with his free hand, he reaches out to touch me on the shoulder—a quick, gentle squeeze before he turns and hurries away.

~

I wake to shouts of laughter—a group of Spanish college students in the grass parking lot a few yards away from where we are parked at the beach. They have a big blue tarpaulin, and they are waving it in the air like a parachute as another girl and boy go racing through the space underneath, ducking so that the heavy plastic does not catch them. Sometimes it does, and they go sprawling onto the grass, and everyone dissolves into shouts of laughter, grabbing each other by the shoulder and clapping each other on the back. *"Otra véz, Otra véz,"* a guy with a video camera keeps yelling. They all take their positions and try it again, slightly different, flapping the tarp higher, or running through in a zig-zag. *Friends.* I try to recall a time when I had some.

Alex and I watch them for a while through the half-open window of the van, each of us wrapped in our own separate blanket. He was grumpy at first to be woken so early, but now he is smiling as he watches them, and I try to keep him in that softness. I say, "This is the kind of stuff that makes me homesick. Having a group of friends to get together with on a Sunday morning and make some kind of weird, funny project. . . ." I'm trying to be light, but there is emotion in my voice that betrays me, and Alex hears it.

His eyes flick to me, disgust in his gaze before he shoves off his blanket and reaches for his pants. "Man, I wish there were some fucking waves," he says.

I get out of the van and go to the bathroom and cry a little, and when I come back, he is already out surfing. *I can't do this*, I realize. *And I don't have to.* I tear a page from my journal, and I write him a note. "You were right." And then I take my bag, and I walk to the road. I stick my thumb out for a car, and I leave him.

⇌

I have no idea what I am going to do. I have about twenty euros in my pocket and am pretty sure nothing in my bank account—I've been waiting for money from an art modeling job I did in Germany, but have been unsuccessful in getting ahold of the school that owes me.

A gap-toothed, old farmer in a beat-up, brown truck picks me up and drives me seven kilometers down the road, leaving me at the edge of the bridge that leads into the town of Ribadesella. I thank the farmer, and he grasps my hand in his wrinkled, brown hand. Something in his grip is too tight, too wanting, and I pull away quickly, throw my shoulder into the creaky door to get out, fast. "I would take you home with me, but my wife would not be happy if someone as pretty as you showed up," he says through the window as I am taking my bag from the back. I turn to catch his eyes as they run up and down the length of my body. I feel the witch in me, her rage rising up into my eyes so fast, the old man sits back, as though slapped with it. I thank him again, this time with no smile, and storm away, across the long bridge, into what feels like a city of men, in a world of men. For the first time, I understand that the witch is not actually blind in her destruction. Rather, her fury is the culmination of thousands of years of fury toward all that has demanded women be smaller, less threatening, more complacent, tolerant of incredible mistreatment. I realize that it is the witch who keeps kicking through the boundaries of my life, allowing it to transform, again and again, into something bigger, even as I beg her to let me stay small, stay quiet, stay comfortable. *There is something more for you*, she persistently insists, as she destroys every artificial safety I try to cling to.

No power is stronger than hers, I realize, and when I am with her, I do not have reason anymore to be afraid. And so to her wild and steady presence I whisper, "Thank you."

⇌

I find a bench next to the sea on the outskirts of Ribadesella, and I sit and watch the water push its way to the shore and then out again. I sit for a long time, allowing myself to know absolutely nothing about what comes next. *Yes to the moment*, I tell myself over and over, like a mantra. *Yes, yes, yes.*

Then I look up and see Alejandro.

He is leaning against the streetlamp on the corner, eating a hard-boiled egg and smirking at me. When he sees me see him, he straightens and ambles over, his dark eyes shining. His long legs turn out slightly when he walks, bowing out a bit from his purple swimming trunks with each step. He stops in front of me and says something in Spanish like, "Are you following me?"

"I'd ask the same of you," I return in English, and his eyes wrinkle in that way, that amused and confused look at my lips, waiting for translation. In all of my years of traveling, in all of the countries, I never had friends who didn't speak English. English was the vehicle everyone knew and used, meanwhile keeping their own language for themselves, their Greek and their German and their Hebrew a secret, private room that they could duck into, speak rapidly and intensely. They knew that I would never know it as well as they knew English, for never was I forced, as they were, to go beyond my own native tongue.

But here I am—forced, with very few words to venture out and over to this new person in front of me. So I simply shrug. He looks down at me, his eyes bright with held laughter, and despite myself, I laugh too. "*Estamos aqui*," he says. Here we are.

⇌

He hoists my heavy backpack onto his narrow shoulders, and we just start walking. He leads me on a meandering path through the little red-roofed town of Ribadesella. Every now and then, he stops to motion me forward with little *come* wiggles of his fingers, waiting for me to grab his hand. When I do, he lets go and keeps walking, along the *ria* and then up, around a small green mountain, the bushes strewn with toilet paper and Mahou beer bottles. He talks to me steadily in Spanish, and some of it I catch, his sentences like a rain-smeared newspaper, so many words unknown to me and therefore blurred out. He is reading Faust, he says, and Mephistopheles, he was this guy who . . . and he really likes him because . . . and the women! Ha! As he talks, I watch his long-fingered, brown hands motioning me forward. I watch his animated lips when he turns back to see if I am still with him, and his rich dark eyes. His dark hair lifts off his forehead in the wind from the sea. The longer part in back, the coleta, the chunk of hair a couple of inches long on the leftish side of his neck, tucks into his red T-shirt every time he turns to look at me.

On the top of the hill, there is a little stone church and a 360 view of the sea, the village, the river. We sit down and look out over all of it. He says, "What do you have in here, your bag is like. . . ." He leans it gently against the stone bench beside us. "You have books? You must have books in here?"

"Yes." I unzip the top pocket and show him the precious books I carry everywhere, Carl Jung and Arnold Mindell, selected essays by Edward C. Whitmont.

He reaches over and picks up my journal, and with his eyes, asks if he can open it. I nod. He can't understand the words, of course, but he stares at them for some time. "The lines," he says. "I am looking at the lines of your hand." He runs his fingers over the drawings, and he asks if he can do a drawing, also, in my book.

I fish out my plastic bag of pastels, and he moves closer to me, his thigh against my thigh, his arm against my arm and starts making big, long curving marks in green with his left hand. I tell him that he should use his other hand, if he is left-handed, that it is a method I learned in an art therapy training, to use the nondominant hand to circumvent the mind and better express the unconscious thoughts of the body. I don't know how I manage to say all those things—I haven't studied Spanish since high school—but somehow I do. He nods gravely and switches hands so that now his drawing arm is the one against my arm, and it bumps and rocks my body slightly as I stare out at the blue-gray water.

When he finishes, he puts the book down, open, beside me and goes off to the other side of the hill to pee. He has drawn a mountain and some wild curving lines that look like a storm, and the sea, and a big man's face hovering in the sky with sad eyes and a sad mouth and underneath the picture he has written *alegría*. Happiness.

He comes back and straddles the stone bench, facing me. He presses the tip of his nose lightly to my cheekbone and stays like that for a second as I look out at the water. "*Hombre*," he says eventually in a very quiet voice, and I smile. He's calling me "man," just like Quin. "What are you going to do?"

I press my lips together, think for a while. I have a week until I need to be in Bilbao for my flight to Rome. "I need to get to Bilbao," I say.

"Bilbao."

I nod. "I need to get to the airport."

He pulls back and stares at me with amusement in his eyes. "That is also where I am going," he says. He shakes his head and says a word that I imagine means "synchronicity," and he stands, dusting his hands on the front of his purple swimming shorts. "*Vale*," he said, "*Vamos*."

He hoists my backpack onto his shoulders and offers a fast string of words in which I catch "uncle" and "driving" "air conditioner" and "Bilbao." When he sees my confusion, he slows down. "We can go to San Vicente de la Barquera. I have a friend. To sleep. From there to Santander. Then train to Bilbao."

"I don't have any money."

"Then how will you get a plane?"

"I have a plane ticket. Just no money to get there."

He stares at me in silence for a minute. I chew on the skin around my thumbnail as my heart beats hard against my chest wall, my brain spinning out hamster-on-speed kind of thought wheels such as, *No way in hell will you put yourself in a situation where you are dependent on a man again, Dayna. But what if he is different? You always think that. What are your other options?* And so on. Alejandro surveys my face with his deep brown, concerned eyes. Finally, with a giant sigh, he digs into his faded red satchel and pulls out a hard-boiled egg, which he hands to me. "Eat," he commands. "You will need your strength for the one or two banks we will rob along the way." He reaches out his hand to grab my other hand, and as he pulls me toward the path, he says, "There is nothing to do but continue."

⇌

Turns out, the friend he has in San Vicente is an eighty-some-thing aunt of a second cousin who he'd met once when he was six, but whatever. When he calls her, she says some effusive words into the phone and then greets us at the train station with much bustle and cluck, fluffing his hair away from his face and waggling my hand in her gnarled old hand as she exclaims and questions—not a word of it I understand. I realize, for the first time, how slow and concise Alejandro must be speaking for me to be able to understand him. After an onslaught of rapid-fire questions pointed in my direction, Alejandro explains gently that I am "learning" Spanish, so she commences to communicating solely via even more waves of her hands and one or two words shouted really loudly in my direction. She leads us up the stairs to an apartment over her house—something special she keeps for special people. "*Especial!*" she shouts as she unlocks the door and ushers us in, showing us a tiny kitchenette, a bathroom with a deep green bathtub, and a room with two twin beds pushed up against opposite walls.

The windows look out on the river where it empties into the sea, and she points out the thin paths that are just visible crisscrossing their way over the green hills to our left. "*El Camino,*" she says, and then the word "*pelegrinos,*" which I take to mean hikers, or pilgrims, since she is pointing at a couple of people walking down below us with dusty backpacks and scruffy hair. By the time I am done piecing this much together, she is onto the next thing, whirling to the closet, all elbows and paisley-print housedress, to show us the towels and extra pillows. Then she is apologizing profusely and kissing my cheeks. She says something to Alejandro and wags her finger and kisses him, and is gone.

Alejandro kicks off his sandals and flops down on the bed closest to the window, folding his arms behind his head. "She apologizes, her great-great-granddaughter is being born right now, and she has to go. She said congratulations to me, because you are beautiful."

I blush and flop down on the other bed. We turn on our sides to look at each other across the room. Outside, the day is softening into evening, the light lavender and deep green. We study each other for a while, the frogs outside the window singing. "Dayna," he says, practicing my name in his mouth. "Dayna. *Dime tus cuentas.*" Tell me your stories.

I close my eyes, and I open my mouth. And if exhaustion hadn't at that moment curled over me like a palm extinguishing a candle, I think I would have. I think I would have told him everything.

⇌

We need a strategy. There are several trains to catch, four nights to sleep somewhere. Alejandro shows me the contents of his wallet—a couple five-euro bills crumpled against each other. "This is ours," he says. "And I am sorry, it is all I have." He'd been traveling since I last saw him at the fete in France, meandering his way toward Bilbao in order to meet an uncle who did something that sounded like driving air conditioners back and forth from Bilbao to Madrid. I asked him to repeat that one a few times, but in the end I had to be content with understanding the basic idea. His uncle was his only hope for getting back home to Madrid and to more work, because he would not be able to pay for any transport home. The uncle would only be in Bilbao for one day—Friday—and today it was Saturday. "We will have to steal as many things as we can," Alejandro says as we sit at the train station in San Vicente, our backpacks stacked at our feet. He pulls a can of baby clams from his pocket that he had apparently nicked in the supermarket while I was in the bathroom. His great aunt or cousin or whatever she was had given us a loaf of fresh bread before we left, and we tear into it, dripping oily red clam sauce onto the white Spanish *pan* in the early morning sunlight. An old man at a bench beside us is sipping a bottle of wine as he sings softly under his breath, some sad, rolling melody.

A brown length of leather, aged by sun and sea and knotted several times, is twined around Alejandro's narrow wrist. I touch it lightly with my index finger, search in my brain for Spanish words. "This is from a girl?" I ask finally. He nods, popping the last bite of bread into his mouth.

"A girl you love?"

He smiles out into the empty train tracks. "For sure I love her. But I don't know anything else. I don't know nothing."

He stands abruptly, wiping his hands on his purple shorts and strides purposefully away from me, from the conversation. Later he will tell me all of it, of the lovely Maria who he'd spent the last six years of his life with, but who had recently: (a) developed a brain tumor, (b) started having psychotic episodes, or (c) been raped in childhood, or maybe last week. All or any of these three options lead to some kind of situation in which he could not touch her or talk to her. Here, my faulty understanding could be *in part* due to my faulty Spanish but could also be due to Alejandro's own round-the–mulberry-bush way of saying things, having both a penchant toward drama and discretion at the same time. "There are these connections in her brain that will never happen again," he was to tell me, while crammed in the bathroom of a train to elude yet another train conductor, our hands locked and folded in front of our chests as we bumped into each other and tried not to bump into the filthy bathroom wall. "She is *crazy*. But it is not her fault. But it is. You know?"

He had gone up to France to work for some months to get away from their relationship, which had ended, he would assure me. But even still, "If she saw you, oh my God, if she saw you, with me, Dayna, she would *kill* you." This sentence leads me toward assuming (b) psychotic episodes, and causes me to look over my shoulder often with an obsessive kind of nervous twitch whenever I sensed a Spanish girl behind me.

At the train station, Alejandro strides away and disappears into the bushes on the other side of the tracks, emerging some minutes later with two paws full of blackberries. I suck the clam juice off my fingers and try not to bite my nails to quell what is rising in me. It's a familiar sensation of vertigo, as though sitting on the top of a very high ladder, the whole wide world suddenly too wide around me, me and my backpack and some boy, with nowhere to go but further along the path that so often dead-ends at a cliff edge.

A blackberry pelts me on my nose.

"*Oye!* Dayna. Stop thinking," Alejandro shouts from the middle of the tracks. He throws three blackberries into the air and catches them successively in his mouth. The old man at the neighboring bench applauds with weak, shaky hands. Alejandro grins. He has a slight underbite, which gives his smile some undercurrent of mischief, like a mad sorcerer. The old man offers him some wine, and even though it is eight-thirty in the morning, Alejandro climbs up off the tracks and takes a few gulps. He smacks his lips. "*Que vida!*" he bellows up to the sky as the train rumbles into the station. Indeed. What a life.

For the next several days, we hide in train bathrooms, hop turnstiles, or—once—fake language incompetence. Or Alejandro does, pretending to be mute, while I am my normal, bumbling foreign self, getting all red-faced and tearful and talking fast in English when the conductor asks for my ticket until, flustered and apologizing, he leaves me alone. "*Que mujer!*" Alejandro congratulates me, clapping me on the shoulder and shaking me.

The countryside is green, hilly, and largely unpopulated. *Pelegrinos* hiking the Camino enter and exit the trains, shrugging off their backpacks in a heap and then heaving them up onto their shoulders again. They are mostly quiet, a few whispers of their own language between them—German, Dutch,

Norwegian. *Pelegrinos*, I have figured out from a few minutes of Internet time in the train station in Santander, indeed means "pilgrims." *One who walks in the fields of strangers.*

Through the fields of strangers, the train rumbles on, as Alejandro teaches me Spanish ballads, singing a line and then making me repeat it. "Dayna, you sing terrible! Terrible!" he gasps with laughter as I do my best to yodel after him, "*Besssaaaaaameeeeee.*"

In villages, between trains, we study each other's languages, legs tucked up under us on benches beside the sea. I conjugate verbs on shreds of napkin. "*Esta-RE, esta-RA, estar-AS,*" Alejandro explains, waving his hand in front of him as though digging up handfuls of air and offering it to me as he illustrates the future tense—the sound, the pause and suspension of it, so clearly signifying some promise of what has not yet come.

We sleep on beaches, using our jackets for blankets, our bags for a pillow. We lie side by side and stare at the stars. "*Como era tu cuando tu era una niña?*" he would ask, and listen to me with utmost patience as I pieced words together, one to the next to the next.

Other nights, when exhaustion makes speaking completely impossible, we just look at each other. Sometimes this goes on for hours, sharing some mutual fascination in the layers of each other's eyeballs, some comfort in whatever light we can see there. We keep things strictly platonic between us, though the memory of his kiss in the stampede still vibrates through me. In a village close to Santander, he leans over to kiss my cheek good morning, and I turn my head fast to lick his cheek instead. A loud honk sounds from a passing boat, loaded with tourists, a few feet off the dock we have slept on, all of them crowded to the railing and gaping at us. Alejandro grabs my hand and waves it at them. "A true Spanish kiss, señores, not to be confused with the French kind!" he shouts. Then he pounces on me and licks me back from chin to temple. "You taste like gazpacho," he says in my ear, giggling, as the boat honks again, once, twice, three times and disappears around the bluff.

In the afternoon sometimes as he naps, his head on my lap on some bench, some train, his dark hair damp around his forehead and at the nape of his neck, I watch him sleep, my fingers curled around his coleta. "You are a good man," I whisper to him in English and feel my eyes burn with tears as our last train pulls into the city of Bilbao. My flight is tomorrow, and his ride to Madrid is leaving the same night.

He smiles, waking slowly, rubbing at his hair. "A good what?" he tries in English, the syllables difficult, cut too sharp and pushed from his mouth. He notices my tears and rises quickly to kiss them off my cheeks. "*Guapa*," he says. He takes my hands in his long brown hands. "You know I would take you to Madrid with me if I could. But I must focus now. No girls. I must live a *vida de monje*." A monk's life. He is studying to be a *bombero*, a fireman. They only take twenty men out of five hundred applicants, he claims. His room is full of study manuals and training guides, he has told me. His life is studying. And Maria. "Really, I think she would kill you."

I smile and squeeze his hand, pull the tears back in my throat, away from him. He wraps me into the crook of his arm and sings me Spanish *canciones* as the train lumbers its way toward the station. His voice is thin, withholding, but comforting still because I can feel how much he loves to sing.

⇌

There is a festival in Bilbao, and the streets are packed—food stalls and T-shirt stalls and beer stalls and whiskey-Coke stalls. Rock music competes with punk music competes with folk, and everyone is dancing or clapping or singing along while motor boats spin circles in the river under the massive metal fortress of the Guggenheim museum. Teenagers sit in clumps in the dirty grass with jugs of wine and Coca-Cola that they mix together in those white plastic cups and drink down with gusto. My palms begin to sweat.

"What's wrong?" Alejandro feels my hand go cold within his. Everyone is wearing green and white this time—more Basque flag colors.

"Oh, just . . . remembering the last Basque festival I was at. . . ."

Alejandro grins his mad-sorcerer grin. "Don't worry, *guapa*, you can kiss whoever you want."

He leaves me with the bags on a bench beside the river and wanders off to find some kind of arrangement for the night—the city is too big and too rough to chance sleeping outside, so he hopes to find a restaurant or a bar that wouldn't mind stashing our bags for us. Then we will try to pull an all-nighter at the festival until dawn. I am dubious about all of this, both the staying up all night—we'd been going to sleep at sundown—and finding a trustworthy bar that wouldn't mind our huge mochilas stashed in their space. But within thirty minutes, he returns, trailing a small, highly intoxicated Spaniard who he introduces as Luigi. This is not really his name, and for some reason Alejandro introduces me as Olga and himself as Sancho. When I stumble later over the man's fake name, Alejandro instructs me to just call him *el fontanel* —the plumber—which might or might not have been this man's real profession. At any rate, the man tells us not to worry, he has a friend who will help. After buying us a few *cañas* at a bar on top of a hill, the plumber sends us along with this friend, a ballroom dance teacher who unlocks the lavender-painted door to his studio and hands us the keys with a wide smile. "It is an honor to have you here," says the skinny ballroom dance teacher, whose name is *M*-something or *N*-something, and that might not be his real name, either.

The studio is painted the same sickly lavender as the door, and it smells of green potato peelings and coffee grinds. "How in the world did you get them to give us this?" I ask Alejandro once the man has left.

"I told them you are a famous Russian *bailarina* and you desperately need a studio to rehearse in tonight." Alejandro is practicing pirouettes on the polished wood floor. "Olga Dobrowoczi."

"Is that a real person?"

"I don't think so." He does a few more pirouettes until he stumbles and has to hold his head to stop the room from spinning. "*Bailarina!*" he shouts. He peels his shirt off, sweating and grinning. He stomps his foot and spreads his arms wide. "Dance with me!"

I skate over to him, sock footed on the slick floor. I stop when I am close enough to smell the nutmeg of his hair, the faint, sweet musk of his skin. "*Bailarina,*" he says again, softer, his dark eyes pools of shadow in the dim light.

I turn my mouth away from his leaning kiss and hold his wrist, Maria's leather thong under my finger grip as I spin him outward, across the studio and away from me.

⇌

In honor of Russia, I suppose, the plumber and the ballroom dance teacher stop by to drop off a ten-kilo bag of potatoes and a bottle of vodka. I come out of the shower to find Alejandro intent on cooking all of them, up to his forearms in peelings in the studio's tiny kitchen. Oil is popping in the pan, and a mountain of white, glistening potatoes is rapidly diminishing beneath his flurry of knife chops. It is late afternoon, the sky high and white, and he has the window open to let the smoke from the oil out. I sit at the table with a cup of tea.

He looks back over his shoulder to grin at me. "I am making my grandmother's tortilla," he explains. "For your trip. You shall never go hungry." He drops a plate full of sliced potatoes into the hot oil and then leaps back from the hiss and pop. He is still shirtless. My eyes rest on his brown back, his narrow waist reminding me of a calf, belonging to farmland, hills of wild pasture. "My grandmother makes the best tortillas in the world." He waves his spatula.

"Does your mother make them like her too, or does your mother have her own style?"

He smiles. "My mother had her own style."

I catch the past tense and raise my eyebrows.

"My mother is dead." He turns back to the potatoes and starts chopping again.

"How?"

"Car crash."

"When?"

"Three years ago."

I watch the knife in his hand, the muscle moving across his shoulder blade, the slight, tight shift in his weight with each cut. Even if I knew the Spanish words, I still wouldn't know how to use them. How *long* the path is, where we each come from. Finally I say, "I guess that changed your life."

"*Sí.*"

He pours the fried potatoes into a bowl of whisked eggs on the counter and turns quickly to tend to a tortilla cooking in the other pan. With an expert flick of his wrist, he flips the pan upside down onto a plate, and from the plate, eases the tortilla back into the pan so that it can cook on its opposite side. A minute later, he is putting it down in front of me, a plate-sized egg masterpiece, glistening with oil. He hands me a fork.

"And your mother?" he asks after I have taken a few bites. "She is alive?"

I think of my wise mother, how long it's been since I've seen her, how much I miss her. My mother, who says, "Dayna, someday you'll realize that your relationship to Quin is not gone. That your relationship to Alon or Falk is not gone. That your relationship to your father is not gone. That in fact there are just many, many different kinds of relationships that you have and will always have, none of them lost, all of them for you, with you, helping you."

Tears pull a little at my eyes. "Yeah," I say. "She is."

Alejandro spears a chunk of potato and egg on his fork but pauses halfway between carrying it from the plate to the bread in his hand. "*Y tu Papa?*" he asks.

"Dead."

"When?"

"I was two."

He puts down his fork.

I meet his eyes and smile reassuringly. I keep putting

bites of tortilla into my mouth, even though I don't taste it. "*Vale*," he says after some minutes of silence. He sits back and nods. "*Dime*." Tell me.

I shrug. Even if I knew the Spanish words, I would not know how to use them. "He killed himself," I say. I pause. "And someone else too. He murdered our friend. And then killed himself."

"*Joder.* And now?" Alejandro is watching me with his hands folded in front of him on the wooden table. "Do you know why he did it?"

"No."

"*Joder.*"

"Everyone knew him as a good person. He *was* a good person. And then he turned into the opposite of that."

"Are you looking for him?"

"No," I say. And then, "Yes." I let Alejandro's dark eyes meet mine. His stare is unwavering. I am the one who looks away first, to the open window, the gulls wheeling. "In my own way. Yes."

⇌

It is nearly dark, and soon there will be fireworks, the plumber has told us. We sit in the street, stomachs full of tortilla, our backs against the lavender door. Down the hill and across the river, police stand in full, black riot gear, gripping guns and Tasers, watching the crowd. The plumber warned us when he dropped off the potatoes that tensions between the ETA—Basqueland's terrorist organization—and police are running high these days. That some food stands had been flying ETA sympathetic banners, and yesterday, the police had shut them down. The ETA have killed over eight hundred people in the last thirty years, Alejandro told me later when I asked, most of them police. Their mission was to fight for Basqueland's independence, and they believed that armed bloodshed was the only means to this end. "I wish I knew more," Alejandro said apologetically and made me promise not to ask anyone else about it. "It is one of those things. Dangerous, and secret."

Alejandro offers me the bottle of vodka. He is already a quarter of the way through. I shake my head, feeling nervous.

He shrugs and takes a pull from the bottle, then a swig of Coke. "I am getting drunk tonight, Dayna."

"Okay."

"I have to, sometimes."

"Okay."

"I cannot always be. . . ." I do not understand the word he uses, and I wrinkle my eyebrows, waiting for an explanation. He turns and writes something in the dust of the studio's window: *100%*. He says, "I cannot always be this."

There is a whistle, and then the shout of the first firework, as it explodes lime green above the river. I pull his narrow body over to mine and kiss the sweet, burnt brown of his neck. Then I let him go—quickly. He stares at me, a quizzical smile on his lips, lips I have not kissed since the fete in France. He shakes his head, just slightly.

"*Guapissima*," he says as he stands and offers me his hand up. "That means super, super *guapa*," he explains. "You are *guapissima*, Dayna. But. What a lie you are."

He is getting drunk fast, and the slurred Spanish is difficult to understand. I smile. *Night Alejandro.*

"You women," he continues as we walk down the hill into

town. "You just create a good feeling." He swings the vodka
bottle by its neck, my hand in his other. "You give a good
feeling, and then you take it away. Like your purpose is to
give absolute pleasure and then the opposite. The pure pain.
Muy puro."

We find a bare spot of grass in the midst of the crowd,
and we lie down to watch the fireworks, white-hot flowers in
the blackness of the sky. "Then again," he says, squinting his
eyes, thinking. "This must be life's purpose too." He turns on
his side to look me in the eye. "I am very sorry about your
father."

And then from the ground, an explosion. Not different
from that of the fireworks per se, the same largeness, the
same to-the-bone noise of dynamite, so that I would not have
noticed if not for the sudden ripple in the crowd, the craning
of necks this way and that.

Alejandro touches my arm and squeezes—"*Mira.*" A line
of black-clad, masked police with machine guns is running
through the crowd in the direction where the blast had come.
This makes the crowd really restless now, and the firework
watching is abandoned as everyone begins to stand and hurry
in opposing directions, like a sea confused by multiple tides.

"*Joder.*"

"What is it? Should I be scared?" I say.

"You can be scared if you want to, *bailarina.* I am scared.
Because you know why?" He is pulling me hastily to my feet
to avoid getting trampled—*Déjà vu*, I sing in my head. "I am
scared because I really have to pee. And where can I do that?
In this crazy crowd? On her ankles?"

"At least it would give us some breathing room."

"*Bailarina!*" He arranges his face into mock seriousness,

pulling me and taking pulls off the vodka bottle simultaneously as he pushes his way forward through the crowd. "This is an emergency! *Vale, vale, vale.* We must run!"

The restlessness of the people is quickly escalating into panic. Those who were walking fast begin to push and yell as they struggle to move against each other and around the people who have chosen to stand stock-still, who are, with much vehemence, yelling things that seem to be likening Spaniards to Nazis, and "the only way to win independence is through fire." Alejandro winds his way through all of it, tugging me behind him, raising his voice only to command, "Move, move, move, *las rinones, las rinones,*" which my back storeroom of Spanish words informs me means "the kidneys, the kidneys." I grab the vodka bottle from him and take a healthy chug as we plow through a lot of people who are screaming under a sky that keeps exploding, green and red and white-pink plumes as though to claim it all—this tight, panicked whorl of humanity struggling to unknot—as merely something to celebrate.

My own bladder begins to throb. I push at Alejandro's back, hoping to help propel him through the crowd. "Dammit, Alejandro, now I have to pee."

He casts an agonized look back at me. "What? Then we actually have to find a real bathroom."

"I'm sorry. I have a very sympathetic bladder."

"A what?"

"A sympathetic bladder," I shout, except I realize this time that I've said it wrong, that I've said *simpatico,* which isn't the word for sympathetic, like it sounds, but actually means "nice," so I'd just said, "I have a nice bladder." I try again as he looks back at me with confused eyebrows. "I have a bladder *genial,*" I say, then cringe because *genial* is just another way to say "nice." With all the vodka flooding my system suddenly, the pushing and the yelling and the firework explosions, my head begins to spin. Whatever word I have been trying for, in Spanish or in English, flies up and away from me like a wild bird racing for the sky. Alejandro stops in the middle of the crush of the crowd to squint at me.

"I love you," I say, everyone jostling and pushing past us. My shoulder is bashed, and I fall forward into him. He catches me without taking his eyes from mine.

"Well," he says. "I love you too."

And then we run.

⇌

Side by side we race, ducking and weaving through the crowd, sprinting across brief spaces of emptiness and then plunging down into bodies again, bare arms, shoulders, the smell of sweat, fire. We are running for the bridge, which will take us across the river and out of the main plaza, back to the narrow streets of bars and cafés, all hopefully empty since most of the city is here, intent on moving in the opposite direction as Alejandro and me. We push and run, past women in white, their faces ashen; green-clad grandmothers clutching blankets and picnic baskets; young boys in white shirts with green scarves; a tall man holding two crying daughters in green-and-white dresses in his arms. In an instant I see why our direction is not a majority decision—a line of police is advancing at a run from the other end of the bridge, shouting, gripping guns that glint in the dirty yellow light from the streetlamps. I yell to warn Alejandro, but he is ahead of me, turning his narrow body sideways as he launches himself through a gap in the crowd. I try to change directions, but my legs buckle. I grip my knees to steady them, my heartbeat rattling the cage of my ribs. Then all of me starts to shake, trembling bone as my stomach heaves its contents toward my mouth; simultaneously, I am ravenous, longing for a brick of meat, some solid thing to shove into my body, quick, before my body is annihilated.

"Dayna!" I turn to see Alejandro disappearing behind the oncoming press of people. I yell for him, and then the police are in front of me, these men wrapped in black rubber, shields of darkness over their faces. Something deep within me bears down, as though to give birth. I open my eyes wide. I dig my feet into the ground, blood moving fast, throbbing in the fingertips, ready to lash out at anyone who touches me. I am the witch, and the witch is me. When they see that I am not running with the rest of the crowd, they bellow, waving their arms and their weapons. One cop separates from the others and marches toward me, screaming, the language all *x*'s and knife swipes. And it is poetry, somehow, the arcs and dips of his rage, as though he is reciting some impassioned verse, Shakespeare, or Rilke. *And the point is to live everything, live everything, and the point is to live everything, everything.* And in the ragged circus of my own terror, I begin to laugh.

⇌

He doesn't hit me or shoot me. The streetlamps all suddenly extinguish, plunging us into darkness. I stare into the void of the policeman's face. Maybe he stares back at me. Maybe, I realize, behind that mask there is not a man, but a woman. Time suspends, hovers. Silent, everything silent, before two teenaged boys barrel past, knocking me to the side, into noise again, and the cop charges after them, through the tumbling crowd. The people who have been trampled are scrambling to their feet, shadows picking themselves off the ground and limping away.

On the far side of the bridge, I find Alejandro sitting with his back to the railing, his knees pulled to his chin.

I collapse beside him. Thigh to thigh, shoulders rising and falling as we breathe together. Before us the Guggenheim museum looms, sweeps and curves of shimmering metal over the dull, flat black of the river.

"Do you still have to pee?" Alejandro asks after some time. His body against mine is just slightly trembling. A bruise the color of a storm is spreading across the side of his face.

"Yes. No. I don't know." I press my nose to his neck, breathe in the smell of him, nutmeg and vodka.

"Dayna," he whispers. He turns his head to me, and I say *yes*, and then we kiss. Weightless, streaming, soaring through stars. It is too much, and we pull back dizzy, bleary-eyed. He presses his lips to my ear, and I feel the heat of the inside of him, on my skin. "*Oye*, Dayna," he murmurs. "*Mi amor.* There is nothing to do but continue."

⇌

We climb, slowly, the hill away from the river, past locked bars and dark storefronts, winding our way through the shadowed streets. Typical of Alejandro, he refuses to relieve himself until he knows that I also can go, and we walk for a long time until we finally find a light behind a cracked open, black metal door. Alejandro pushes it open slowly. *"Hola. . . ?"* One old man sits in the corner, smoking hash. The walls are dark green with a neon undertone. "My friend needs to use the toilet?"

The man says nothing, and Alejandro takes this as a yes, pushing me toward the alcove at the rear of the bar. "I'll go in the yard in the back," he whispers.

When I emerge from the bathroom, the old man is gone. My heart is still pounding from our race through the crowds. I stand in the hallway, trying to catch my breath, and find myself staring at a picture of a woman pasted onto the wall—a terrorist who is either imprisoned or dead. Her hair is curly and frames her round face. She is pretty, and surprisingly soft-looking, with a hint of a smile on her full lips. She is not young, but not old—probably my age. I stare at her, a slow understanding beginning in the center of my body, the way I understand Alejandro when he speaks Spanish words I do not know.

The back door slams, and Alejandro comes to stand behind me. "These terrorists. They are also *guapisima.*" He puts his chin on the top of my head. "You see what I am saying about women?"

"It's not only women. But since Eve, we have always been blamed." I don't mean to whisper, but I do.

"Siiii. Claro," Alejandro whispers back. With a burst of energy that startles me, he runs to the middle of the room and climbs up on a chair. He spreads his arms wide, addressing the room: the stale tortillas and tapas in their dirty glass case; the empty, wooden chairs; the many political rebels, the terrorists and the terrorist supporters, who clearly favor this

bar. "*Oye!*" he shouts out to the spinning dust, the dark neon, the hanging smoke from the old man's spliff. "This is not the way to independence!" He spreads his arms wide. "You don't fight your enemies, my friends. You romance them. You dance with them."

I lean against the doorway, heartbeat not slowing, heartbeat hurting. Soon, we will go our separate ways. There is no future tense for us, and we both know it. On the wooden chair, in the dark, empty bar, Alejandro begins to dance, cradling an imaginary partner close to him, swaying his hips just slightly back and forth. I love him, and I will also probably never see him again. Nor perhaps will I ever see anyone I have known and loved again; perhaps I will only continue on, walking in these fields of strangers, loving and letting go. And I can wring my hands and wonder. I *do* wring my hands and wonder. About the vastly different kinds of connections I have in the world. About the mystery of my work. About how full of words and utterly speechless I am, after these years in foreign countries, each day threaded with a throbbing sense of synchronicity and purpose but with no explanation as to what that purpose is or why in the world these relationships are washing into me with such specific questions and no hint of answer nor conclusion.

But watching Alejandro, I feel a sudden bloom of something I have never felt before. Something so true and soft: sadness and gratitude combined, longing and peace combined, terror and pure contentment. For I understand finally that there is nothing more to be done. That I'm not fucked up or irreparably damaged by my father or any of the other things I have accused myself of. I am just young and human and trying to learn about that boundaryless word "love." Trying to understand what to do with a love story—these flash moments of total bliss that transform far before we are ready for them to, and become something much more complicated, longer stretching, uncontainable by any one explanation. The love story shatters, then reforms into a new story. The first story is clear, succinct, the most often told. The ensuing stories as shifting and immense as the multiverse, as challenging to comprehend as distance in space, the size of stars. But how much more beautiful life becomes when we can let the story we want break apart and reassemble as *it* wants—wild, important, imperfect. An infinite kind of truth.

Outside, the fireworks have finally stopped. Alejandro, from his perch on the chair, extends his fingers to me. "*Baila-rina!*" he commands. "Stop thinking. Dance with me."

7.

BARCELONA

2019

Quin knocks on my hotel door just as the sun is tinting the narrow Barcelona streets dark apple red. He is taller than I remember, but otherwise he looks exactly the same as he did the last time I saw him ten years ago. His black T-shirt is frayed at the neck, and his faded jeans could likely be the same ones he used to wear in Greece. He fills the doorway, his skateboard in one hand, an open can of Estrella in the other. He keeps his eyes fixed on my two-year old son, who peeks out at him from between my legs.

"I can't quite . . . I can't look at you yet," he says, keeping his head turned. I pull him to me, kiss his sticky, sweaty cheek. He smells like cigarettes and incense and the bus he's spent the last several hours on. He says, "I just need a minute," and brushes past me to check out our suite. "This is nice, man, nice room," he says, poking his head in the bathroom, opening and closing the balcony door.

My son goes to get his wooden car and hands it to Quin with an eager grin. I'm stunned. Quin's voice is loud, he's strong smelling, and we are both trembling with pent-up emotion—all things that normally overwhelm my shy, sensitive child and make him cry or hide in my arms. But now he is relaxed, trusting immediately. When Quin sits down on the sofa, Colm climbs on him.

"He's not usually like this," I say, mystified.

Quin examines him on his lap. "There's something about him. He's so . . . what is it? Like he knows something. He's looking right into me."

"People say that. They keep calling him an old soul."

"I hate that term, man. It's so weird. Like, what does it mean?"

I laugh. "I don't know. I don't know what people see when they say it. I'm biased obviously; of course I think everything about him is amazing."

"No, no. He is. He *is* amazing, man."

I sit down beside him, and we start to just tumble all over with words, talking about too much to say anything.

I touch his knee finally and tell him, "Hey, it means a lot that you came to see me while we're here. I know it was a long bus ride from Madrid."

He shrugs. "It was worth it to see my best friend again."

My eyes well. "I'm happy you would still call me that. It's been so long since I've seen you."

"Whatever, man, what does time mean? Your best friends are your best friends, forever."

"As Norman Lear said, 'if I'm sitting here talking to you and enjoying it, there isn't a moment that took place that preceded it that wasn't worth it. Good or bad.'"

"Yes. Exactly. Exactly that, man."

We sit quietly for a minute, feeling it, the time that has passed. All that love and pain and the wild fear of losing each other, and then losing each other. For a long time, losing each other. Then coming back, but not with any promise or bond, not like we had. Just sitting here together, hands open.

He says, taking a sip of his beer, "Oh, man, your husband . . . I can't remember his name, shit. . . ."

"Alasdair. He wanted to be here, but he has a work dinner tonight. You know that's why we are here, for his work. . . ."

"Yes. Alasdair, he seems like such a good guy. He's so right for you, he balances you. I realized finally why you and I could never be together. We would implode. You need that kind of balance."

"I told you that," I say. "For literally years."

"I know. I mean. Wait, did you?" he says, laughing. "I guess it took me this long to understand."

We talk for a while about his life in Madrid. He's in between jobs again, sleeping on park benches, so I offer to buy him a plane ticket to England, to come stay with us for a while, have some stability. But then we both agree that flying into England would be too big a risk with his visa situation. He chokes on his voice and says his dad needs surgery on his heart, and he needs to get back to the States to see him. I think about how I would pack up my family and go be with him for as long as it took if he needed it, in a hospital in the country neither one of us live in anymore, and I'm awed by it—the way my love for him is still that deep, that entire.

I squeeze his hand. "I've always got you, and I love you, so think about how I can help you, okay?"

"I love you, man, I know. Thank you." He squeezes my hand back.

The familiar octave of his voice hits the place in me that remembers the good, untamed part of myself, and I have to close my eyes for a second to just feel. For years, I desperately tried to get myself to a safe place so that I could be an anchor for him, and now I'm here, realizing I need his anchorless state just as much as he needs steady, unmoving ground. I want him near me always, near my son, but the only thing I can have from him is the same that I've always had: a reminder of how to let go.

We hug each other hard to say goodbye outside of the hotel, and I cry because it may well be another ten years before I see him again, or else never. "What's important always comes back, Dayna," he says, gripping me tightly. "You can trust that."

I close my eyes and nod. *Begin to understand. Then let it go and begin again. Let something new and deeper find you each time.* "I know," I say. "I learn that best from you."

It is true that everyone important who I once let go of has, indeed, come back again.

Ryan did a landscaping job at my mother's neighbor's house at the same time that I was on a visit back home. He'd left the EMT work long ago and returned to our hometown to have a quiet life full of the things he loved—playing banjo with his wife, coaching his kids in soccer, planting people's gardens. We leaned against his truck in the late-afternoon sun and talked about everything for a good long time, and when we hugged goodbye, we held on. "Somehow you're still one of my best friends, even if we don't see each other or talk," he said, mystified by it, and he huffed out of his nose and put his cheek on the top of my head. "I feel that way too," I said.

Alejandro writes me long, tangled emails in half Spanish, half Google-translated English—about the gossip and politics of the Madrid firemen and his unpaid parking tickets and the songs he's been writing with his beat-up guitar.

I bumped into Dimitris at a fish restaurant on a trip to Mykonos one summer. I'd been avoiding visiting Páros because I didn't know how I'd feel about running into him, seven years since I'd last seen him, but then there he was, on a completely different island. And it surprised me, how good it was to see him. We shared a glass of wine and cried and apologized to each other for an hour for everything, for all of it, and he was shaking and I was shaking when we hugged goodbye.

With that out of the way, I went back to Páros the following week. I had dinner with my old writing teachers, Jack and John Pearl. We sat on the balcony of our favorite seaside restaurant, and over plates of Greek salad and grilled octopus, Jack talked about going with Quin the morning after the glass fight to clean the apartment. "I've never seen so much fucking blood," he said mildly. "Like someone was murdered."

"Why so much blood?" asked Aurora, John Pearl's nine-year-old wonder child who had recently come from New York to live with him.

"Sometimes when people fall deeply in love, it creates a kind of madness," John Pearl explained, pouring me more wine. "And you get to see your real humanity. The whole untamed, honest thing of it."

Aurora digested this with a thoughtful gaze. It seemed to make perfect sense to her. And sitting there beside my two old writing friends, the sun long gone, the blue throb of the sea beneath us, I realized it made all the sense in the world to me too.

That early morning, 4 a.m., an hour before I had to catch my flight back to the states, I asked a tattoo artist to ink the first line of Mary Oliver's "Wild Geese" onto my forearm. As the parlor swelled with the first pink hues of sunrise, the tattoo artist, a slight Greek woman with pale blond braids, murmured to me as she worked, "This is the truth. You do not have to be good."

"You only have to let the soft animal of your body love what it loves."

⇌

Shai returned to me on a crowded street corner in south Tel Aviv on a winter afternoon during Hanukah. He stopped abruptly to pet a dog at the same time I realized I was walking directly behind him. His sunglass-covered eyes swung up to meet mine as I was jostled into his shoulder. He smiled big. We gripped each other in an instant hug. He had gotten married. He showed me pictures of his grinning daughter. And just like that, the darkness between us was gone.

Falk I ran into not once but three times over the course of a year, in various different parts of Berlin until, on the third time, we decided to just hang out. We spent the last four days of my last trip there inseparable again, skipping with linked arms across that flat city, buying matching ironic hats from the tourist kiosks, taking bus tours, tearing up together in the Jewish museum.

Alon and I FaceTime often, and though we do not see each other, we remain woven into each other's daily lives. Sometimes during our conversations he needs to talk about the ways that I hurt him, and I listen and apologize. I tell him I'll apologize forever, if he needs me to. Sometimes the pain from my past choices rakes at me, and he is always the one to remind me how to just let it be as it is—one more thing on the long path that got me here.

The last person to return has been Quin.

His green eyes regard me now as he holds me at arm's length outside the hotel. "Listen, I wanted to tell you something," he says. He has developed a Spanish accent, the lilt specific to Madrid, and it brings back fractions of moments with Alejandro—the green cliffs of northern Spain, the taste of tortilla, the sound of fireworks. His face gets soft, and he says, "I want you to know that everything that happened with us was monumentally important in my life. I feel like you know me well enough to know, or at least sense, that I didn't stop talking to you because I'm not interested in you or out of judgement or hatred . . . you know, my way of processing things and feeling them is just really clumsy. The truth is, there wasn't a day that passed that I didn't think about you."

I wipe the tears from my face with the palms of my hands, and he squeezes my shoulders.

"Goodbye, and I love you," he says, stepping onto his skateboard. "When I'm with you, it's still the only time I don't feel alone. So thank you." He grabs my hand and presses his lips briefly to my knuckles and then he turns and skates away, into the dark of the long city street.

I return to my life in England the next day. The soft hills are lit with autumnal gold, the garden thick with wet chard and spinach, the letter from the fussy neighbors complaining about our new "out of keeping" front fence lying on the wooden table.

I carry my son home from our walk through the fields, the orange evening sun low over the South Downs. In one hand is a fresh, full dirty diaper I have just stripped off of him while he giggled on his back in the tall grass. My other hand holds him to my body as he nurses. This is the *definition* of having my hands full, I think as I walk fast toward home, toward dinner that still needs to be made. The house is strewn with toys and tracked-in grasses, leaves, little piles of stones that my son as deposited in the corners after learning he can get fistfuls of them from the driveway if he lies on his belly and reaches his hand under the gate. I am not worried about encountering anyone looking like I do: my boob out, bearing a shit-heavy diaper. Whatever my body does is okay with me, and I don't care what the stuffy neighbors think. I realize, *I'm an adult now.* And I laugh. Giving silent thanks that this moment has come in an infinitely different way than it once came to my mother, sitting up beside her two babies, terrified of what state her husband would come home in from the bar.

In my arms, my son stretches his hand up suddenly, to a flock of wild geese slicing through the sky above our heads. Their familiar, guttural cry unfolds through the cold autumn air. I stop on the path, and we watch them together, my son and I, quiet with reverence, as we behold the beauty of a world that's always moving.

SWITZERLAND

2015

Dear Dad,

In the months of your disappearance, when we knew only that you had done something terrible and were now nowhere to be found, I woke every morning at 3:00 a.m. to scream. I was two years old. My mother's brother would roll over in the bed we were sharing and watch me, standing near his shoulder, my feet sturdy in the coils of his blue blankets. I screamed and screamed, and he waited, listening, letting me for a while, before he pulled me to his chest, as he did every night, to rock me back into silence.

Many years later, when I was fourteen, I found this line from F. Scott Fitzgerald: "In a real dark night of the soul, it is always three o'clock in the morning." I hadn't heard yet the story of my childhood 3:00 a.m. screaming ritual. I hadn't heard the phrase "dark night of the soul." I didn't know what the sentence meant, but I copied it down onto blue construction paper and taped it to my wall, where I read it every day and felt things that I didn't—and would be trying to for the rest of my life—understand.

Driving across the California desert in a thunderstorm, your middle brother wanted to tell me about you. He wanted me to know you were a good man. "A good man," he said over and over again, as if worried I would protest. Dig up the story. Ask him why.

He pulled off underneath an overpass and rested his hands on the steering wheel as he stared out at the torrential, yellow desert rain. "You know, he was always the favorite brother, out of the four of us," he said. "All of us. We looked to him."

We watched the lightning as it made swift cuts across the dark sky. "And now what?" I wanted to say. "Do you still look to him?" But I didn't ask, because I knew, even after all these years, that none of us could answer that question.

Growing up, you loved music, dreamed of being in a band. When you were sixteen, your father bought you and your brother each a guitar during a vacation in Mexico. The two of you picked out harmonies, played James Taylor, Jackson Browne. You liked to play in the evenings, and after Jamie was born, you sang low and sweet to her, easing her into sleep. "Good night, you moonlight ladies. Rockabye, sweet baby James."

When you died, your brother took your guitar and wrote you a song. He recorded it on a white cassette tape and gave it to Jamie and me, as a present to remember our father. As I grew older, when I missed you and I didn't know who you were or why I missed you, I would take my red Sony tape player out to the backyard and listen to your brother's gentle voice, singing for you.

You. Who took your rifle from its shelf. Who strode out into the evening, into the beginning of a blizzard, who walked, slanted, through the white wind and the dark trees to Tom's house. You who opened the door, you who raised your gun, who did not breathe, or avert your eyes, who said to Tom's screaming wife, "Shut up or I'll shoot you too."

You who pulled the trigger.

I was thirteen, at your mother's house in California one summer, looking at pictures of you. You in a wildflower field, your hand extended to your horse. You on a tractor, dragging logs to build the house Jamie and I would be born in. You blowing out candles on what would be your last birthday cake. Thirty-two years old.

Your youngest brother came into the room to see what I was doing. "You know, your dad was the favorite brother," he said.

"I know," I said.

"He's the one who taught me how to water-ski. He was better than anyone else in the family. He would hold me on his skis with one arm, grip the handle with the other." He looked away, smiling to himself. "He also taught me how to drive. I was seven. He steered while I worked the pedals. We drove the car through the garage."

I waited to hear more, but there was no more. Just a sad smile before he turned and left the room.

My mother's brother loved you also. "Your father was a man who could do anything he put his mind to." He told me once about your determination to shoot an elk with a bow and arrow for your wedding. The story is hazy, not quite remembered, except for this —my uncle, a young man of twenty, hiking up to the lip of a yellow plain and seeing you, there across the field, bow at your side, kneeling. Your hand gentle, respectful, on the pearl brown belly of an elk, as it lay in the grass, as it shuddered its last breath and then died.

You left Tom's house, you climbed into your truck. Your hands cold, I imagine you did not feel them. You drove fast into the furious snow. Your truck got stuck on a fallen log on the forest road. Your truck got stuck in that white storm. You could get no further away from yourself. You left the engine running, the heater on, and you began to write, slowly, your last words. "I, Gary Brayshaw, leave everything I own to my wife, Judy Brayshaw, and my daughters, Jamie and Dayna . . . P.S. I owe Rick a six pack."

At 2:53, your engine died. The snow had built itself around your truck in white shoulders, blocking you in. You did not feel your finger on the trigger. You did not feel the barrel against your skull. Your life closed at 3:00 a.m., and we spent months hiding from you, not knowing you were dead, terrified you were coming for us. Your body was not found till the spring.

This one is Jamie's memory:

Bathtub water lukewarm. She was four and afraid, listening to the noise downstairs. You were storming through the house, shouting, and our mother was shouting, then pleading, then shouting again. There was a slam, a crash that made the bathwater tremble. Then the roar of your truck, spinning out gravel as you drove away. Our mother slow-climbed the stairs. "It's time for you to get out, Jamie," she said to my sister tightly. Our mother's eyes wrestling back what she had seen: the shadow that was slowly possessing you, the side that no one else knew.

"Do you remember him?" I asked my sister. She was quiet for a while.

"Only dark hair," she said, finally. "Falling asleep on the

couch, and he would lift me up, really gently, to take me to bed. I'd put my face in his dark hair."

Your bullet hit Tom in the face. He was dead instantly and collapsed into his wife, who had stood beside him at the kitchen sink only a minute earlier, who was trying to stop screaming. The children, somehow, stayed sleeping in the back bedroom.

We spent Christmas one year with Tom's family—they have been our good friends for over twenty years. "How do you know each other?" people ask.

"Well, our dad killed their dad," we say, or "Their dad killed our dad," and we laugh. We are the only ones who think it's funny.

Tom's daughter, Fern, made us soup out of fresh greens from the co-op for Christmas Eve dinner. She added cream to the simmering onions and hummed to herself in the kitchen while her mother, Lila, wrapped presents for her grandson, a wooden boat and a picture book about trees. On the desk in her bedroom, there was a framed photo of her dead husband. He was smiling with a black beard, sitting on top of a mountain.

I do not have anything that was once yours. My mother gave your clothes away. I wanted to know what you smelled like, and my mother told me cherry tobacco and spruce trees. I asked Lila what your face looked like when you shot her husband. She said very calmly, "Wooden and blank."

Your mother, my beloved grandmother, gave me the picture of you with a horse, and I put it up on my bedroom wall. "Who is that?" some people asked. And I wondered if I would ever know how to answer.

*I am now in graduate school in Switzerland, getting my masters
in dance for conflict transformation. I'm the age of your last year
alive. It is because of you that I am here, continuing to try to meet
the shadows of the world head on, these dark nights of the soul—
to embrace them. On my school's break, I meet my mother and my
stepfather in Grindelwald to spend a few rainy days hiking
through the Alps. Before breakfast one morning, my mother tells
me she had a dream about you. None of us dream about you; the
giant question mark that you are will not find form, even in
dream world, so this is a moment. This is one of those times when
the world hushes and leans forward, all things stopped in order to
listen. "What happened?" I ask my mother.*

*"Well, what's interesting," she says, "is that Jamie also
dreamed of him. Last week. He came to her and promised to take
care of her daughter. He said he was watching over Jamie too. He
hugged her for a long time. And now," my mother says, "he came
to visit us."*

*In her dream, you told my mother that you had come to talk
about me. You were digging a hole and burying treasure there for
me. "Tell Dayna she's doing the right thing," you said. "It's good
that she's in school, and this, this treasure is for her." My mother
promised to bring me the message. "And now I have to go," you
said. "I'm also in school."*

*My mother, telling me the dream, shakes her head with a
smile at this. "What's he in school for, I wonder?" she says.*

*"How to be a father from the other side," I say, and we laugh.
We laugh and we laugh, until tears stream. We laugh about this
story that you left us. The beautiful wreckage.*

END

About the Author

Dayna MacCulloch is a Somatic Wellness Coach based near Brighton, UK and Olympia, Washington. You can find out more about her work through her website, WaterStoriestheBody.com, or follow her on IG @waterstoriesthebody.

SELECTED TITLES FROM SHE WRITES PRESS

She Writes Press is an independent publishing company
founded to serve women writers everywhere.
Visit us at www.shewritespress.com.

Brave(ish): A Memoir of a Recovering Perfectionist by Margaret Davis Ghielmetti. $16.95, 978-1-63152-747-0. An intrepid traveler sets off at forty to live the expatriate dream overseas—only to discover that she has no idea how to live even her own life. Part travelogue and part transformation tale, Ghielmetti's memoir, narrated with humor and warmth, proves that it's never too late to reconnect with our authentic selves—if we dare to put our own lives first at last.

Finding Venerable Mother: A Daughter's Spiritual Quest to Thailand by Cindy Rasicot. $16.95, 978-1-63152-702-9. In midlife, Cindy travels halfway around the world to Thailand and unexpectedly discovers a Thai Buddhist nun who offers her the unconditional love and acceptance her own mother was never able to provide. This soulful and engaging memoir reminds readers that when we go forward with a truly open heart, faith, forgiveness, and love are all possible.

A Different Kind of Same: A Memoir by Kelley Clink. $16.95, 978-1-63152-999-3. Several years before Kelley Clink's brother hanged himself, she attempted suicide by overdose. In the aftermath of his death, she traces the evolution of both their illnesses, and wonders: If he couldn't make it, what hope is there for her?

The Tell: A Memoir by Linda I. Meyers. $16.95, 978-1-63152-355-7. Meyers's account of losing her mother to suicide when she was twenty-eight—and of how, determined to give the death meaning, she changed her own life for the better.

The World Looks Different Now: A Memoir of Suicide, Faith, and Family by Margaret Thomson. $16.95, 978-1-63152-693-0. The gripping, intensely personal story of a mother struggling to come to terms with the suicide of her twenty-two-year-old son only weeks before he was due to deploy to Afghanistan.

The First Signs of April: A Memoir by Mary-Elizabeth Briscoe. $16.95, 978-1-63152-298-7. Briscoe explores the destructive patterns of unresolved grief and the importance of connection for true healing to occur in this inspirational memoir, which weaves through time to explore grief reactions to two very different losses: suicide and cancer.